"Evangelical pastors and church lead
Faithful Reading. Irenic and thoughtf
the Christian Old Testament faithfully. Anyone who reads this book will come away with a better sense of how to read Scripture and an appreciation for its beauty and richness."

Nathan MacDonald, professor of the interpretation of Old Testament at the University of Cambridge

"Those who have longed to sit in John Walton's classroom but are unable to do so need look no further. *Wisdom for Faithful Reading* distills over four decades of his Old Testament research and his reflection on responsible interpretation into a scholarly-yet-accessible volume. Exhibiting his trademark attention to ancient Near Eastern backgrounds, Walton argues for key interpretive principles and the importance of rhetorical strategy and genre in interpreting the Old Testament. His deep respect for biblical authority shines through as he guides teachers and pastors to responsibly interpret the Old Testament in a way that will ultimately equip the church to honor and glorify God."

Jennifer Brown Jones, instructor of Old Testament at Liberty University

JOHN H. WALTON

WISDOM *for* FAITHFUL READING

PRINCIPLES *and* PRACTICES *for* OLD TESTAMENT INTERPRETATION

Academic
An imprint of InterVarsity Press
Downers Grove, Illinois

InterVarsity Press
P.O. Box 1400 | Downers Grove, IL 60515-1426
ivpress.com | email@ivpress.com

InterVarsity Press® is the publishing division of InterVarsity Christian Fellowship/USA®. For more information, visit intervarsity.org.

Cover design and image composite: David Fassett
Interior design: Daniel van Loon

ISBN 978-1-5140-0487-6 (print) | ISBN 978-1-5140-0488-3 (digital)

Printed in the United States of America ♾

Library of Congress Cataloging-in-Publication Data
A catalog record for this book is available from the Library of Congress.

29 28 27 26 25 24 23 | 13 12 11 10 9 8 7 6 5 4 3 2 1

Dedicated to all my valued conversation partners over the years,

including family, students, friends, colleagues,

and yes, my pastors.

CONTENTS

PART TWO: GENRE GUIDELINES

Section D—Prophecy and Apocalyptic | 157

PART THREE: A WAY FORWARD

Section A—Characteristics of Faithful Reading | 185

Section B—Living Life | 198

LIST OF FIGURES AND TABLES

Figures

Tables

PREFACE

Most Bible readers could agree that faithful interpretation is desirable. So why this book? Why approach it this way? Over my forty-plus years of teaching, through trial and error in attempts to communicate clearly, I have developed certain brief, catchy phrases that embody important insights into biblical interpretation. Think of them as methodological "soundbites" that offer principles and guidelines. They do not offer a comprehensive or systematic approach to interpretation. Yet I believe they offer valuable insights that can steer us toward faithful interpretation. And that has been my goal in writing this book: to accumulate insights that may set a course for all who take the Bible seriously as we seek to become faithful interpreters.

It does this most importantly by helping us not to perpetuate unproductive habits. When our kids were young, my wife and I used to read a picture book to them titled *Tootle* by Gertrude Crampton, one of the best-selling kids' books of all time. Tootle is a "baby train" learning the rules of being a train, two of which were to "stay on the rails no matter what" and to "stop for a red flag waving." Unfortunately, the little train soon gets distracted and goes off the tracks to chase butterflies, play in the buttercups, and make daisy chains as he enjoys a day in the meadow. Such behavior is, of course, unacceptable, so the school engineers come up with a plan to teach him about staying on the tracks. They all hide in the meadow with red flags so that everywhere Tootle goes, a red flag pops up, spoiling his fun. The green flag is on the tracks.

Many of the guidelines presented in this book can serve as the red flags of the Tootle story. We go happily through the meadow of fun biblical interpretation without considering whether we are on the right track. The guidelines can serve as red flags to let us know that we are not "tracking with the biblical author," as well as to show the green flag when we are going in a productive direction. I will discuss many red flags, but my intention is that in the end we will have a clearer understanding of the green flag as we pursue the message that God has given us in the text. Hopefully, this can help us "stay on the rails, no matter what."

Lest the reader imagine that I am being guided by a toddler's story book, a word from the world of scholarship is in order. Adele Berlin provided seven guidelines for seeking a new path in hermeneutics. One of them was the exhortation to take the historical and social context seriously. She first notes that for those who believe there is an "original stable meaning" (as I do), we should beware of interpreting the text anachronistically. She explains, "One's interpretation should be as true as possible to the world from which the text emerged. This includes the meaning of words, the physical realia and historical events, and the world of ideas." She ends with a statement of her commitment, one which I share: "I must proceed on the assumption that although the original meaning of the text may not in theory be retrievable, I must in practice work as if it were."[1]

Using a variety of guidelines to frame this book offers the benefit of communicating core ideas concisely. The disadvantage is that they largely defy organization and, in their individuality, make it difficult to sustain continuity chapter by chapter. All the chapters reflect a common thread: to be faithful interpreters we need to hold ourselves accountable to the authors' literary intentions. Despite that, I am not attempting to sustain an argument that will eventually lead to an overall thesis. The guidelines are not organized by a logic that leads inexorably from one to the next. They offer discrete concepts.

I have attempted to organize them loosely in categories, first those that pertain to the Bible generally, then those that pertain more particularly to the larger canonical categories of the Old Testament. There is nothing intrinsically essential to this organization; it is simply an attempt to provide a convenient organization (rather than settling for an utterly random one).

---

[1]Adele Berlin, "A Search for a New Biblical Hermeneutics: Preliminary Observations," in *The Study of the Ancient Near East in the 21st Century*, ed. Jerrold S. Cooper and Glenn M. Schwartz (Winona Lake, IN: Eisenbrauns, 1996), 204.

I did not write this book as a textbook—I wrote it to help academically-minded people in the church who are trying to improve and inform their reading of the Old Testament.[2] I think that it will have its best use by people who have taken on the responsibility of communicating God's Words to others. Whether you are simply reading it on your own or with a group, and whether you are participating in a group or leading a group, I hope that you will find this book useful. Students may find that the book gives them direction, but even pastors might find in it some helpful correctives. I hope that teachers will find in it a way to introduce their students to approaches to biblical interpretation. Moreover, it is my hope that pastors will see the need to instruct their congregations in sound methodology and then will model it well.

The last unit of the book does something a little different but no less important. I am committed to the idea that our reading of Scripture cannot stop with understanding the authors' intentions, though it does need to start there. Interpretation alone can become sterile or pedantic. The power of Scripture is not just in the fact that it was given; it is in the reality of being lived. God has given us revelation of how he has been working out his plans and purposes in the world and invites us to become full-fledged, committed participants working alongside him for his honor and glory. We were created for this! Therefore, in the last unit, I have also offered some reflections on living out what we have learned from faithful interpretation of Scripture.

This book could be used in many ways. It could be used for a small group study or for an adult Sunday school class. It could be used in a Christian K-12 school curriculum. My hope is that in whatever context it is used, the result will be that readers will have a clearer idea of how they should think about the Old Testament and how it functions as God's Word so that it can be reclaimed for the church, which has grown to neglect it.

---

[2]A brief word about footnotes is in order. A few footnotes throughout the book cite a source for the information presented, as most footnotes in most books do. However, many of the footnotes in this book are given to point to further reading, generally in books that I have written. They will be marked "for further reading."

ACKNOWLEDGMENTS

In many ways this book is the work of a lifetime, and it would be impossible to name all the colleagues and students who have contributed to my thinking over the decades. So I can only cite the most important contributions to this stage of development. Most prominent among them is my wife, Kim, who has been my conversation partner for my entire adult life and has helped me shape my thinking in many ways. She also read this manuscript and offered many suggestions for improvement that help the book communicate better.

Second, though all three of my kids (Jon, Josh, and Jill) have contributed to my thinking in different ways, Jon's interaction is most noticeable in this book. He and I have collaborated on three previous books (he writes under the name J. Harvey Walton), and he read sections of this book and contributed clear and distinctive ideas that helped me communicate important content better.

Third, conversations with colleagues and friends have played a significant role. I offer particular thanks to Jeff and Aubrey Buster and to Adam Miglio, who help me think more deeply and therefore enable me to communicate more clearly.

Finally, I am grateful to my TA, Lori Petrie, who edited the manuscript for me and provided the indexing. Thanks also must be given to the phenomenal team at IVP, particularly to Jon Boyd, who gave me the chance to write this and shepherded it through the process with invaluable suggestions along the way.

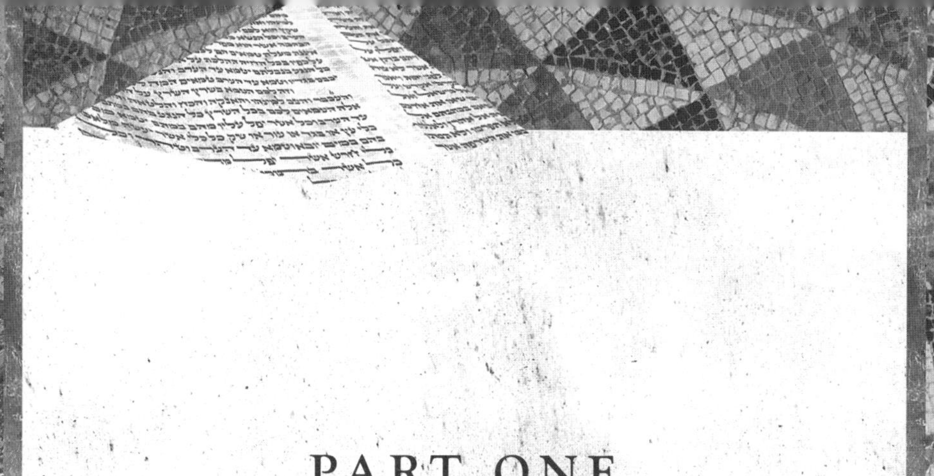

PART ONE

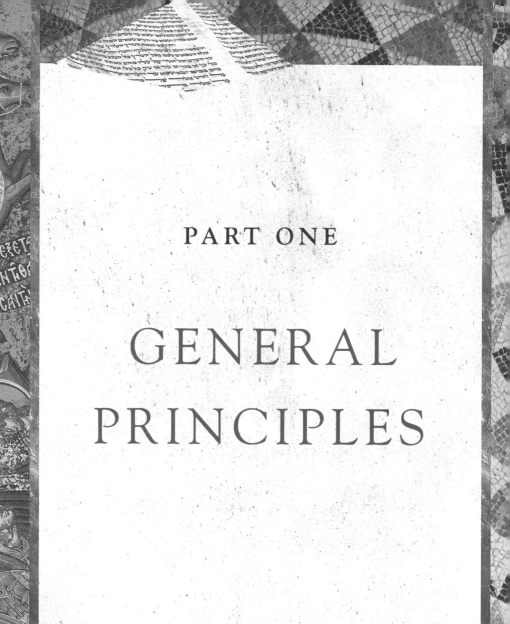

GENERAL PRINCIPLES

SECTION A

INTRODUCTION

1—One Quest

The world looking in on Christianity has little understanding of the Bible. This is reflected in the questions skeptics pose interminably in the blogosphere. One permutation of it is reflected in the Peacock television adaptation of Dan Brown's *The Lost Symbol*. In one scene, Dr. Peter Solomon talks about the Bible to his protégé, Harvard Symbology professor Robert Langdon: "It's a bizarre book of stories filled with contradictions, with outdated beliefs, with outright absurdities. . . . People sense there is a power in them that we have yet to understand."[1] Christian insiders often do no better. It is not unusual for insiders to begin looking for a special code, just as Peter Solomon did. Many find it difficult to figure out what they should expect from the Old Testament and how what is purportedly the Word of God has relevance to their lives. They want to be faithful interpreters, but they don't know how.

Faithful interpretation—that is the essential quest for anyone who takes the Bible seriously. If we believe the Bible is God's revelation, carrying God's message, then we must receive it as a trust over which we have a certain stewardship. When we talk about being faithful, we are acknowledging that we must submit to the authority that is inherent in the Bible—because it was given by God. Submitting ourselves means that we recognize

[1]A similar conversation takes place in the book (chap. 131), but the television version puts it more succinctly.

our accountability to God and the human instruments that he used. We are not free to pursue our own meanings and message. We cannot be content with "what this passage means to me" as we seek to appropriate the message that is inherent in the text itself. God's message is in the text, so we are accountable to the text. Nevertheless, the message was communicated by Spirit-led authors, writing with purpose and intention. So our accountability to the text cannot be separated from our accountability to the literary intentions of its authors.

2—Two Caveats

"FAITHFUL" RATHER THAN "RIGHT"

Note that I frame this quest by the word *faithful*—not by the word *right*. People who take the Bible seriously have perhaps spent too much time and energy trying to insist that their interpretation is right and the interpretations of others are wrong. This is not to say that interpretations cannot be right or wrong. Nevertheless, in the cases of the most controversial issues, "right" is precisely what is under discussion. Everyone cannot be right, but we should recognize what commends one interpretation over another. That is why I have framed this as "faithful" interpretation. Our methodology should be faithful even though sometimes we might arrive at different answers.

Simply put, an interpretation is the result of identifying evidence (for example, linguistic, literary, historical, theological, cultural) and assessing that evidence, then applying it to a base of presuppositions one holds. Such presuppositions may pertain to what readers believe about the Bible or to the theology they deduce from the Bible. They may be presuppositions held consciously, by choice, or subconsciously, adopted through long years of passive reception and tradition. In the process, interpreters prioritize and shape the various pieces of evidence to accord with their presuppositions and cultural locations to arrive at an interpretation. That interpretation, then, reflects what the interpreters consider having the strongest evidence in light of their governing presuppositions.

Unfortunately, it is common for all of us to consider the interpretation that we prefer, given our perspectives and presuppositions, as simply "right." It is logical to conclude that the interpretation with the strongest evidence carries the highest probability. But for another reader who has different presuppositions, or who prioritizes the evidence differently, or who is not persuaded that one piece of evidence is legitimate, a different interpretation will take pride of place and be considered as having the strongest evidence.

Using the adjective "faithful" instead of "right" humbly recognizes that we all fall into the pitfalls of blind presuppositions and overlooked evidence. We can only seek to be as faithful as possible. No interpreter is infallible. Maybe sometimes we will even be right, but that is not our claim to make. Certain interpretations may be *disproved* by evidence, but interpretations cannot be *proved* true. Evidence *supports* an interpretation and therefore lends it a higher degree of *probability*.[2] The greater the evidence that supports a particular interpretation, the higher the probability we are understanding God's message, and the higher our confidence in our conclusions can be.

COMMUNITY

Even though individual scholars often introduce an interpretation, I would contend that interpretation is ultimately the responsibility of the community. Unquestionably, communities can be misguided and misled just as individuals can. The point I want to make is that we all need each other. No person alone can make every observation that is needed for a strong interpretation. No person alone can assess all the evidence well. No person alone can rise above his or her blind spots and prejudices. Everyone in the community can make observations that others might not make—or can contribute important insights. I have experienced this over the years as I have interacted with my students.

The community should also be valued for vetting the results of a proposed interpretation, though consensus is not required. This is not to say that the community must approve all conclusions, because that would

[2]I am grateful to my science colleague, Kristen Page, for these important distinctions.

make the community the authority, not the evidence from the text.[3] As a cautionary note, history has shown that at times the Christian community has been in general agreement on an interpretation that has later been recognized as inherently flawed.

We need the entire worldwide community of faith to achieve the desired faithfulness most successfully. Still, we can proceed with some modicum of confidence if we are making every attempt to ground our interpretation with three essential commitments: accountability, consistency, and controls.

3—*Three Essential Commitments*

ACCOUNTABILITY

First, and most importantly, readers of Scripture are accountable to God because we want to discern the message he intended to give, not our own message superimposed on his. But there is another link in the chain. God chose to use human instruments—including tradents, authors, editors, and compilers—through whom to communicate his message. For simplicity, I will group all these human instruments in the designation "author."[4] God vested his authority in these human instruments and therefore, since we wish to be accountable to God, we must be accountable to them. If we believe that their message was given and guided by God, our first line of accountability is to understand what those authors intended to communicate to their immediate audience. To turn that around, if the author cannot be shown to have a particular point in his message, then we should not have it in our interpretation.[5] We are accountable to the author more than to our

[3]I recognize the early Christian community eventually recognized and designated which books carried authority, but I nevertheless believe that the authority they recognized was God's authority imbued on the authors.

[4]Though some of the traditions that eventually find their way into the Bible would have been passed down orally, and scribes doing various tasks may have been included, we attach authority to the end literary result that became part of the canon. For further clarification, see chap. 14.

[5]When referring to the authors of Scripture (as broadly defined above), I will be using masculine pronouns since there is no hint that any females were part of the literary process. This simply reflects the realism of the ancient world.

modern communities or traditions. One way to express this is to speak of being tethered to the author's literary intentions. This wording recognizes that we can neither get "inside his head" and read his mind, nor do we attempt to do so. Instead, we assume that he is a competent, effective communicator and that we can receive the communication he intends.

CONSISTENCY

Once we adopt the author's literary intention as the focus of our accountability, we must consistently and mercilessly engage in purging our interpretation of anything that cannot be defended as a part of his intention. This is arguably the most important statement in this book. For example, if there is no indication that the author would have been aware of a possible connection between Abraham's near-sacrifice of Isaac and the crucifixion of Jesus (see below, chap. 15), then consistency and accountability demand that we not make that part of our interpretation of Genesis. If the Old Testament authors show no awareness of the idea that the serpent is Satan (see below, chap. 6), consistency and accountability demand that we not make that part of our interpretation of the Old Testament. Whatever connection the New Testament author makes between the serpent and Satan (itself subject to variable interpretations) would become part of our interpretation of the New Testament texts, not superimposed on the Old Testament. In other words, we should do a contextual reading before we do a canonical reading.

CONTROLS

We therefore need to accept controls on our interpretation willingly. Such controls are found in the methodology that I am proposing throughout the book. Doing so does not mean that we are restraining the Bible; we need to restrain ourselves. Without controls, interpretation becomes more subjective than it inherently is, and we risk losing God's message entirely. Christian history is filled with examples of when this happened with devastating results: consider the Crusades, the Inquisition, Manifest Destiny, antebellum slavery, and the Holocaust, just to name a few of the more prominent cases—all justified by biblical interpretation without adequate controls.

4—Four Fundamental Concepts for Interpretation[6]

CONTEXT IS EVERYTHING

We all know that to understand a communication, we must take it in context. Most of us have experienced the discomfort of a situation where someone takes a few words that we have said and twists them into something that we never intended, with negative consequences. In the field of journalism, the journalistic ideal is that quoting someone will take account of the context. Words, phrases, and even paragraphs and narratives can be subject to misinterpretation if they are not considered in the context in which they are given.[7] A classic example of taking a biblical phrase out of context is when Genesis 31:49 is used for a benediction. The familiar text reads, "May the LORD keep watch between you and me when we are away from each other." When we consider the context, easily understood from the surrounding passage, this verse is an expression of distrust that calls on God to monitor Jacob's behavior for treachery and betrayal. The words cannot be commandeered and used for a blessing. Consider how much more disastrous this is when a couple has it engraved on their wedding rings!

Readers simply must consider contexts of various sorts. Here are summaries of the four most basic: linguistic, literary, cultural, and theological.

1. The *linguistic context* pertains to the task of understanding what a Hebrew, Aramaic, or Greek word meant to the person using that word and to the audience they addressed. Sometimes that cannot be reflected in a single English word. Moreover, sometimes there are particular nuances to its use in specific contexts, that is, authors and genres can each lend specialized meaning to particular words.

---

[6]These ideas are commonplace, but I was introduced to them as an entry point for interpretation by Nancy Bowen, Professor of Old Testament, Earlham School of Religion.

[7]For further reading, see Richard Schultz, *Out of Context: How to Avoid Misinterpreting the Bible* (Grand Rapids, MI: Baker, 2012).

Example A—*Hesed*: The Hebrew word *hesed* is translated in many different ways.[8] The 1995 NASB renders it "lovingkindness" while the NIV uses a variety of English equivalents, such as "unfailing love," "kindness," "acts of devotion," "favor," and "mercy."[9] The problem here is a common one in translation. It is not that translators disagree over the meaning of the word. Rather, to our frustration, there is no true English equivalent to *hesed*. Consequently, no choice can be considered entirely accurate. To represent the word well, we would need a whole sentence, such as, "*Hesed* is an act that fulfills an obligation; whether formal or informal, stated and agreed upon or inherent in the normal expectations of human interaction or protocol. It involves conforming to an understood expectation and, as such, reflects commitment to propriety." The closest English rendering may be "commitment,"[10] but even that fails to do it justice. Any English word chosen to translate *hesed* adds nuances that are not in the Hebrew word and also loses nuances that are inherent in the Hebrew word. This cannot be helped—it is a hazard of translation (and, therefore, of interpretation). As faithful interpreters, we need to be aware of this variable.

Example B—*Torah*: The Hebrew word *Torah* is often translated "law." A detailed analysis, however, recognizes that cultures in the ancient Near East were regulated by custom rather than by written legislation. This, added to linguistic analysis, suggests that Torah has more affinity to instruction that leads to wisdom than to legislation.[11] Again, the Hebrew word carries an array of nuances and connotations that are not present in any English word. These and many other examples that could be discussed demonstrate how important it is to understand the linguistic context of a text so that our understanding of the words coincides with what the ancient author and audience would have understood.[12]

2. The *literary context* pertains to issues of genre (such as proverbs), of form (for example, poetry), of rhetorical devices (such as metaphors), of

---

[8]Just check the variety of translations of Psalm 136, where it is used thematically in every verse, to see the variations.

[9]For a few examples, see Genesis 19:19; Exodus 15:13; 20:6; 34:6; Joshua 2:12; Ruth 1:8; 2 Samuel 7:15; 9:7; Psalms 23:6; 100:5; 136; Proverbs 19:22; Isaiah 54:8; Daniel 1:9; Hosea 6:6; Micah 6:8.

[10]John Goldingay, *Daniel*, 2nd ed. (Grand Rapids, MI: Zondervan, 2019), 463.

[11]For further reading, see John H. Walton and J. Harvey Walton, *The Lost World of the Torah* (Downers Grove, IL: IVP Academic, 2019).

[12]For a list of sixty such words, see the *NIV Cultural Backgrounds Study Bible* (Grand Rapids, MI: Zondervan, 2016), xix-xxvii.

discourse analysis (how a section is arranged to make a point), and of rhetorical strategy (how a writer will string together individual narratives to develop his purpose across the book—for example, the cycles of the book of Judges). When we read English literature, we are correct to have different expectations of epic poetry, like Tennyson's "Charge of the Light Brigade" versus a journal article on the Battle of Balaclava during the Crimean War, which Tennyson immortalized. Likewise, Longfellow's "The Midnight Ride of Paul Revere" must be evaluated differently than a college textbook's account of the beginning of the Revolutionary War.

> **Example—Job:** Consider the story of Job. The first observation is that this is a piece of Wisdom literature. Wisdom literature can use a variety of genres, and by its nature is not tied to the use of historical report (note that the parables are a form of Wisdom literature). Likewise, however, Wisdom literature could potentially use a historical figure. At the first level, then, a commitment to read literally does not resolve the issue of whether Job is a historical figure or not. Wisdom literature could go either way. But this is already an important observation in that it demonstrates that literal reading does not demand a commitment to the idea that Job is a historical figure.
>
> Some have considered Job to be a parable, and that is not impossible, though it is not common for a parable to name its characters.[13] An alternative is to consider the book of Job to be a "thought experiment." Thought experiments engage a complicated discussion through the use of a hypothetical scenario. Parables are a form of thought experiment, but Job could be a thought experiment that is not a parable. Using a thought experiment is a legitimate rhetorical device for engaging in philosophical discussions.

Beyond the question of genre, narrators make choices when telling a story—which details are important and how should the story be told? Furthermore, in a series of stories, such as those found in most narrative books of the Old Testament, the stories have been selected and recounted with a purpose in mind. Consequently, an individual narrative should be considered in relationship to those around it, not just as an independent

[13]The only possible exception in the Gospels is the story of Lazarus and the Rich Man, though some interpreters are reluctant to consider that a parable precisely because of the named character, Lazarus.

story (see chap. 25). All of these considerations and more are essential to understanding the literary context.

3. The *cultural context* pertains to the shared culture between the author and audience. It is particularly of significance when readers are not part of that culture and are not well-informed about it. Every communicative act between cultural insiders benefits from a multitude of "things that go without being said."[14] The problem is that when cultural outsiders attempt to step into that conversation, ignorance concerning those things that go without being said can undermine their ability to understand.

> **Example A—The Tower of Babel:** The story of the Tower of Babel is only nine verses long (Genesis 11:1-9). Interestingly, at one point, explanation is given to the original reading audience about building materials, presumably because that was important information that they did not intuitively know. Nevertheless, numerous other elements in the narrative are left unsaid, presumably because the original readers did not require explanations. Trouble arises when they are elements that we, as modern readers, do not know. Readers throughout the history of interpretation have, for example, been inclined to believe that the builders were constructing a tower to allow them to climb into heaven—that they were going to use the tower to go up. The author does not address this question of the function of the tower because his audience is well aware of its function—it is built for God to come down. Furthermore, outsiders have been inclined to think that "making a name" reflects an arrogant pride on the part of the builders. Here, however, the builders are guilty of greed more than of pride. If God comes down to dwell among them, the people believe that they will be able to take care of the God's needs and that he will therefore shower them with blessing and prosperity.[15]

Many passages in the Old Testament have been misinterpreted because we are outsiders to the ancient Israelite culture and therefore important cultural nuances are lost to us. In our ignorance, we are inclined to read into such texts our own understanding based on our own culture.

---

[14] A phrase used by E. Randolph Richards and Brandon O'Brien, *Misreading Scripture with Western Eyes: Removing Cultural Blinders to Better Understand the Bible* (Downers Grove, IL: InterVarsity Press, 2012).

[15] For further reading, Tremper Longman III and John H. Walton, *The Lost World of the Flood* (Downers Grove, IL: IVP Academic, 2018), 129-42.

> **Example B—The Sun in Joshua:** When we read Joshua 10:12-15, where the Israelite general requests that the sun and moon "stop" or "wait," we are immediately inclined to interpret in terms of physics and the laws of motion. Moreover, we assume that they have reached the end of the day and Joshua requests more daylight to complete his victory. We have missed the detail that the sun is over Gibeon and the moon over Aijalon—thus, sun in the east and moon in the west. It is therefore morning, not approaching evening. If we read this in its cultural context, we will set aside issues of physics (heavenly bodies coming to a grinding halt) and read it in light of divination literature. Several omens from the ancient Near East describe the position of the heavenly bodies as "waiting" or "stopping" at particularly significant locations in the sky when observing conjunctions or oppositions. These omens were understood as a means by which the gods communicated their will and intention. Joshua 10:12-15 is describing an event that would have had the significance of a divine omen to its original audience.[16] An insider audience would have recognized that; it did not need to be said.

We must recognize how distant our modern culture is from the ancient culture of Israel. In the globalization that is now characterized by more frequent interactions between cultures, we have recognized how challenging it is to communicate across those cultural boundaries. Furthermore, cultural change is happening so rapidly that we would find ourselves culturally challenged if we were to go back to live fifty years ago.[17] How much more should we then expect that reading literature from the ancient Israelite culture will present significant challenges that we must seek to overcome.

4. The *theological context* pertains at this level not to the theology of the whole canon or to the theology of the interpreter, as important as they are. Neither does it refer to systematic theology (the collection of our modern theological conclusions). Rather, I am referring to the theological

---

[16]For detailed interpretation and evidence, download the free appendix from www.ivpress.com/the-lost-world-of-the-israelite-conquest.

[17]This concept was developed in a TV series in the first decade of the twenty-first century titled "Life on Mars." A police detective in 2006 has been struck by a car and is in a coma. He nonetheless finds himself living in 1973 serving as a police detective. The plots frequently turn on how different police work and police conventions were in 1973—often producing a cultural vertigo for him.

presuppositions in the mindset of the ancient human author that often need to be distinguished from modern or New Testament theological ideas.

Example A—The Hope of Heaven: Though not all interpreters agree, many maintain that through most of the Old Testament, Israelites held no hope of salvation from sins or eternal life with God. If this is true, and I believe that it is, then Old Testament passages should not be interpreted with an assumption that Israelites had a hope of heaven (some individual passages will be addressed in chap. 29).

Example B—"The Devil": Contrary to popular assumptions, Israelite theology had no knowledge of the figure that we refer to as the "devil." The Hebrew term *satan* ("adversary") eventually was adopted as a proper name for the devil, but that was not the case in the Old Testament. Consequently, the interloper in Job 1–2, called "the satan," cannot be assumed to be the devil.[18] Israelite theology had a different idea in mind. Furthermore, passages like Isaiah 14:12-15 cannot be interpreted as referring to the fall of the devil. The devil is not known to them and therefore there is no fall of such a being to discuss.[19]

INTERPRETATION MATTERS

Interpretation cannot be considered just a hobby or something that we can do without. Our translated versions had to be interpreted before they could be translated. Any reader is automatically and inevitably interpreting. Meaning can only be identified through an interpretive act. If we were just reading Shakespeare or Homer, it might not matter that different readers would arrive at different interpretations. But for those who consider the Bible to be God's Word, interpretations of it can become the basis for life and faith, for action and belief, for values and priorities. Different interpretations and different methodologies can have significance not only for how an individual lives, but for how societies and movements take shape. The cost is high, and we cannot afford to treat interpretation lightly or to be nonchalant about it.

---

[18]The use of the definite article "the" serves as evidence that *satan* is not a proper name.

[19]For further reading, see John H. Walton and J. Harvey Walton, *Demons and Spirits in Biblical Theology* (Eugene, OR: Cascade, 2019), 212-28; John H. Walton, *Old Testament Theology for Christians* (Downers Grove, IL: IVP Academic, 2017), 196-207; John H. Walton and Tremper Longman III, *How to Read Job* (Downers Grove, IL: IVP Academic, 2015), 50-56.

Example—The Ten Commandments: One of the topics I often speak about is the Ten Commandments, and one of the first points I make is that the Bible never calls them that. They are the "Ten Words" (thus "Decalogue"). Does this mean that they are not "commandments"? If they are "words" instead of "commandments," how are we supposed to respond to them? We understand that "commandments" should be obeyed—but what about "words"? And it gets even more complicated when we begin looking at each of the ten "words." When the text says that no other gods are "before" me, does it refer to priority ("more important than me"), chronology ("existed earlier than me"), or location ("in my presence")? Most modern popular interpretation follows the first; the Hebrew favors the last. When the text says not to take the Lord's name in vain, does that mean that we should not treat it as having no real power (as people do when they use it in an exclamation, such as "Oh my God!") or that we should not seek to exploit its real power (as people do when they seek to use it in magic or ritual)? Modern interpretation is inclined toward the former; Israelite context toward the latter. In these cases, we have vastly different interpretations of something as basic as the "Ten Commandments"—which arguably play a central role in our understanding of ethics and morality.[20] Interpretation indeed matters!

MIND THE GAPS

Interpretation calls for us to fill in some sorts of gaps, while attempts to fill other sorts will only lead us astray. Some of the gaps that we must be aware of have already been mentioned. For example, as cultural outsiders, we will experience gaps that an insider would not. As interpreters, we need to be aware of such gaps and do our best to fill those gaps by research into the culture as we become aware of things that go without being said.

Another type of gap is the result of the author's focus. Authors are by necessity selective. They have chosen the story with a purpose, and they will tell it in such a way as to achieve their goal. That means that some elements of any reported event will be left out—with a reason. Interpreters may well be curious about some of those omitted details, but the

[20]For further reading, John H. Walton and J. Harvey Walton, *The Lost World of the Torah* (Downers Grove, IL: IVP Academic, 2019), 231-57.

interpretive task must focus on what the author *did* communicate. Trying to recover, or worse, speculatively provide that which the author has chosen *not* to communicate can mislead us. For example, we may be very interested in knowing how Abraham explained to Sarah what he was doing when he took Isaac to be sacrificed. But the author has not told us, and any ideas that we might have will not lead us to better interpretation.

Finally, we will encounter some gaps that represent literary art. Narrators at times purposefully leave something unsaid because they are expecting the audience to connect the dots successfully and draw conclusions. It takes careful assessment of subtle nuances to know how to fill these gaps because we can easily engage arguments from silence. Nevertheless, we want to do everything that we can to track with the author. That means that some gaps we work hard to fill, while others we resolutely allow to stand so as not to follow our own tangents.

IT'S COMPLICATED

Faithful interpretation is hard work because we cannot depend on our intuition. Interpretation of an ancient document written in another language and by those with a different culture is rarely straightforward. The task is complicated by many factors that must be considered, many of which this book addresses. Furthermore, many significant elements in interpretation depend on technical information. Some interpreters will be unaware of such technical issues and therefore not even know what they are leaving out of their consideration. Others will be aware of those elements but will find the details inaccessible to them. To some extent, this goes back to the idea of reading in community. Some members of a community may have more knowledge of technical issues than others will, but everyone will have something to contribute to the interpretation process. At the same time, we all have our own limitations.

> **Example—Genesis 6:1-4:** When we consider the brief passage in Genesis 6:1-4, we discover how complicated interpretation can be. Obvious questions arise: Who are these sons of God? Why does it call the women "daughters of men"? Who are the "Nephilim" in verse 4? Are they the sons of God

> referred to in verse 2? Are they their offspring? Who are the heroes? Other questions are less obvious. Most readers assume that the described events are taking place just before the flood and wonder how the flood is connected to them. Alternatively, the narrative style used in Genesis suggests that these verses take us all the way back to the time of Seth ("When human beings began to increase in number").[21] And it gets worse. In Yahweh's short speech in verse 3, presumably indicating the explanation for what is happening, two of the key words are unknown to us.[22] Furthermore, to what do the 120 years refer? Then we get to all the questions concerning the event itself. Are the sons of God heavenly beings who are marrying humans? Can that happen? Are we dealing with incubi? Are these heavenly council members? Are such beings real or mythological? The questions are unending and, for the most part, insoluble—and this is just a four-verse passage.[23]

Interpretation *is* complicated, but that must be weighed against an important point: the message of the Bible as a whole is clear. Any reader at any level can grasp the essentials of who God is and be drawn to follow him. Thankfully, then, the most important message of the text regarding God's plans and purposes, what he has done, and how we can become participants with him is all very clear for anyone who opens the Bible. The next section offers an introduction that focuses on what Scripture is doing and how it goes about doing it, which is developed in more detail throughout the book, and eventually revisited in the conclusions.

5—Five Principles for Faithful Interpretation

The basic ideas leading to faithful interpretation, which have been introduced in the preceding sections and will be developed in the remainder of the book, can be summarized as the following five principles.

---

[21]For further reading, see Tremper Longman III and John H. Walton, *The Lost World of the Flood* (Downers Grove, IL: IVP Academic, 2018), 122-28.

[22]The two unknown words are the verb describing what God's Spirit will not do and the preposition that leads into the sentence about being mortal.

[23]See the three-hundred-page monograph exploring the interpretive issues, Jaap Doedens, *The Sons of God in Genesis 6:1-4* (Leiden: Brill, 2019).

1. The author's message carries the authority of Scripture, and of God. When we depart from his literary intentions, we are no longer submitting our interpretation to the authority of the text.

2. The author's message is couched in his language and culture. We therefore need to be alert to the dangers of reading Scripture through our contemporary language and culture. We may not be able to recover certain details of his language and culture, but we can often recognize when we are driven by our own language and culture.

3. Our accountability in interpretation is to track with the author in the text that he has produced. It is what he says and what he means—his message—that matters because that comes with the authority of God.

4. Our interpretation should be supported with evidence that can identify the author's literary intentions. If an interpretation that we are considering cannot be defended as something the author could have meant, we should reconsider. As I have noted, that evidence is typically derived from analysis that is linguistic, literary, cultural, historical, and theological.

5. Our task is to find our place in God's story, which he has communicated so that we can know him and be in relationship with him, thereby becoming whole-hearted participants in his plans and purposes as he has revealed them in Scripture. Sometimes Christians wonder, "How can I know God?" We can find an answer to that if we think about how we come to know people in our lives. When you first meet someone, you introduce yourself—by telling a little part of your story. As you spend more time together, you each tell more of your story to each other. We know people through their stories—stories of their past, present, and future. The more of their story we know, and the more of ours we share, the deeper we grow in relationship. In the Bible, God has given us his story, and we come to know him and grow into deeper relationship with him as we encounter his story and share ours with him.

To be clear, in this book I am differentiating between "interpretation"—the process of determining what the authors of Scripture intended to communicate—and "application"—what we *do* with the message that is actually in the text once we understand it. We need to engage in interpretation to the best of our ability, using all the evidence that we can garner. Once we have identified the message the author intended to communicate (interpretation), we then need to appropriate it for ourselves and prayerfully seek wisdom to apply it to our lives and our world. Such application derives specifically from the message of the text—it is tethered to the text.

There is, however, a second type of application that is tangential to what the author was communicating rather than derived from it. Such untethered application may represent the Spirit's leading and can have great benefit. Much about Christian belief and the Christian life of faith is not addressed in Scripture, but it is important and should be addressed. My intention, therefore, is not to cut off all the insightful or inspiring thoughts that people have about Scripture that may not track with the author. But those thoughts should not be mistaken for biblical interpretation. The danger is that they will take the place of biblical interpretation and lead us to neglect the messages that carry the authority of the author and text.

If we neglect giving attention to the author's intentions and seek application only based on our intuitive reading of our translations, we risk running off the tracks to wander in the beautiful meadows of our own imaginations (see the illustration of *Tootle* in the preface). We may enjoy the meadows, but they don't get us where we need to go if we seek to understand the authoritative message of the Word of God (following the tracks). In contrast, so much stands to be gained when we follow the tracks laid down in the message of Scripture. Readers might understandably be interested in how we should go about doing application, but that is not what this book is about—I am going to focus my attention on doing interpretation.

SECTION B

GENERAL BIBLE

This unit will discuss a dozen phrases that all have to do with how we arrive at the meaning of the text. The introduction laid out the challenges of discerning meaning as well as the importance of doing so. It introduced the idea of tracking with the author's intentions. What follows will unpack a variety of perspectives pertaining to this quest. These phrases are not intended to sustain a single line of argumentation. Instead, they offer perspectives on different aspects of interpretation, including diverse elements connected to cultural awareness, reading approaches, literary sensitivity, translation, literary production, the role of Jesus in the Old Testament text, and the role of the Holy Spirit in our reading. These guidelines are only loosely connected to one another but each offer insights that are essential for faithful interpretation.

6—A Text Cannot Mean What It Never Meant

I originally encountered this caution in the classic volume by Gordon Fee and Douglas Stuart, *How to Read the Bible for All Its Worth*: "Biblical texts first of all mean what they meant. That is, we believe that God's Word for us today is first of all precisely what his Word was to them."[1] Fee and Stuart

[1]Gordon D. Fee and Douglas Stuart, *How to Read the Bible for All Its Worth* (Grand Rapids, MI: Zondervan, 1981), 13. Note, these page numbers are from the original edition; subsequent editions

then present the inverse of that statement as what they call the "basic rule": "a text cannot mean what it never could have meant to its author or his readers."[2] As Fee and Stuart clarified decades ago, this phrase refers to the first step in interpretation. It does not deny that there are other steps to be taken as we then appropriate the Bible's message for ourselves and seek application. Nevertheless, the success and effectiveness of all the other steps depends on and is controlled by that first step. To the extent that the other steps diverge from the first step is the extent to which the authority of the text is potentially compromised.

These "other" steps are variably labeled re-appropriation, reception, relevance, application, or contemporary significance. (Note that the kind of appropriation I will address throughout this book is distinct from "cultural appropriation," which can arise when there is power differential between a dominant and an oppressed culture, as in colonial or imperial systems.) These steps, however, are more accurately understood as dealing with "significance" for our lives rather than "meaning." The confusion between the two is reflected in the question so often posed in modern Bible studies, "What does this verse mean to me?" This expression is unfortunate because it could imply that "meaning" is purely subjective. In contrast, the "meaning" that we seek in faithful interpretation attempts to avoid subjectivity as much as possible. It is well recognized that subjectivity cannot be avoided entirely, or, to put it another way, that total objectivity is impossible. Nevertheless, we strive for something approaching objectivity, not by successfully erasing all aspects of our culture and presuppositions, or by eliminating our personal biases, but by basing our interpretations on evidence rather than impressions or feelings.

Evidence is the foundation for faithful interpretation. As indicated in the introduction, the strongest interpretation is going to be the one with the strongest evidence. If the authors carry the authority vested in them by

---

(the fourth edition was in 2014) may have different pagination. I should note that many of the ideas in this present book were already being articulated by Fee and Stuart. I learned much from their book early in my career and would recommend it to anyone seeking to be a faithful interpreter. Many aspects of my interpretation methodology began with them and have been filtered now through forty years of teaching.

[2]Fee and Stuart, *How to Read the Bible*, 60.

God and we are therefore accountable to them, the "meaning" that is of most interest to us is the author's meaning, not what it means to us. To put it another way, the meaning for those *to* whom it was originally written has significance *for* those of us interested readers in other times, places, and cultures (see next chapter).

This phrase also conveys another important implication: the *meaning* does not change, even though the application and contemporary significance might. When we understand the meaning as located in the intentions of the authors, we realize that it therefore does not take a new shape for every reader or every era. It is always worthwhile to explore ever-new significances that a text might have, but any assertion of significance must be rooted in that one, original meaning. Otherwise, the identified significance would forfeit its claim to represent the Word of God.

This concept remains true as the New Testament authors work with Old Testament texts, even prophecies. The New Testament authors are indicating a contemporary *significance* to the Old Testament texts; they rarely seek to unpack the *meaning* of those texts from their original contexts. Nevertheless, when the New Testament authors do this, their words carry authority as they have new inspired messages to offer—new affirmations. Consequently, as we will discuss in detail later (chap. 34), the fulfillments identified by New Testament authors constitute identification of significance of the prophecies, not identification of the meaning of the prophecies. As the New Testament authors unfold the fulfillments of prophecies in ways that the Old Testament authors could not have imagined or intended, they are not changing the meaning. Consequently, when we are interpreting Old Testament texts that are later addressed in the New Testament, our first level of commitment is to the intentions of the Old Testament authors and the meaning that they intended. What the New Testament authors did with them will become the focus at later stages of studying the passage.

We are now able to expand on this guideline. The text can never mean what it never meant, yet its significance can transcend that original meaning. If the *meaning* is discovered by seeking out and weighing evidence, how is a proposed *significance* of a text validated? When the significance is presented in the New Testament, it is validated by virtue of the authority recognized for the New Testament authors. When other interpreters who do not possess an innate authority (such as any of us who are not New Testament authors!) present a new significance, the proposed significance does not carry the authority attributed to the biblical text, yet it still may be deemed true based on any number of criteria.

Figure 6.1. Truth and authority

This statement suggests yet another distinction to be made: When we recognize the authority of the text, one of the implications is that we accept it as true. But when we accept something as true, that is not the same thing as considering it authoritative. Truth is a larger concept than authority, but authority is totally encompassed in truth.[3]

Our applications may reflect keen insight and ring true in every respect, but that does not mean that they have authority. In fact, even our interpretations do not carry authority—they represent only our best attempts to discern the authoritative meaning of the author. They are based on evidence, but they are subject to any number of possible misconceptions and are undermined by the imperfect degree of our evidence. We are not native speakers of the language; we are not members of the culture; we are often hampered by unrecognized preconceptions. Consequently, we may have good reason to consider a given interpretation true, but that does not mean that our interpretation carries authority.

By now the reader has recognized the problem: How then can we ever claim to understand or speak the authority of the text? If any reference we make to the text reflects an interpretation of the text, then we can never make unqualified statements concerning its authoritative message. This is not as hopeless as it sounds. It calls for humility, rather than despair; for an

[3]Here, I am using authority specifically within the realm of biblical affirmations. One's government or one's employer (even one's parents) may have authority, but they are not always true.

attitude of open-mindedness, rather than an unrelenting fanaticism on minutia. We can be committed to orthodoxy, sound doctrine, and the innate authority of Scripture while at the same time recognizing that we may occasionally have to change our mind about the interpretation of a particular passage. Another way to say this is that we ought always to be in a frame of mind in which we welcome being surprised by the text and maintain a willingness to see new evidence to factor into our interpretations. We make every attempt to track with the author and to gather all available evidence and weigh it carefully. Hopefully the basic theory is clear, but a few examples can illustrate the potential pitfalls.

Example A—Genesis 3: In Genesis 3 we are introduced to the serpent in the garden. When we read that text through Israelite eyes and in the context of the Old Testament, we find no evidence that they considered the serpent associated in any way with Satan. It is neither identified as Satan nor understood as somehow empowered by Satan. Since this is true, our interpretation of this passage should not be based on the idea that Satan is the serpent or behind the serpent's actions. The text can never mean what it never meant. That does not mean that the New Testament references that draw associations between Satan and the serpent (Revelation 12:9; 20:2) are misguided. There Satan is portrayed with the metaphor of a dragon (by definition, as a serpent). It is likely that John is drawing a parallel to Genesis 3 as he builds his apocalyptic imagery, but this hardly offers interpretation of that passage. Whatever we are able to draw from John's imagery, it does not change the meaning of Genesis 3. Discerning what an Israelite reader would have inferred about the serpent is not a matter of consensus among interpreters. One recent option has suggested that they would have viewed it as a chaos creature.[4] Regardless, its role as a catalyst is clear in the passage. Its comments instigate the decision of Eve, then Adam, to eat the fruit in order to be like God. This stops short of accusing the serpent of being the cause of sin, which in turn can fine-tune some of our theological discussions about the origin of evil.

[4]Richard E. Averbeck, "Ancient Near Eastern Mythography as It Relates to Historiography in the Hebrew Bible: Genesis 3 and the Cosmic Battle," in *The Future of Biblical Archaeology: Reassessing Methodologies and Assumptions*, ed. J. K. Hoffmeier and A. R. Millard (Grand Rapids, MI: Eerdmans, 2004), 328-56.

Example B—Genesis 3:15: Genesis 3:15 has traditionally been interpreted as a Messianic prophecy,[5] so we might explore the evidence for such an interpretation, first in the Old Testament, then in the New Testament. In the context of Genesis, one of the first questions that is typically asked concerns the use of the singular with regard to the seed. It is a complicated question, since the Hebrew term translated "seed" is a collective term, which means that it can legitimately use singular grammatical forms even if it refers to a large group. Interpreters have been divided on this issue.

More important for our current discussion is the question of the verbs that are used to convey the conflict between the two parties at the end of the verse. The NIV translates them as "crush" and "strike" respectively. The ESV and NASB render both as "bruise" and NLT and NRSV render both as "strike." Those translations that render both verbs the same are reflecting the Hebrew, which also uses the same verb in both clauses. Presumably, the NIV has chosen to use different translations to account for the combination of the verb with different nouns (head, heel) in the context. For our purposes, it should be noted that not only are the verbs the same, but both attacks constitute potentially mortal blows; the serpent may be killed when someone steps on its head, and a person may be killed when a poisonous serpent bites their heel. What is important about this is that the text does not indicate who will win. Consequently, when we consider what the verse meant to the author and audience, we find no reason to think that it indicates an act of deliverance from the power of Satan. Recall from our last example that the Old Testament audience would not have considered the serpent to represent Satan anyway. The conclusion of all of this is that there is nothing here that would indicate that the Old Testament author or audience would have understood this verse as messianic, or even hopeful. It expresses instead that the conflict that has now begun will be ongoing.

But what about the New Testament? Readers may find it odd to learn that this verse is never referred to directly in the New Testament. If Genesis 3:15 were to be considered the first proclamation of the gospel in the Bible (as has been often claimed), it might seem curious that the New Testament did not

[5]See many discussions and a strong defense in P. Williamson and R. Cefalu, eds., *The Seed of Promise: The Sufferings and Glory of the Messiah: Essays in Honor of T. Desmond Alexander* (Wilmore, KY: GlossaHouse, 2020).

draw attention to it in some way. A verse that is sometimes offered as a possible reference to Genesis 3:15 in the New Testament is Romans 16:20. There, in his final greetings (and therefore not in a teaching passage), Paul indicates that "The God of peace will soon crush Satan under your feet." Given this translation, it is no surprise that some have drawn a connection to Genesis 3:15, but important qualifications are called for. First, if it is a reference to Genesis 3:15, it actually refutes the idea that Genesis 3:15 is messianic. In Romans 16:20, the foot that crushes Satan is the church at Rome (empowered by "the God of peace"), not Jesus. But second, and more importantly, the connection to Genesis 3:15 is not as clear as it may seem on two counts. First, the Greek word Paul uses for the verb "crush" in Romans 16:20 is not the same one that his Greek translation of the Old Testament used in Genesis 3:15. If Paul wanted to make the connection, it would have been logical that he would use the Greek verb familiar from that passage. Second, Paul does not speak of crushing under the *heel* as Genesis 3:15 does, but under the *foot*. That is actually an important distinction because the idea of placing enemies under one's feet is a widespread idiom throughout the ancient and classical worlds (see Psalm 110:1). Consequently, Paul may not be referring to Genesis 3:15, but if he is, he is not interpreting it in a messianic way. But even if someone might still believe he is, the Old Testament text can never mean what it never meant. Consequently, when we read Genesis 3:15 as a messianic prophecy, we are not tracking with the author's intentions, and we may not even be reflecting a New Testament interpretation.

7—The Bible Is Written for Us but Not to Us

Most Bible readers know that when they are reading the Bible, they are reading a translation from ancient Hebrew, Aramaic, or Greek. That reality, however, does not always lead to the recognition that therefore the Bible was not written to us. That is, the audience assumed by the author is one that shared his language and culture. Nevertheless, since we believe that the Bible is God's revelation to all people everywhere, we can affirm that it is written for us—for everyone.

Consequently, however, a significant gap exists between that original audience (to them) and all the thousands of other audiences (for us) who have received it. An author may hope that his work will have an audience that extends beyond his initial target group. For example, many of my books are translated into other languages, so I anticipate that my reading audience may extend beyond those in my own culture. Even with that in mind, however, I cannot write to those audiences. I cannot write in their language, and I cannot tailor my content to all of those cultures. Furthermore, should any of my work last into future generations, I likewise cannot anticipate the issues and concerns of those future generations. In this regard, the biblical authors were no different. Ancient Hebrew authors would not be expected to include content that might address social networks, climate change, party politics, capitalism, individualism, evolutionary biology, an expanding universe, nihilism, communism, consumerism, and so on—all the varied aspects of our modern world. They could not anticipate Christianity, Islam, Hinduism, Buddhism, or any other religious system. We could not expect them to address modern values, philosophy, medicine, economics, or politics, or to understand how we think about history, science, or law, let alone our views about reality or existence. Our values and sensibilities, even our categories of thinking, would be as foreign to them as theirs would be to us.

It is important to accept that God did not somehow mystically bridge this gap and implant culture-specific messages to "outsider" readers without the awareness of the authors. The authoritative message of God was understood by the author who was communicating it and he expected his audience to be able to understand it and respond to it.[6] We can therefore say that even though the message was culturally bound in some ways, it also has the capacity to transcend culture. If we desire to receive the full impact of the message that transcends its cultural context, we cannot expect the author and text to traverse the distance to us; we must make every attempt to approach the text through the language and culture of the author.

---

[6]Fulfillment of prophecy is no exception. It is true that the prophets did not know how their prophecies would be fulfilled, but the fulfillment is different from the message (see below, chap. 34), and the message was always known to the prophet.

For the language, we have gotten used to closing the distance through the act of translation. Though translation will always be an imperfect instrument, it bridges the linguistic gulf adequately. Our efforts, however, cannot stop there—we also need to bridge the gap culturally. Just as the ancient Israelites would have been ignorant of our culture, so we are not able to penetrate their culture intuitively. Bridging the language barrier requires a translator; bridging the culture barrier requires a cultural broker. A cultural broker has familiarity with both cultures engaged in cross-cultural communication.

The conceptual world of the Israelites would have been more similar to that of the ancient Babylonians or Egyptians than to ours. Consequently, it is ineffective to begin with our modern culture as the default and try to adjust to the ways an ancient Israelite culture would be similar or different. It is more prudent to start with those ancient cultures as the default for Israel and then make adjustments for the ways in which God's revelation transformed them. In other words, we should proceed by assuming that Israelites would think more like those around them instead of assuming that they would think more like us. We can then identify differences between Israelites and their neighbors based on the revelation that God gives them.

> **Example A—Equality:** Modern Western readers feel very strongly about equality—equal rights and equal status (race, gender, etc.). It is a value to which we give high priority, and it intuitively strikes us as proper. We maintain that order can only be achieved when prejudices and inequalities are eliminated. But this is not how people in the ancient world thought. For them, hierarchy brought order. Ruling structures in the nation, village, and family were desired and represented normality. Attitudes that we may consider misogynous they would consider as representing legitimate roles. What we decry as slavery they would defend as essential to a functioning agro-pastoral economic system. Not only must we avoid imposing our values on them, we should be slow to criticize them for the values that they hold in high esteem. Though we may find much to critique about human institutions, we dare not allow our interpretation to become a form of cultural imperialism. If we can agree that the Bible is not written to us, we recognize that we must discern as

clearly as possible what it meant to them before we can understand what it means for us.

Example B—Samuel's Call: When we read the story of Samuel's call in the night (1 Samuel 3), we can easily miss an important aspect of the narrative. God's call to Samuel is not a general call to be a faithful follower that any of us might experience. This is Samuel's call to a prophetic ministry, evident from the fact that he is given a prophetic message to give to Eli. The word of the Lord was rare in those days (1 Samuel 3:1), and Samuel is being called to fill that void. Consequently, the message for us cannot be construed as reflecting on how important it is to listen to God when he calls. True as that might be, that is not the message to them. The incident is critical to the case that is being made by the narrator of 1–2 Samuel, that David is God's chosen king. Any king would claim that he is chosen of God, so how can an observer reach such a conclusion? For the narrator, the evidence that David is God's chosen king is that he was anointed by Samuel, and Samuel is a legitimate prophet. Samuel's credentials also include his unlikely birth and his priestly training.

The message to them concerns Samuel's impeccable credentials as a bona fide prophet whose anointing of David came at the command of the Lord (and against Samuel's intuitive judgment), thus validating David's claim to being Yahweh's sanctioned king. The message for us must therefore be based on that understanding. As we track with the narrator of the books of Samuel, we acknowledge Samuel's prophetic credentials, accept therefore that it is truly God's leading for him to anoint David, and accept that, despite David's lack of credentials and various shortcomings that will eventually become all too clear, he is God's choice for king. We therefore should not find in the message some exhortation that we should all listen for God's voice in the night. The authoritative lesson is that God is working out his plans and purposes through Samuel and David. We discover that God is able to do his work even through confused or flawed people.

Example C—Job 19:25: Consider the well-known passage Job 19:25, where the suffering Job declares, "I know that my redeemer lives!" Many English translations through the centuries have capitalized Redeemer, as they have interpreted the term to refer to Jesus. Christian readers, seeing the capital letter, can therefore be excused for understanding the text to refer to Job's hope, anticipating the redeeming work of Christ. Nevertheless, if we are accountable to the author's intentions, such an interpretation cannot be sustained. The Hebrew term Job uses, *go'el*, refers to a particular social role within Israel. When someone in the family was wronged (generally in legal matters, but not limited to that), the *go'el* would work to set things right, usually by recovering that which had been taken.

Job cannot possibly have Jesus in mind, nor would his immediate audience have any knowledge of Jesus. We cannot broaden out further and suggest that this is a general reference to Messiah as redeemer, because that role of Messiah is not easily identified in the Old Testament. We cannot even say that Job is expressing the need for someone like Jesus. In contrast, when we attend to the words and culture of the author, we recognize that Job is not looking for someone to take the punishment for his offenses. He has steadfastly insisted on his innocence. He is looking for someone who will vindicate him—to demonstrate that he is righteous, not to impute righteousness on him. He is looking for vindication, not justification, and the work of Christ is not designed to bring about vindication for people.[7]

The message for us cannot focus on the role of Jesus because that is not the message to them and, in fact, goes an entirely different direction. The message to them concerns the complex issue of Job's vindication. In one sense, Job is vindicated already in the opening lines of the book, both by the narrator and by God. In like manner, Job's restoration at the end of the book could stand as vindication. Nevertheless, Job's quest for vindication in the midst of his suffering is not commended, because the vindication that he imagines would come at God's expense. Job demands a hearing with God to prove that Job's suffering was undeserved and that therefore God was in the wrong. That is what his *go'el* was supposed to demonstrate. Job's insistence then reflects a flawed view of God. The ultimate message is that we should not follow Job's example and press claims against God when we feel that he has treated us unfairly. We cannot domesticate God to conform to our unfounded beliefs about what he owes us. In this interpretation we can see that not only is the message not about Jesus; it warns us against acting like Job by pitting our own self-righteousness against God. Job 40:8 makes it clear that Job is not commended for this behavior, and we should beware of it in ourselves.

[7]For further reading, see John H. Walton and Tremper Longman III, *How to Read Job* (Downers Grove, IL: IVP Academic, 2015), 74-78.

These examples help us to understand how different our interpretation might be in some instances from what the ancient Israelite audience would have had. If our interpretations depart from those that the original author and audience would have had, we are no longer tethered to the text. In such cases, there could be no claim to the authority of the text since we have wandered away from its affirmations—the subject of the next chapter.

8—Reading the Bible Instinctively Is Not Reliable and Risks Imposing a Foreign Perspective on the Text

Once we recognize that the text never means what it never meant, and that it is not written to us but to those of a different culture and language, we realize that our intuitions for reading Scripture may not serve us well. Many people read their Bibles the same way that people read their horoscopes. They look for some phrase to jump out at them that they can use as a bridge to their circumstances or to the thoughts running through their minds that they can then mine for working through the issues that they face. They are often then inclined to consider this something that "God gave them" or that "the Spirit impressed on them" to give them guidance. Maybe it is; but that is not what interpreting the Bible means. Someone may be able to claim that God gave that thought to them (and who could say it isn't so?), but God could give them similar prompts when they are reading Tolkien, Shakespeare, or even the Sunday comics. The point is, whatever happened in that moment of insight is not what Scripture is for, nor is it how Scripture delivers its truth or authority.

The truth of Scripture is not delivered to readers when they simply open their minds to any random thought that passes through it. Our instincts are unavoidably modern and therefore our search for relevance and meaning will inevitably reflect our context. It is true that since the message of the Bible is for us, we eventually want to understand its relevance in our modern context. The problem is that if we proceed directly to that question without first interrogating the text as to its meaning in its original context, we run the risk of imposing ideas on the text that are foreign to it and thereby missing or at least distorting the message that was there.

To return to an example that we used earlier, if a reader opens to the account of the tower builders in Genesis 11 and interprets the building project as an act of pride, he or she may feel convicted that they have been guilty of pride and resolve to nurture humility in their attitudes. It may well be that the reader suffers from pride and that they would do well to address it. But if, as I previously suggested, the offense of the builders is not pride, then the reader has not received the message of the text. Instead, they have imposed their intuitive reading on the text (a combination of tradition and the interpretation of translators), which, as it turns out, is foreign to the text rather than representative of it.

Our own culture and context do not feel foreign to us, so we often do not recognize that our reading can introduce distortion. In contrast, the ancient context seems foreign to us. So, for example, when I speak of understanding the Old Testament in light of the ancient Near East, people at times argue that I am imposing something foreign on the text. After all, the Old Testament is distinct from the polytheistic mythology of the ancient world. This is true, but I am not claiming that the Bible should be read on a par with other literature from the ancient world.

The Israelites lived in the ancient world and thought like people of their time thought. Consequently, it would be impossible to impose that culture on them. At the same time, we recognize that Israelites were supposed to be learning to think differently from the cultures around them in certain very specific ways.

> **Example—The Temple:** Israelites built temples for the same reasons that Babylonians or Egyptians built temples (housing the presence of God and interacting with him). That is not anything like why Jews today build temples or why Christians today build churches. Moreover, the Israelite rituals and worship in those temples would have looked very similar to the Canaanite or Assyrian worship in their temples. Nevertheless, even though they built temples for the same reasons, and their worship practices looked quite similar,

the Israelites were supposed to think about their God in very different terms. It is not imposing something foreign on the Old Testament text to understand how their temples and rituals were similar to that of their neighbors. Modern readers do not intuitively understand those systems, so we are likely to misunderstand the texts by imposing our foreign ideas on it. But we would also be imposing something foreign to the text if we failed to recognize how Israel was different from her neighbors.

As an analogy, consider the Hebrew language in which most of the Old Testament is written. Calling attention to the meanings of Hebrew words is not imposing something foreign on the text of the Old Testament. Hebrew cannot be imposed on the text—it was written in Hebrew! Resolutely maintaining the shape of our English translations even when Hebrew suggests a fine-tuning would be imposing something foreign (our English translation) on the text. At the same time, if we were to insist that we modify the Hebrew and read as if it were written in Canaanite, that would likewise result in distortion. Yet, if we could learn more about an obscure Hebrew phrase from information that we had about Canaanite, that could be helpful.

Example—Genesis 1:2: In Genesis 1:2 the NIV, ESV, and NLT all indicate that the spirit of God was "hovering" over the waters. A modern reader might immediately begin to meditate on a derived promise of God that the Holy Spirit "hovers" over us. But that jump already betrays several disconnects. First, it is a serious mistake to take Genesis 1:2 as a promise—nothing in the text suggests that. Second, it does not say that the Spirit hovers over us. In fact, that would be a theological misunderstanding since the Spirit dwells in us. Third, it may well be that the reference is to the Holy Spirit, but that is not a given. Evidence is lacking to demonstrate that the Israelites considered the spirit of the Lord to be the third person of the Trinity (see chap. 29, example one, for the discussion of "spirit of the Lord"). If we are interpreting with accountability to the author's intentions, we could not work with that assumption.[8] Fourth, however, the translation "hovering" is much in doubt. An alternative is that in Genesis 1:2 the Spirit of God (however that is understood

[8]Note that the NRSV says, "a wind from God swept over the face of the waters."

> theologically), might be waiting and preparing in anticipation of involvement in creation.[9] There is no good English word for that, but careful study would alert the reader that focusing on the Holy Spirit in our lives, or on the verb translated "hovering," would not lead to the message of the text. Furthermore, we are given no information regarding what role is being played by the spirit, and we cannot rely on our speculations to lead us to truth.

It would make no sense to claim that Hebrew is being *imposed* on the Old Testament—since it is written in Hebrew. Similarly, we can hardly *impose* the ancient Near East on the Old Testament—since Israelites are ancient Near Easterners. Nevertheless, sometimes false assumptions could be made in the process (for example, assuming that since ancient Near Eastern creation accounts are mythological, Israelite creation accounts must be mythological).

We can avoid creating problems by making an important distinction. We have seen that the Israelites and the Old Testament are *embedded* in the ancient world (their cultural context), and we should not be surprised by that fact. That, however, does not mean that the Old Testament is *indebted* to other pieces of ancient literature. Here I am referring to an often-heard claim that some parts of the Old Testament have drawn heavily on particular pieces of Babylonian or Egyptian literature, adopting it and adapting it to be their own.[10] Indebtedness is a more complex position than embeddedness and requires much more evidence to demonstrate, which is often not available or is, at least, highly interpretive. We can safely set the indebtedness question aside and focus on the unquestionable issue of embeddedness. This can help us to realize that we need to resist the easy approach of just reading the text intuitively from our own cultural worldview and make whatever attempt is possible to read it from an ancient worldview.

---

[9]This is based on a technical linguistic study. For more detail see my more extensive discussion in "The Ancient Near Eastern Background of the Spirit of the Lord in the Old Testament," in *Presence, Power, and Promise: The Role of the Spirit of God in the Old Testament*, ed. D. Firth and P. Wegner (Nottingham: Inter-Varsity Press, 2011), 38-67.

[10]Most often this is claimed for the creation account (Genesis 1), the flood account (Genesis 6–8), Psalm 29, and Proverbs 22:17–24:22 (see Instruction of Amenemope). For further reading, see John H. Walton, *Ancient Israelite Literature in Its Cultural Context* (Grand Rapids, MI: Zondervan, 1989), 34-42; 165-66; 192-97.

We can never hope to achieve full knowledge of the ancient world, but we can nurture an awareness that reading from our own culture can introduce distortions. This can lead us to the regular discipline of trying to set aside those elements in our interpretation that reflect our modern questions and issues. The more we can accomplish that, the more successful we can be at asking their questions and seeking the answers that they have given. We will be more faithful interpreters if we can avoid imposing our foreign, modern perspectives on the text as we try to be more accountable to the author's focus and intention. In this way, his affirmations can be free to emerge with the authority God has given him. To circle back to Genesis 1:2, that means that whatever actions are included in the spirit's (Spirit?) action, what we draw from it is that God's plans and purposes were being actively carried out even as God crafted the cosmos—designed to serve God's own purposes.

9—Literal Reading Means Being Accountable to the Ancient Author's Literary Intentions

The introduction proposed that readers' accountability is to the author's literary intentions, or what could be called his communicative intentions, and the previous chapters indicated that those intentions are founded in the author's language and culture. This chapter moves to the next insight into accountability: any talk about reading the Bible "literally" properly refers to tracking with the author's intentions. A "literal" reading will take account of the literary, linguistic, and cultural aspects of the author's communication.

Many Bible readers today declare that they are committed to reading the Bible literally. That is a value that I would also espouse, but we must all unpack the idea carefully. One of the most important elements in literal reading is that we should be careful to read a text in light of its genre and rhetorical devices (consider the example of the book of Job already discussed above in chap. 4). When we claim to read the Bible literally, we are not claiming that it contains no rhetorical devices or figurative genres. To ignore those would constitute a "flat" or "wooden" reading.

> **Example A—Parables:** A parable is a figurative genre. Jesus used the genre to good effect, yet it required careful thought. We could say that his message is literally true, but it is contained within a figurative device. He did not expect his listeners to search far and wide for the Good Samaritan and interview him about what he did. There is no Good Samaritan, although all should aspire to be like him; there is no prodigal son, although perhaps we might catch glimpses of him in the mirror. We read these literally when we recognize that they are parables and treat them as the sort of literature they were intended to be.
>
> **Example B—Psalms:** The psalmist uses many rhetorical devices. When he praises God for being his rock, literal reading does not lead us to ask whether God is sedimentary or metamorphic. If something is a metaphor, reading literally requires that we read it as a metaphor and interpret it in accordance with its metaphorical meaning.

In another sort of contrast, a literal reading is to be distinguished from one that sees pervasive codes or secret symbolism and would include allegorical readings (of works not written as allegories). The Reformers referred to this as the "plain" reading of Scripture.[11] We do not want to make the mistake of reading a historical report as a metaphor. Faithful interpretation would not reduce the parting of the Red Sea to a figurative idea if it were not intended that way by the author. Literal reading reflects a commitment to read the text as the author intended for it to be read—the plain reading (as opposed to mystical readings or spiritualizations). Often this is straightforward, but not always.

> **Example—Daniel 11:** A particularly tricky example of understanding rhetorical devices is found in Daniel 11. Here it is clear that a rhetorical device is being adopted by the narrator as he recounts a number of events of the fifth through second century BC. The question is whether (1) the rhetorical device features a series of selected events of the future framed prophetically and in

[11] For further reading, Iain Provan, *The Reformation and the Right Reading of Scripture* (Waco, TX: Baylor University Press, 2017), 81-106.

vague terms (for example, a king of the north will arise) or (2) the rhetorical device features events of the past framed as future. In either case, it is unlike any other piece of literature known in Scripture and, therefore, without biblical precedent. If it is the second, it is well-attested in both ancient and classical literatures of antiquity, whereas the first is not. Those who favor the first view claim that the second view would constitute deception and would therefore be unacceptable in the Bible. Those who hold the second view contend that it is not deception if it is using a well-recognized rhetorical device, and that if we fail to read it as events of the past framed as future and instead read it the way those who favor the first view insist it was intended to be read, then we are not reading the text literally. Regardless of which rhetorical device one identifies as the author's, the point is that one has to make every attempt to understand the rhetorical devices that are used in order to interpret properly.

All of this means that as readers, we must do the necessary work to understand how the author intended his work to be read. As already mentioned in the last section, our own intuition might work against us, especially since we might not intuitively recognize ancient genres and the conventions that they use. We need to set our cultural ideas aside and do all that we can to understand what the author is doing. Again, that may mean that we need to learn more about how certain genres work in the ancient Near East and what rhetorical devices they tended to use. For example, we cannot use our own inclinations about what apocalyptic literature is and how it should be read. We need to understand how apocalyptic literature was used and functioned in the ancient world (more about this in chapters 32 and 33).

Compounding the challenge, certain genres might not work the same in the ancient world as they do in ours. When we think about historical reports, we do so with a certain idea of what "history" is and why people would write about the past. Upon further study, we may discover that people in the ancient world had a far different set of conventions and purposes as they wrote about the past. We are not doing justice to literal reading if we are imposing our conventions and purposes of history writing on the ancient authors. We must try to think about the past as they thought about the past. Literal reading means tracking with the author in every possible way.

When we move from the question of genre and rhetoric to the words themselves, our task gets even more complicated. It does not take much thought to realize that at the level of words, we cannot really read the text literally if we are reading it in translation. Words in a target language (for example, English) are only rough approximations of the words in the source language (for example, Hebrew). We will discuss the challenges of translation below (chap. 12). For now, it is important to recognize that reading the words of the English translation literally will not necessarily result in sound interpretation and may even mislead us.[12] We have already encountered a few examples (such as *redeemer* in Job 19:25). As rough approximations, the English word in a biblical passage may be only one of a number of words that could have been chosen by translators. Perhaps in some contexts, one option would suit better, whereas in another context we might choose a different option.

Example: *'arum*: Consider the Hebrew word *'arum* in Genesis 3:1, describing the serpent.

- KJV: more subtle
- NIV, ESV, NRSV: more crafty
- NLT, JPS: shrewdest of all
- NASB: more cunning
- CEB: most intelligent
- GW, Message: more clever

Which one are you going to read "literally"? It will not do to just read literally whatever your translation has. It is natural that we would want to ask, What does the *Hebrew* term actually mean? All ten other occurrences of this Hebrew word are in Wisdom literature (two in Job, the rest in Proverbs) and, as in the above sample translations, contexts can suggest a positive, negative, or neutral trait. That must be taken into account. We may also find that some of the above translations will suit some contexts better, while others will seem more appropriate for other contexts. This is not unusual. Nevertheless, none

[12]This practice is represented when someone says, "If we look up the word in Webster's dictionary, we will find . . ." This is not productive—we are not interested in the English word and Webster's will not help us interpret the biblical text better.

of those English words is a perfect equivalent for Hebrew *'arum*, though all catch pieces of it. There is no English word that is a perfect equivalent that works in all contexts and that covers all the exact nuances of the Hebrew. Therefore, no matter which English term our translator chose, interpreting that particular English term literally will be unproductive. Literal reading requires an understanding of what the Hebrew communicator wished to communicate with the word he chose.[13]

Understanding a word like this accurately requires a paragraph description since no English word carries the same combination of nuances. On this word, Ziony Zevit proposes the following explanation (note, not possible in a simple word translation):

> People who are *'arum* conceal what they feel and what they know. They esteem knowledge and plan how to use it in achieving their objectives; they do not believe everything they hear; they know how to avoid trouble and punishment. In sum, they are shrewd and calculating, willing to bend and torture the limits of acceptable behavior but not to cross the line into illegality. They may be unpleasant and purposely misleading in speech but are not out-and-out liars. They know how to read people and situations and how to turn their readings to advantage. A keen wit and a rapier tongue are their tools.[14]

If we desire to read literally, that is the sort of meaning that we must understand. But none of the various English interpretations say this. This is not to say that it would be preferable to put a whole paragraph like this in our translations; it is only to point out the challenge that translators and translations face. Comparing translations can be helpful, but it would not resolve issues like this one.

Another problem that can arise in trying to interpret words literally is that at times several different Hebrew words are translated by one English word, yet each of the Hebrew words has a slightly different nuance. If the

[13]As a further complication, even though we can be confident that the Hebrew author chose his word carefully, he may have made his choice based not only on the meaning of the word, but because it stands as a wordplay on the word for "naked" (also *'arum*, though appropriately plural), in the previous verse.

[14]Ziony Zevit, *What Really Happened in the Garden of Eden?* (New Haven, CT: Yale, 2013), 163.

same English word is used for each of them, the nuanced differences between them will be lost.

> **Example—Deceive:** The English word *deceive* is used to translate eleven different Hebrew verbs in only about thirty occurrences.[15] Each carries different nuances. In Genesis 3:13 Eve accuses the serpent of "deceiving" her. What would it mean to read that literally? It all depends on which nuance that Hebrew word carries. As it turns out, the Hebrew verb *nsh'*—used here in Genesis 3:13—is used in contexts in which the one being accused of deceiving is not aware that what they are saying is deceptive and, in fact, would not agree that they were deceiving. Consequently, one could not claim that a literal reading of Genesis 3:13 would conclude that Eve portrayed the serpent as intentionally trying to deceive her. The verb used carries no implication of the speaker's intent. Other Hebrew verbs could have been used to convey an intent to deceive.

As a final category, consider words that could potentially be read either casually (that is, intuitive reading of English translation) or rhetorically.

> **Example—All:** Sometimes when the Bible uses the term "all" it refers to a totality with no exceptions. When Pharaoh states in Genesis 41:40 that "all" his people are to submit to Joseph, one can imagine that there are no exceptions. A casual, perfunctory reading leads in that direction, and that would be a literal reading. Yet, in other passages, the same term is used rhetorically and should not be read in the same way. When the narrator in Genesis 41:57 says that "all" the world came to Joseph for food, no one would interpret the verse in light of populations of people crossing oceans to get to Joseph, nor would they assume that Joseph met each one personally. We would not be tracking with the author if we tried to read his rhetorical statement casually. That would be a flat reading and would not be literal, because the author intended it rhetorically.
>
> The two uses of *all* in Genesis 41 are generally unarguable, but not all examples are so straightforward. When Genesis 7:19-23 repeatedly use the word *all* to describe the flood, it is not as clear whether the author intended us

[15]The Hebrew roots are *gnb* (Genesis 31:20-27); *shqr* (Leviticus 19:11); *rmh* (Genesis 29:25; Joshua 9:22; 1 Samuel 19:17; 28:12), *pth* (2 Samuel 3:25; Proverbs 24:28; Jeremiah 20:7-10; Hosea 7:11); *nsh'* (Genesis 3:13; 2 Kings 18:29; 19:10; 2 Chronicles 32:15; Isaiah 19:13; 36:14; 37:10; Jeremiah 4:10; 49:16; Obadiah 1:3); *tll* (Job 13:9); *t'h* (Job 15:31); *kzb* (Prov 14:5); *kḥš* (Zechariah 13:4); *'qb* (Genesis 27:36); *shgg* (Job 12:16).

to read the word casually (a flat reading) or rhetorically (a nuanced reading). A literal reading would entail reading it the way the author intended it. But how can we tell in a case like this?

We may get a lead from noticing what type of literature it is. The flood was a cosmic cataclysm. Does that sort of context lead to casual usage or rhetorical usage? Fortunately, we have other biblical examples to help us. Another great cosmic cataclysm was the destruction of Jerusalem and the temple by the Babylonians. When we read that sort of account, we notice that again, universalistic terms such as "none" or "all" are used rhetorically (Lamentations 2:22; Zephaniah 1:2-3). This may not conclusively resolve our questions about Genesis 7, but these examples demonstrate that a rhetorical use would be reasonable in the flood account. Reading the apparently universal language in Genesis 7 as rhetorical would be reading literally if that is what the author intended. We can find further examples from ancient Near Eastern literature at large that use this sort of rhetoric in cosmic cataclysm contexts.[16]

Whether we are dealing with words, rhetorical devices, or genres, reading literally requires some awareness of what the author is doing. Our instincts will not always serve us well. We must track with the author, and it can involve some work to discover what the author is doing.

10—We Are Accountable to the Author's Literary Intentions, Which Constitute the Affirmations of Scripture

Besides insisting on reading literally, many Christians adhere to the idea that the Bible is inerrant. The most common articulation of this belief is found in the "Chicago Statement on Biblical Inerrancy," which indicates that the Bible is true, inerrant in all that it affirms.[17] Such a qualification implies that there are some statements in the Bible that the Bible does not

[16]For further reading, see Tremper Longman III and John H. Walton, *The Lost World of the Flood* (Downers Grove, IL: IVP Academic, 2018), 30-41.

[17]See www.etsjets.org/files/documents/Chicago_Statement.pdf.

affirm.[18] It is the task of the interpreter to discern what the affirmations are in each portion of Scripture. For example, the book of Job is not affirming the logic of his friends' arguments, though it could be understood to affirm their inadequacy.[19] Readers distinguish, therefore, between what is being affirmed in each statement and what is not, that is, "affirmation" versus "reference."[20]

> References are references because they mean things to the audience who heard them, and because they mean things, they are used as a vehicle to convey the author's message, which in turn contains the text's affirmation. What that message is can only be determined by understanding what the references mean. This in turn requires that we be attentive to the meanings of the words as the ancient audience would have understood them, but it also requires that we be attentive to the features of composition and discourse which also determine meaning.[21]

Every part of the Bible contains references, and they all work together to offer some affirmations. Many references should not be counted as affirmations, but all affirmations are also references, because they were spoken into an understood worldview and culture.

In our modern context, we often assume that the major affirmations of the Bible pertain to moral or ethical behavior and theology. Indeed, it is true that such affirmations can occasionally be found in the Bible. In fact, what we see in 2 Timothy 3:16 affirms such an inclination: "useful for teaching, rebuking, correcting and training in righteousness." Nevertheless, what Scripture is "useful" for may not be the same as what it was "given" for. In Timothy's context in Ephesus, he and his congregation encountered many false teachers. Paul is therefore reminding his protégé that, since Scripture has its source in God, it can provide him with a resource to lead his people on the right path. Paul is not making a general statement about

---

[18]Minimally this would refer to the words of the satan or the false assessments offered by Job's friends. But once the possibility for such material is acknowledged, other types of examples cannot be ruled out.

[19]Thanks to my colleague, Aubrey Buster, for this example and nuance.

[20]For a full discussion of these terms and the implications of them, see John H. Walton and J. Harvey Walton, *Demons and Spirits in Biblical Theology* (Eugene, OR: Cascade, 2019), 16-18.

[21]Walton and Walton, *Demons and Spirits*, 18.

the purpose for which Scripture was given by God or indicating the main functions that it has. Scripture unquestionably has implications for teaching doctrine and training people in righteous living. But it would be a mistake to consider Scripture to provide a systematic theology (concerning, for example, doctrines of original sin or of the relationships within the Trinity) or a comprehensive moral system. It has moral and theological insights to offer, but its larger and more significant message relates to communicating God's plans and purposes in the world. Those plans and purposes are initiated at creation, pursued through the covenant, demonstrated in the history of Israel, praised by the psalmists, articulated by the prophets, realized in Christ, promoted by the church, and will find their ultimate expression in new creation. God's people, whether Israel or the church, are to find their place in God's story and as eager participants in his plans and purposes. The most important affirmations of Scripture are connected to this metanarrative—a metanarrative the writers of Scripture are well aware of and to which they are intentionally contributing.

In light of this, it should occasion no discomfort concerning material we find in the Bible that falls into the category of "reference" rather than "affirmation." Note the following examples.

- The Bible's focus on communal identity is reference to how people thought back then; it does not affirm a mandate that all people must find their identity in community (thus denouncing individualism).
- The Bible's language indicating acceptance of the ancient idea that cognitive processes took place in the heart, liver, kidneys, and so on, is a reference to how people thought back then; it does not constitute a divine message affirming a physiology that would discount the role of the brain.[22]
- The Bible accepts without objection or qualification that there is a solid sky, that the sun is moving, and that the earth is a flat disk; and people continued to believe some of that even up to the

[22]While it may seem possible that the ancients simply used the organs as metaphors like we do, that possibility is diminished when we observe, for example, what is reflected in the Egyptian practice of mummification and the Mesopotamian practice of extispicy.

Reformation. Despite the fact that such biblical passages were used to refute Copernicus and Galileo, these should be understood as reference, not affirmation.

- Both Old Testament and New Testament operate in a world where hierarchy was valued and where women played a subservient role to men. Statements indicating such social constructs and calling for God's people to conform to them reflect references to the contemporary culture and need not be taken as affirmations of how all cultures should be shaped.
- The practice of arranged marriages, whose purpose was producing the next generation, and the occasional necessity for polygamy, are all references to how things worked in those cultures at that time. As such they are references and should not be picked up as affirmations.
- Minute details such as Jesus' claim that the mustard seed is the smallest of all seeds (Mark 4:31) should be classified among the references, not among the affirmations. It reflects how people thought then and is not a botanical claim.
- The Old Testament makes occasional reference to a divine council (1 Kings 22; Job 1–2; Psalm 82; generally also believed to be implied by the plurals in Genesis 1:26-28 and the Sons of God in Genesis 6:2-4). Some believe that such references constitute a truth claim that affirms such a divine council is in operation. Alternatively, this could be taken as reference, reflecting how people thought in Old Testament times.

Many readers may now be feeling distinctly uncomfortable. If what I am saying is true, then where does it all stop? Do we also imagine that Israelites only *believed* that God parted the Red Sea—that it is therefore only a reference and not an affirmation? What about the resurrection? Where are the lines to be drawn?

In the cases of the Red Sea and the resurrection, we note that in both biblical discussions, the reality of the events is vouchsafed by eyewitnesses. None of the above bullet point examples pertains to the reality of reported events. Instead, they refer to how the world is perceived and how society is shaped. Furthermore, the examples given above are not connected with

God's plans and purposes in the world, whereas the events reported in Scripture are documenting those very plans and purposes. If the events did not happen, then the revelation of God's plans and purposes would be undermined. The nature of the Bible's affirmations can be best identified as we track with the author.

This is not the same as saying that some of the Bible is inspired and some is not. It is likewise not saying that some of the Bible is God's Word and some is not. The traditional view of Scripture is represented by speaking of "verbal, plenary inspiration": every word contributes, and all parts are included. Since inspiration is the affirmation that Scripture finds its source in God, we are affirming that each word ("verbal") finds its source in God (as it is used to communicate the message that he is giving). This view also affirms that all parts ("plenary") find their source in God (for example, we cannot exclude genealogies or parts of Song of Solomon). The belief that every word and all parts find their source in God does not suggest that every word and all parts are independent affirmations. Rather, they all contribute to the affirmations Scripture makes.

Though Christian readers' ultimate interest may be in the affirmations, we cannot understand them well without paying attention to the references. The importance of those references to that which is familiar to the ancient author and audience can be understood by considering what is called "relevance theory."

Relevance theory explains how people tend to process information. Hearers or readers will follow the path of least effort to achieve expectations of coherence and sensibility and adopt that interpretation of what they have heard or read.[23] All sorts of information will dictate what factors contribute to that process, including general aspects of culture as well as influences that have been recent or particularly significant (for example, ones that carry emotional weight or that have had a meaningful impact). Optimal conclusions depend on how accessible the connections are and what cognitive benefit they are considered to have. "Relevance theory's strength is its focus on how discourse relies on contextual assumptions for

[23]John Hilber, *Old Testament Cosmology and Divine Accommodation* (Eugene, OR: Cascade, 2020), 12-13.

meaning."[24] But when those contextual assumptions are not accessible to us, we may substitute our own cultural assumptions for them and unsurprisingly therefore decipher the meaning differently. In such cases, greater processing effort is required. When a text is situational (for example, a prophecy or an epistle), the principle of relevance is complicated. Hilber notes that prophetic oracles "can be resignified when edited for final canonical presentation to a secondary audience."[25] That is, given new contexts, an audience will have more recent events more readily accessible and will interpret in light of the newly unfolding circumstances.

How does relevance theory pertain to references and affirmations? References are valuable because they aid the original audience in accessing the affirmations from the context of their own cultural and contextual assumptions. The references do not hold status as affirmations (then or now). They helped the original audience perceive the affirmations, but they can be obstacles for our own perception of the affirmations because the references are not equally accessible to us. Relevance theory helps us to understand why references are important in the communication of affirmations, and it also helps us to realize why our attempts at interpretation can easily go astray. One of the important ways to distinguish between references and affirmations is whether the information was previously known or widely recognized.

> **Example A—Some Commandments:** When the Decalogue indicates that the Israelites should not commit murder, adultery, or theft, we might logically inquire whether this is new information. Would the Israelites have been unfamiliar with such ideas during the centuries in Egypt prior to their arrival at Sinai? Would earlier Babylonians, Egyptians, or Canaanites have found these strange or restrictive? The answer is "no" on all counts.[26] This being the case, it becomes arguable to label these as "revelation." They are common knowledge both inside and outside of Israel. The statements of the second part of the Decalogue reflect common legal wisdom about characteristics of

---

[24]Hilber, *Old Testament Cosmology*, 2.

[25]Hilber, *Old Testament Cosmology*, 15.

[26]Evidence from the legal collections of the ancient world, almost all pre-dating Moses, attests to this fact, as does the fact that Moses had to flee Egypt after he murdered an Egyptian.

ordered society in the ancient world. The message being revealed to Israel must extend beyond that. It *refers* to what is commonplace in the ancient world but then *affirms* that in the covenant with Yahweh, Israelites are expected to conform to those universal sensibilities. The divine affirmation goes beyond the common cultural sensibilities. The message regards the way in which covenant order in Israel corresponds with the low bar of what is universally expected in ancient cultures, though it also extends beyond them at points (the initial elements in the Decalogue).

Example B—The Flood Account: This is also true of a narrative like the flood account. It is not new information that there was a flood—everyone in the ancient world knew this. In that sense, the fact of the flood is affirmed at one level, but it primarily exists as reference to a known event rather than an attempt to reveal a previously unknown event. The affirmation concerns not the widely recognized event itself, but the narrator's claim about the reason for the flood and Yahweh's intentions in sending it. That is, the narrator's explanation of the flood event is what constitutes the essential affirmation rather than the fact of the event (which was a given). Clearly, the author's interpretation would have no meaning if the event did not occur. Nevertheless, his interpretation differentiates it from any other ancient Near Eastern report of the event.

In both of these cases, the truth claim is not found in the base statement (for example, "don't murder" or "there was a flood"). Although those are true, they do not need the authority of Scripture to identify them as such. The actual affirmations are more complicated.

The Bible's literary purpose is not for God to "confirm things as true." This kind of thinking comes from reading the Bible as a sort of instruction manual. For example, consider the health and safety handbook at a workplace. All employees are expected to read it, and it understandably consists of information that the employers want employees to know. Some of these directions are intuitive and would be known by anybody, such as "run away from a fire" or "don't lift with your back." Some of them are admonitions to do things that might be annoying (like wearing earplugs) or to prohibit things we might find expedient or convenient (like standing on chairs instead of ladders to reach high shelves). Some of what is included in the handbook we would have no way of knowing otherwise, such as who the fire marshal is or where the exit routes for the building are. The point is that, when employees read this book, they are reading a list of things that their employer wants them to know, and it is important to receive all this information regardless of whether or not they previously knew it.

The Bible, on the other hand, is not like an employee handbook. It is the communication of a *message*, not a list of directives that the reader is expected to internalize. Communication, by its very nature, consists of using information that is known to convey information that is not. When we receive a communication, we are (usually subconsciously) looking for what it is telling us that we did not know, since conveying that knowledge is what the communicative act is for; it is why the speaker chose to talk in the first place. When we read the Bible, then, we are not looking for a list of divine commands or sayings; we are looking for what it is telling us that we did not already know. More accurately, however, since the communication is not to us personally, we are looking for what it is telling its *original audience* that *they* did not already know. God was not giving them a list of things they ought to know; he was trying to tell them something that they did not know—something that was important enough to be worth taking the trouble to say. Because God thought it was worth the trouble, we consider it a valuable enterprise to try to figure out what it was. Those are the affirmations that we are seeking.

For the modern reader, we are not supposed to internalize an idea that God wants us not to murder (which most people know already based on their culture). Instead, we are supposed to understand why telling the Israelites about the terms of their covenant (and the consequences of breaking it) was important enough for God to take the time to say. We may also conclude that we would do well not to murder, but we knew that already, and that is not the point.[27] The affirmation is bound up in the message God had for those original readers.

[27]Three previous paragraphs derived from comments from J. Harvey Walton via email, September 17, 2019.

11—A Genre Discussion Must Precede an Authority Conversation

Earlier chapters have made the point that the authority of the text and its affirmations are tied to the author's literary intentions. The next step, already referred to a couple of times, can now be addressed in more detail. The author's literary intentions are realized in part from the genre that he uses. Genre is one of the main factors in deciphering a communication properly.

Example—Psalm 139: Psalm 139 presents an interesting opportunity to consider the importance of genre identification. The various genres found within the book of Psalms have received much scholarly attention, and there is widespread agreement about the categories that exist, though sometimes labels may vary. Among the most common genres are Hymns of Praise (individual or communal) and Songs of Lament (individual or communal).[28] Each genre has formal elements that help the reader to identify it. For example, communal Hymns of Praise generally begin with an imperative call to praise (such as, "Shout to the Lord!"). Songs of Lament typically begin by invoking the name of the Lord.

Psalm 139 has often been intuitively read as a Hymn of Praise with its verses that comment on the praiseworthy attributes of God (vv. 1-13). The psalmist's praise is mentioned explicitly in verse 14, and overall, the psalm contains many assertions that can be identified as praising God. Yet, when we examine the psalm closely, some observations may lead us to raise questions about the genre of the psalm.

First, we can immediately notice that it begins with an invocation. This fact is obscured by translations like the NIV that put "Lord" halfway through the verse. Most translations reflect the Hebrew order well by putting the name first. As previously noted, opening with such an invocation is characteristic of

[28]For a convenient introductory discussion, see Tremper Longman III, *How to Read the Psalms* (Downers Gove, IL: IVP Academic, 1988), 19-36. For classification of each psalm, see John H. Walton, *Chronological and Background Charts of the Old Testament* (Grand Rapids, MI: Zondervan, 1994), 47-50.

lament psalms, but that is not the only such indicator in this psalm. Like lament psalms, Psalm 139 includes an imprecation against enemies (vv. 19-22) and ends in a petition (vv. 23-24).

Furthermore, it includes some complaint, though it is not easily recognized as such. For example, Psalm 139:5 in the NLT reads, "You go before me and follow me. You place your hand of blessing on my head." That makes God's involvement sound very positive—a matter for praise. Most other translations have something like the NIV, "You hem me in behind and before, and you lay your hand upon me." This represents the Hebrew well, though a reader could interpret the statements either positively or negatively. The Hebrew reader would find no such ambiguity. The Hebrew behind the phrases to "hem someone in" and to "lay your hand upon me" have decidedly negative use. "Hemming in" is oppressive and is used for laying siege to a city in almost all of its thirty-five occurrences. The second phrase, "laying on a hand," is more uncertain since this combination occurs nowhere else. If it referred to a hand of blessing, we would expect the word for hand to be *yad* (see Genesis 48:14, 17), but here it is *kap*, often understood as the palm. Given this noun, and a verb that often refers to imposing something, it is possible that this expression conveys being heavy-handed, not conveying a blessing.[29] Psalm 139:10 speaks of guiding, and that verb can be used positively, but given the negative verbs used previously, it should probably be understood in its other sense—to lead captive. Finally, the word often translated "precious" in Psalm 139:17 refers to something being rare and inaccessible. The psalmist struggles to understand what God is thinking by treating him the way that he has.

Once these verbs are recognized as being in the negative spectrum, the imprecation against enemies (vv. 19-22) makes sense. Furthermore, the first twelve verses can be seen as incredulity rather than wonder. Since God knows all and sees all, he should recognize that the psalmist is innocent of wrongdoing and vindicate him. In this way, Psalm 139 is very similar to Job's complaint in Job 7:17-21. This interpretation, in turn, leads to a very different understanding of the final petition in Psalm 139:23-24. Instead of a sinner's plea to be shown hidden faults, it would be understood as a resolute claim of innocence: "Check me out thoroughly—you will find nothing offensive!"

---

[29]Compare Job 41:8, which uses *sim* + *kap*, and Psalm 32:4, which complains of God's heavy hand.

For our present discussion, it does not matter whether you are inclined to interpret Psalm 139 as a praise psalm or as a lament psalm—follow the evidence. The point is that the psalm will be interpreted differently depending on which genre it is. Therefore, we cannot determine what the authoritative meaning of the psalm is until we make a decision about the genre.

Determining the authoritative meaning of a biblical text not only involves discernment about what the genre is; it also entails how a genre works. We need to recognize that what we expect from some genres may not be the same as what an ancient Israelite would expect from a similar genre.

Example A—Genealogies: It is one thing to affirm that Genesis 5 or 1 Chronicles 1–9 are genealogies, but we also must investigate what genealogies meant to the original audience and why they were of significance to them.[30] For example, we cannot assume that a genealogy must represent every generation (note that Matthew skips some generations between David and Jesus). We cannot assume that the numbers they use have no significance other than chronology. We cannot even assume that in those cultures, the numbers or the order of the names was static; evidence suggests they were fluid.[31] In sum, we cannot make demands on how their genre of genealogy works based on our experience of how we use genealogies in our culture. As is the case with genealogies, other similar genres may have other forms and functions in different cultures. They are meant to establish continuity and a family story but are not constrained by some of our modern conventions and significances.

Example B—Telescoping in Daniel 1: What we believe to be essential for a reliable historical report of past events today may be very different from what an ancient reader would consider essential. This is also a genre issue—that is, it asks, what conventions and expectations does a particular genre entail?

For example, some interpreters have been troubled when reading Daniel 1:1 that Nebuchadnezzar came to Jerusalem and besieged it in the third year of

[30]It may even be that the genealogies that begin Matthew and Luke function differently in Greco-Roman culture than the genealogies in the Old Testament function in Israelite culture and literature.

[31]Unfortunately, this evidence is complex, and the possibilities derive mainly from ancient Near Eastern texts.

Jehoiakim, king of Judah. A detailed study of the history both from the Bible and from contemporary Babylonian sources leaves no room for Nebuchadnezzar coming to Jerusalem in the third year of Jehoiakim (605–604 BC), and he did not lay siege to the city until Jehoiakim was dead (597 BC).[32] The issue is resolvable when we recognize the convention of telescoping that is used in ancient historical literature.[33] Once we account for telescoping, we find that the first couple of verses of Daniel 1 take place over a twenty-year period. This passage is therefore not the historical problem that interpreters have worried about when they unwittingly expected the text to meet modern criteria.

Example C—Hyperbole in the Conquest Accounts: Consider the frequent use of hyperbole in conquest accounts. Understanding the message of the conquest account in Joshua requires us to understand how the genre of conquest account operates in the ancient Near East. There we find fluidity regarding details in parallel documentation. One of the most notable characteristics is exaggerating the magnitude of the victory and the scale of the casualties. Readers understood these conventions and would not have considered them deceptions but would have recognized that the details were couched in rhetorical hyperbole. The main interest of these accounts is in interpreting the event.[34]

Recognition of rhetorical devices such as hyperbole is not only good reading strategy, it is very helpful to us when we encounter what may otherwise present difficulties in reading texts. The book of Joshua gives the impression of a total conquest of the land, but Judges 1, in contrast, highlights all that had not been accomplished. Once we recognize the use of hyperbole in conquest accounts, we can read Joshua with a different perspective. The universalistic impression that it gives can be recognized as hyperbole that is appropriate to the genre. If we are accountable to the author, we must read his narrative with full awareness of the conventions that were open to him.

---

[32]Note that the statement in Daniel also appears to contradict what we are told in Jeremiah 25:1 (though the difference can be reconciled).

[33]Telescoping refers to compressing a series of events that happened over a longer period of time into a concise statement. "The American colonies broke free of British rule and wrote their own constitution."

[34]John H. Walton and J. Harvey Walton, *The Lost World of the Israelite Conquest* (Downers Grove, IL: IVP Academic, 2017), 178. For further reading, see K. Lawson Younger, *Ancient Conquest Accounts* (Sheffield, UK: Sheffield Academic, 1990), 242-66. Consult this work for many examples that document hyperbole in ancient conquest accounts.

Marc Zvi Brettler has stated the issue clearly, and he represents a consensus of thinking among scholars working with ancient historical documents.

> I do not believe that the ancients understood the writing of history as we now do. There was little, if any, interest in narrating the past for its own sake. Stories were set in the past for a variety of reasons, but antiquarian interest was not one of them. Though sparks of such interest developed in the Renaissance, it came to fruition only in the nineteenth century, and it would be a grave mistake to read the biblical books as the products of those German universities with an interest in recreating history . . . how it really was. Instead, the historical traditions of the Bible should be understood broadly within their ancient context, and more narrowly within their ancient Near Eastern context.[35]

The points he makes are important for us as readers who want to interpret the Bible faithfully. Since we are accountable to the ancient authors of Scripture, we need to set aside our own expectations of certain kinds of literature and readily adopt their perspectives. This can actually be quite helpful since it means that passages that may have been considered contradictory or inaccurate using our own criteria will not be problematic when we recognize the ancient conventions for writing about the past.

If we do not make some attempt to recognize the genres of the biblical literature and to understand the authors' ideas of how they are communicating within those genres, we risk losing the voice of the biblical author among the presuppositions that we bring from our own culture.

12—All Translation Is Interpretation

Moving on from what the authors are doing in their texts, this chapter considers how Bible readers gain access to what the authors are doing. For

[35]Marc Zvi Brettler, "The Tanakh as History," in *The Believer and the Modern Study of the Bible*, ed. Ganzel, Tova, Yehudah Brandes, and Chayuta Deutsch (Boston, MA: Academic Studies Press, 2019), 229-30.

most of us, the first step in interpretation has been done for us when someone translated the text into our language. If we were not able to access the Old Testament through translations, many readers would be stranded without being able to benefit from God's revelation. It is right to be grateful for translations, but at the same time, we must recognize how inherently limited they are and how they can lull us into an unrealistic confidence that in them we have the unfiltered Word of God. In other words, we need to be fully aware of the challenges that translating poses to those who do it, as well as the obstacles it poses for interpreters.

The Italian phrase *traduttore traditore* indicates (using a wordplay) that translators are traitors, an overstatement (driven by the desired wordplay) of the principle this chapter explores. This is not intended to criticize competent, conscientious translators, but to recognize the underlying concept: in order to translate something, one first has to interpret it. Therefore, a translator cannot help but to betray the original language in some degree. Translation involves offering in one language a meaning that was expressed in a different language. To do so, translators must determine what they believe the meaning is, and thus, interpretation has to take place. Unfortunately, this means that when we are reading our English Bibles, we are actually reading someone's interpretation of the text, not the text itself. This can be disconcerting because most Bible readers have no choice—they have not had the opportunity to learn Hebrew, Aramaic, or Greek, though comparing translations can helpfully alert them to places where further research is called for.

No translation is perfect, because no interpretation is perfect. People often ask me what the best translation is, but that is the wrong question. I can only address the strengths and weaknesses of any given translation—and all translations have both. Translations differ in their translation strategies. Some determine to remain as close as reasonably possible to the source language. Others determine to work within the confines of the source language but to communicate as clearly as possible to the target language group. Both approaches are defensible and can be valuable.

Some translations adopt particular positions regarding their translation values. For example, some will prefer to use inclusive language where they believe it is appropriate to do so, while others will use whatever gender designations exist in the source language. Translations will also differ with regard to how they are managing the textual variants that occur in the manuscripts or even whether they are inclined to prefer the Hebrew Masoretic Text or the Greek Septuagint tradition. Finally, translations often are inclined to favor traditional readings over more recent proposals because they realize that the intended audience will feel more comfortable with what is familiar. At the same time, that approach can err by not being open to new advances in research concerning words and meanings.

All of these are interpretive issues. Just as commentators will differ in their interpretations of passages, so translators will bring their interpretive inclinations into their translation. This is not a criticism—in fact, it is unavoidable. Likewise, theologians will bring their interpretations to passages that they use in their construction of doctrine. The various positions in the myriad of "Four Views" books are often built on such differences. John Goldingay has rightly observed, "Every translation is a collection of the compromises that someone is choosing to make."[36] Moving ideas from one language to another always has a cost—something is always lost, added, or both in the process.

All of this information highlights the important point that a translation does not end the discussion ("the Bible says . . ."); rather, it opens the discussion and calls for more study. A faithful reader's commitment to accountability calls us to try to understand what the words and phrases mean that the authors used to communicate to their audiences. The meanings of words and combinations of words (collocations) are determined by usage. Studying the usage of words in a time, culture, and context is called "synchronic analysis." This type of analysis is far more important in interpretation than studying the history of a word (for example, analyzing its component parts or its etymology), called "diachronic analysis."[37]

---

[36] "Will the 'First Testament' Grab Your Attention?" interview of John Goldingay by Glenn Paauw, *Christianity Today* (May 18, 2018), 74, https://www.christianitytoday.com/ct/2018/june/first-testament-translation-john-goldingay.html.

[37] A full discussion of these approaches along with their strengths and weaknesses is given in John H. Walton, "Principles for Productive Word Study," in *The New International Dictionary of Old Testament Theology and Exegesis*, ed. W. VanGemeren (Grand Rapids, MI: Zondervan: 1997), I:161-71.

Since the meanings of words often change at least in part over time, studying the history of a word is not a reliable method of interpretation. This can be clearly illustrated by the words of a British king concerning Christopher Wren's restoration and redesign of St. Paul's Cathedral in London about 1700. The king purportedly described the majestic cathedral with its new dome as "amusing, artificial, and awful," and he was being complimentary.[38] "Amusing" meant pleasing, "artificial" identified it as a spectacular artifice, and "awful" indicated that it was awe-inspiring. It would be of no help at all today to declare that "awful" means "full of awe." Some biblical examples can help illustrate the concept further.

> **Example A—Daniel 1:** In Daniel 1, the Jewish young men in Babylon take a bold stand. In circumstances in which their identity is being reshaped by their captors in multiple ways, they decide to boycott the king's food, opting for a different diet. This is described as a determination not to defile themselves. This much is clear, but when we seek to discover what food they are rejecting and what they want instead, the issues become very complex because of the two Hebrew words describing those foods. The food they reject is the word *patbag* (NIV "royal food," ESV "king's food," NRSV "royal rations"), a Persian loanword that is used only in Daniel in the Old Testament (Daniel 1:5, 8, 13, 15, 16; 11:26), and rarely in Persian and Greek literature. The food they request in its place is represented by the word *zeroʿim* (Daniel 1:12, 16; NIV, ESV, NRSV all render it "vegetables"), a plural form of the word commonly translated "seed."[39] It is essential for these two problematic words to be understood correctly to interpret Daniel's decision and the message of the text accurately. Interpreters who conclude that Daniel is refusing the king's food because it violates Israelite dietary laws, or because it has been sacrificed to idols, or because he is choosing a

[38]The details of which king said this in which context are uncertain, see https://quoteinvestigator.com/2012/10/31/st-pauls-cathedral for detailed discussion. Regardless of which king it was, or even if it is an apocryphal account, the point remains that these three adjectives had a very different meaning in 1700.

[39]Daniel 1:16 adds further complication since it manifests an apparently variant form with an additional /*n*/. The noun can refer to agricultural product or human descendants. It is a collective term so does not appear anywhere else in the plural. It can best be compared to an English word like "people"—a term that is collective in itself but can be used in the plural to refer to people groups ("peoples").

healthier vegetarian diet, have all worked under the assumption that *patbag* is a meat dish. Available evidence suggests that is not the case.[40] It is easy to understand how that mistake might be made if *patbag* stands in contrast to "vegetables," but there is no reason to conclude that "seeds [of various kinds]" should be equated to vegetables, though it is evident enough that "seeds" would not include meat. Furthermore, Daniel and his friends also reject the king's wine, an aspect of the scenario that does not fit these interpretations.

When we move on to an analysis of the term *zero'im*, we can suggest that this refers to cereals and grains more than to legumes. Daniel's preference for this form of ration becomes significant considering Ezekiel 4:9, where a list of such cereals and grains describe the diet of the exiles. This opens the possibility that Daniel and his friends are choosing the diet of exiles over the *patbag* diet (whatever it consists of) connected with their status in the palace. In this way, they are asserting their identity, which has been compromised in so many other areas. Meat is not part of the picture, nor are Israelite dietary restrictions. Whether this interpretation is accepted as reflecting the best assessment of the evidence or not, the example makes clear how the interpretation of the passage has been determined in large part by the translation choices that have been made.

Example B—Genesis 3:16: Genesis 3:16 is a passage that has played a central role in the discussion of gender roles. The NIV rendering, "Your desire will be for your husband, and he will rule over you" (similarly, NRSV) retains a certain ambiguity regarding the specific nature of the "desire" (*teshuqah*). Other translations offer an interpretation of what sort of desire it is.

- "Your desire shall be contrary to your husband, but he shall rule over you" (ESV).
- "You will desire to control your husband, but he will rule over you" (NLT).

[40] A more detailed analysis is offered in Aubrey E. Buster and John H. Walton, *Daniel*, New International Commentary on the Old Testament (Grand Rapids, MI: Eerdmans, forthcoming). Athenaeus's reference to the Persian *potibazis* (Greek cognate of *patbag*) describe the food provided in terms of baked barley-and-wheat bread. Athenaeus 11.110.503, where he cites Dinon's *Persica*, found in F. Jacoby, *Die Fragmente der griescher Historiker* (Berlin-Leiden, 1923–1958), 690 F4.

- "You will want to control your husband, but he will dominate you" (NET).

Note that in the latter, the translation not only offers a negative understanding of "desire" but also of "rule" (*mashal*). These are obvious examples in which the translation is interpretive.

As already mentioned, our best understanding of Hebrew words is founded on usage determined through synchronic analysis. This procedure encounters problems when a word is rarely used. That is exactly the case with *teshuqah* (desire), a word that only occurs elsewhere in Genesis 4:7 and Song of Songs 7:10. In the former, the context suggests a negative nuance, but in the latter, it suggests a positive nuance. The two contexts are very different, and most interpreters of Genesis 3:16 choose one or the other as a guide to understanding this verse. Translations that retain some neutrality are less interpretive, yet even the English word *desire* has some interpretation implied. For example, what if the word *instinct* would better capture the Hebrew term? The connection to Song of Songs 7:10 allows the possibility of sexual desire. Alternatively, might the "desire" in this context be the desire to have children, despite the drawbacks (such as indicated in the first half of the verse)?[41] Could it be a desire for her husband as the one who can establish order for her despite all the possible disruptions posed by childbearing? In the latter case, the husband's role (*mashal*) would reflect a positive situation (as the verb generally does in the Old Testament) rather than a negative one. Contrary to our modern impulses, in the ancient world people found a comfortable order in hierarchy.

Example C—Daniel 10:13: Consider some representative translations of Daniel 10:13, where a man in awe-inspiring garb appears to Daniel with a message that includes an explanation of his delay:

- "The prince of the Persian kingdom *resisted* me twenty-one days" (NIV)
- "The prince of the kingdom of Persia *withstood* me twenty-one days" (ESV)

---

[41] A further determination is whether the obstacle is "pain" as often translated, or "anxiety" as a defensible alternative. Despite the tendency of translations, the beginning of the verse refers to the woman's experience of conception, rather than of childbearing. Conception is not painful, but it is fraught with anxiety in the ancient world, suggesting that "anxiety" would be a better translation. For further reading, see John H. Walton, *Genesis*, NIV Application Commentary (Grand Rapids, MI: Zondervan, 2001), 226-29.

- "The prince of the kingdom of Persia *opposed* me twenty-one days" (NRSV)
- "for twenty-one days the spirit prince of the kingdom of Persia *blocked* my way" (NLT)

The verb (observe italics) is of great interest here, particularly because this verse has been used as the primary proof text for a view of spiritual warfare featuring territorial powers. It therefore calls for scrutiny concerning whether the translations have overreached. That is, does the verb represent a conflict between parties?

The author of Daniel uses the Hebrew collocation (verb plus preposition) *'md* + *leneged* ("stand before"), which is used in a number of other contexts (Joshua 5:13; Daniel 8:15; 10:16) but is never confrontational.[42] So it is more likely that the prince of Persia is standing in audience before the envoy who now speaks to Daniel. We might consequently conclude that God's envoy is allied with the prince of Persia (just as Yahweh allies himself with Cyrus, the Persian king). This analysis shows the traditional translation to be not only an interpretation, but an indefensible one given the data. The situation is lamentable since such far-reaching theological conclusions are based on this translation.

The examples we have offered here are extreme and obvious cases where translations reflect interpretations that nudge us in a particular direction as we try to understand the message of the text. Nevertheless, we should not imagine that such is the case only in a handful of passages. All translation is, by nature, interpretation. That fact cannot be avoided, but acknowledging it alerts us to important issues as we seek to be faithful interpreters. One way that we can make ourselves more aware of the possible interpretive options is to use multiple translations side by side. That practice can make us aware of controversial translations, even if it will not always identify potential problems.

[42]See full treatment in John H. Walton and J. Harvey Walton, *Demons and Spirits in Biblical Theology* (Eugene, OR: Cascade, 2019), 189-90. These are all the occurrences. Note that David Clines (ed.) *Dictionary of Classical Hebrew* (Sheffield: Sheffield Phoenix, 2008), VI, 466a likewise indicates that the collocation means to "stand before."

13—Words That Are Roughly Comparable in Two Languages Often Carry Different Nuances

This observation is in some ways an extension of what has preceded and, to some extent, offers one reason why all translation must be considered interpretation. The more specific idea pertains to the fact that different languages compartmentalize ideas in different packages. This is not a question of *correct* translation but of the *inadequacies* of translation itself as an undertaking. Inevitably, unintended nuances are added or lost when a particular word in the target language is chosen to represent a word in the source language. In some extreme cases, no word in the target language adequately captures the sense of the word in the source language. An example of this, the Hebrew word *hesed*, was already discussed in the introduction.

The focus in this section, however, will be on Hebrew words that *do* have an adequate representation in English, but nevertheless where some aspects that are inherent in the Hebrew word are not reflected in the English word, or, conversely, where some aspects usually included in the English word are not part of the Hebrew word.[43]

> **Example A—*br'* as "Create":**[44] Creation can take place at many different levels and in many different ways. Even though we use the English word for a variety of these,[45] when we think about God creating the world, we most naturally think in material terms. When we use the verb "create" in that sort of context, the word has a material focus. And it is true that God is the Creator of the material world. "Create" is still the best translation of the Hebrew verb *br'*, and while the Israelites would include the material aspects in God's work, I would contend that their primary focus of God's creation pertained to his ordering of the cosmos. This sort of creative act often entails giving

[43]This list is excerpted and adapted from *The NIV Cultural Background Study Bible* (Grand Rapids, MI: Zondervan, 2016), xix-xxvii, which I prepared as Old Testament general editor. Significant parts of it are direct quotations.

[44]Genesis 1:1.

[45]Consider examples such as "creating" a curriculum, a committee, a masterpiece, or a mess.

something a role, purpose, or function in an ordered system. Its emphasis is therefore on God acting with purpose and giving things a purpose rather than on simple materiality. It is more like creating a home rather than creating a house.[46]

Example B—*tardemah* as "Deep Sleep":[47] The use of the adjective "deep" in many translations indicates that this is not to be equated with a normal activity of sleeping. When we examine the contexts in which this word is used, we discover that it has one of two possible connotations. In such a sleep, one is either (a) unaware of threatening circumstances or (b) prepared to receive a vision. These nuances are not expressed by simply calling it a "deep" sleep.

Example C—*nwh* as "Rest":[48] When modern readers encounter the word *rest* we often think of relaxation and disengagement. The Hebrew word can pertain to relaxation or refreshment, but more often refers to experiencing stability, security, and equilibrium—everything as it ought to be. God's rest is associated with his presence in the temple and his rule of the cosmos. Rest is the opposite of unrest, and when God rests, he is not disengaging but engaging. God rests on his throne. The rest he offers to people does not involve downtime but a sense of security and order that he provides when we adopt a kingdom perspective.

Example D—*ht'* as "sin":[49] It is not uncommon to encounter the statement that "sin" in the Old Testament means "missing the mark." It is true that this verb can refer to failing to achieve an objective (Proverbs 8:36; Isaiah 65:20), and once it is even used for slingers who do not miss their target (Judges 20:16). There is no reason, however, to think of these uses as reflecting the "original" meaning of the word that is translated "sin." We can see that different meanings can attach to different contexts, but in most contexts, this verb simply means "to sin" and is not necessarily limited to the idea of missing a mark or failing to achieve an objective. Sin can be seen

---

[46]For further reading, see John H. Walton, *The Lost World of Genesis One* (Downers Grove, IL: IVP Academic, 2009).

[47]Genesis 2:21; 15:12; Judges 4:21; 1 Samuel 26:12; Daniel 10:9; Jonah 1:5.

[48]Exodus 20:11 (as a reflection on Genesis 2:1-2, which does not use this word); Deuteronomy 12:10; Joshua 1:13-15; 21:44; Psalm 132:7-14.

[49]Genesis 20:6; Joshua 7:11; Judges 11:27; 1 Samuel 2:25; Job 1:22; Psalm 51:4-7.

as a threat to relationship with God—it results in alienation because offense has been committed against God. Regarding this Hebrew word, the translation "sin" is straightforward, but the more "in-depth" explanations sometimes offered can be misleading.

Example E—*yr'* as "Fear":[50] In everyday English, fear is a negative feeling and is therefore considered undesirable. That creates confusion when readers encounter the word in positive contexts that exhort them to nurture this feeling (for example, the familiar "fear the Lord"). That disconnect easily alerts readers that there must be more going on here than what the English word communicates. This Hebrew verb and its associated noun have broad usage with either people or God as direct object. In the latter cases, it can refer to being afraid of God, particularly of his anger or judgment when sin has been committed. This matches familiar English usage. Translation problems arise from the misunderstanding that is created when the word serves as a positive and necessary response to God, a nuance not expressed by the English word *fear.* It refers to holding God (and occasionally humans of authority) in high esteem and therefore treating him (and them) with respect. That respect can at times be motivated by the consequences of failing to do so, but in the end, it should operate independently of consequences. "Fear" of the Lord accords God his proper place and role and is a response to his authority. By way of example, when someone today works with radioactive material, there is potential danger in the interaction that calls for respect.

Example F—*hokmah* as "Wisdom":[51] This concept in Hebrew has a different focus than the English word used to translate it. It does not pertain to intelligence or common sense (though both of those could be expressions of *hokmah*). *Hokmah* is intimately connected with the concept of order because wisdom is the pursuit of order, and Yahweh is the source and center of both. *Hokmah* perceives what constitutes order and pursues, preserves, promotes, and practices order in every area of life. Relationship with God is primary, but *hokmah* seeks order in family relationships, response to civil authorities, making good choices, controlling one's tongue, and so on.

---

[50]Genesis 3:10; 15:1; 32:7; Exodus 1:17; Leviticus 19:3; Deuteronomy 10:20; Job 1:9; 28:28; Proverbs 1:7.
[51]Exodus 28:3; Deuteronomy 34:9; 1 Kings 4:29-34; 2 Chronicles 1:10-12; Job 12:13; 28:28; Psalms 104:24; 111:10; Proverbs 1:7; 2:6; 8:12; Isaiah 11:2; Jeremiah 9:23.

Example G—*'hb / sn'* as "Love/Hate":[52] In normal English usage, these are primarily emotive terms, though sometimes used hyperbolically ("I love this new app!"). Though the Hebrew terms can carry emotion or sentiment, they pertain primarily to either being in positive relationship or not. They can refer to preference and favor or the opposite. They can also refer to political alliances and the formal aspects of marriages. Therefore, for example, we should not perceive that there is a theological inconsistency when God says, "Jacob I have loved, and Esau I have hated." Our misunderstanding derives from a failure to recognize that these are not inherently emotive terms.

Example H—*'ebed* as "Slave, Servant":[53] In Hebrew, *'ebed* is not a derogatory term that compromises personhood or degrades one to the status of a possession. It is an appropriate designation for a slave, but also for a servant or even a high-ranking royal administrator. Slavery in ancient Israel and in the ancient world at large showed little similarity to the ethnic dehumanization that is characteristic of the slavery of American history. Some of the distinctions result from Israel being a communal society; others point to the reasons for slavery (for example, managing debt in an agrarian society). Consequently, the word cannot be understood simply through our modern lenses and sensibilities, though we may still find good reason to critique it.

Example I—*shophet* as "Judge":[54] Broadly speaking, this label is used to refer to someone who helps establish justice. In modern English usage, it often pertains to an elected office and a formal role within the judiciary system. In Israel, a *shophet* could at times be engaged in deciding cases (Exodus 18:22), but in the book of Judges, they filled military roles, bringing about justice for the people of Israel who were oppressed by enemies. We must not think that our current idea of judges and what they do is the same as the role they fulfilled in the book of Judges.

---

[52]*'hb*—Genesis 22:2; 24:67; 25:28; 29:20, 30; Exodus 20:6; Deuteronomy 4:37; 21:16; Judges 14:16; 1 Samuel 16:21; 18:1-3; 2 Samuel 1:26; 1 Kings 5:1; 11:1; Esther 2:17; Ecclesiastes 3:8; Jeremiah 2:25; Hosea 2:5; Mal 1:2; *sn'*—Genesis 26:27; 29:33; Exodus 20:5; Deuteronomy 21:17; 22:13; Proverbs 19:7; Mal 1:3; 2:16.

[53]Genesis 9:25; 14:15; 19:19; 40:20; Exodus 21:2; 32:13; Leviticus 25:39, 44; 26:13; Deuteronomy 5:15; 1 Samuel 16:17; 2 Samuel 3:22; 1 Kings 9:22; Job 1:8; Esther 1:3; Isaiah 20:3; 52:13; 53:11.

[54]Exodus 18; Judges 2:16-18; 1 Samuel 7:6.

In the twentieth century, the Amplified Bible tried to address the problem of finding the correct word by offering not just one word in translation of important words but numerous overlapping synonyms in an attempt to broaden the nuances made available to the reader. Unfortunately, this only compounded the problem. It gave readers the idea that they could choose whichever of the options fit best with the interpretation they wanted to give. Rather than isolating the proper nuance, it gave more options from which to choose.

Even those who have had the opportunity to learn Hebrew and Greek rarely progress beyond learning English equivalents to represent the vocabulary words in the original language. So what is to be done? The first important step has been provided by this chapter: be aware of the problem. Such awareness will hopefully help readers avoid the tendency to dig deeply into an English word in an attempt to penetrate the meaning of the text when what really needs to be done is to dig deeply into the Hebrew word. The first step to getting help is to realize that we need help.

The second step is to acknowledge that some reference works that seem as if they might be able to provide help might not in fact do so. Many popular word study resources, including some found online, may be overly influenced by theological agendas or are offering devotional thoughts. The most help will be found in works that are linguistic in nature, rather than theological or devotional, and written by trained, competent linguists. Furthermore, because of the continuing work in linguistics in general, and semantic analysis of Hebrew and Greek in general, it is important to use recent, up-to-date resources that employ synchronic analysis (as described in the previous chapter), minimizing diachronic analysis.[55] Unfortunately, for most readers, these sources are not easily accessible.[56] Nevertheless, if we can be aware of the issues involved, many potential problems can be

[55]At times Hebrew exegesis requires diachronic analysis when the data are insufficient to reach conclusions solely on synchronic analysis.

[56]Accessibility is limited because these resources are costly and often communicate in technical terms. The most important resource for the Old Testament is the sixteen volume *Theological Dictionary of the Old Testament*, edited by J. Botterweck and H. Ringgren and published by Eerdmans. One can also often find help of this sort in technical academic commentaries, but even there, it is surprising how little semantic analysis takes place.

prevented because we will have adjusted our presuppositions and expectations about translation. We can be aware that we should not push controversial or technical interpretations based on English words. When we realize the technical knowledge that is necessary but not known to us, we will restrain ourselves from overreach based on English meanings and modern sensibilities.

14—In a Hearing-Dominant Culture, There Are No Books or Authors as We Know Them, and "Book" Is the Last Step, Not the First

So far, this part of the book has discussed what the Bible is, how readers should approach it, some reading strategies, the importance of literary awareness, and the problems presented by working in a translation. Now the attention turns to several areas where Bible readers often make assumptions that can have a significant impact on our interpretation. Specifically, most readers hold preconceived ideas about how the Bible was produced, about the importance of Jesus in the Old Testament, and about the role of the Holy Spirit in our Bible reading. Three chapters will now address each of these issues in turn.

Often when we begin to study a biblical book, the first questions we ask concern date and authorship: Who wrote the book and when did they write it? This is a logical question and when we ask it, we are following the example of a multitude of study Bibles, Bible Handbooks, Old Testament surveys, and even biblical commentaries. It represents an attempt to understand context. As logical as it is to our own cultural inclinations, it is actually problematic when we are dealing with an ancient Israelite context.

In the ancient world most information, traditions, and memory were communicated orally. Writing was not their first impulse, and most people were largely illiterate. In our culture, we often associate illiteracy with the primitive, the unschooled, or even the ignorant. It would be a mistake to carry those cultural prejudices into our understanding of the ancient world.

The cultures of the ancient world were designed to operate without the assumption of literacy. Compare today to how computer use is designed to operate without the assumption that users are literate in computer programming language. Consequently, the transmission or communication of ideas in the ancient world took place largely by word of mouth—speaking and hearing. This sort of culture is designated "hearing dominant," as opposed to a culture like ours that is "text dominant."[57]

In hearing-dominant cultures, a tradition did not begin by someone writing it down. Note that the prophets spoke (they are rarely said to have written), and even Jesus spoke—he never wrote a book. Memory of the past was preserved and enshrined in culture through continual retelling.

In the ancient world there were no books. On the rare occasions when things were written down, they were written on materials like clay tablets, wax tablets, papyrus, parchment, or ostraca. Formal written documents were stored in archives, often associated with the temple or palace, where they were available to a handful of specialists and sometimes served in the scribal curriculum. They were not accessible to common people who, as mentioned, could not read or write anyway.

The literature that we refer to as "books" of the Bible only actually became books through a long process of transmission and compilation. Even though Israelites at the time of David may have been aware of many of the early traditions we have in the Old Testament, they would not have had "books" of Genesis, Joshua, or Judges. Furthermore, the traditions and memories that are preserved in those books were not first written down to then become traditions. They were oral traditions that eventually were written down. Since they did not start as "books" we cannot attach them to "authors." By the time these traditions became documents and eventually books, it would have been impossible and meaningless to identify an author. Traditions do not have authors. The people who compiled the traditions and shaped them into books are not technically the authors, though they had important creative input into the books we now read. Nevertheless, they would have been reflecting ancient, authentic material.

---

[57]For a book-length discussion of the significance of this concept and its implications, see John H. Walton and D. Brent Sandy, *The Lost World of Scripture* (Downers Grove, IL: IVP Academic, 2013).

Consequently, if in the ancient world there are no books and no authors in the way that we think about them, we cannot really address questions like "Who is the author of this book?" and "When was this book written?" Yet being accountable to the authors' intentions is a main theme throughout this book. So now it's clear that what that means is that we are accountable to all of those who had a role in shaping what we have received as the books of the Bible. The most important step in this long, complicated, and untraceable process is the person or group who gave the book its final rhetorical shape. That was the person who selected what to include or to leave out, who combined the narratives so that they worked together in the communication of a particular literary purpose.

Technically, Christian doctrines consider the *text* to be inspired (2 Timothy 3:16), not the people, though they were moved by the Holy Spirit (2 Peter 1:20-21). Those texts have a communicative purpose, and that purpose was achieved through the work of combining materials (whether narratives, psalms, proverbs, or prophecies) to create a single literary product. That purpose provides the message of the text that we embrace as the authoritative Word of God.

Once we recognize the complexity of the process involved in giving us Scripture, we can see that our questions about date and authorship of books are just not the right questions to introduce the study of a biblical book. The historical process by which a biblical book was compiled is important, but not at this stage of interpretation. There is no reason to doubt that much of the information that is included in the books of the Old Testament traces back to the times that the book describes (narratives or prophets). But time works on traditions, as memory selects and shapes a culture's understanding of its roots and identity. This happens in every culture, and it must happen for traditions to survive and for history to have its effect. It happens in Egypt and Babylon; it happens in Israel, Greece, and Rome; it happens in the United States, China, Nigeria, and Argentina.

Consequently, the actual biblical books are not as old as the traditions that they comprise. Moreover, in most cases, the ones who gave final shape to the books are not those who were involved in the initiation of the traditions. Furthermore, the message found in the purpose and rhetorical shaping of the book would not have been present through much of the history of transmission of the traditions—it is established in the final compilation.

A commitment to the authority of Scripture with its purposes and message, therefore, must be focused on those who gave each book its final shape. These are the "authors" with whom we want to track and to whom we are accountable. On the way to that final form, tradents, scribes, and those involved at every stage of transmission, composition, and compilation were involved, all, as we believe, under the direction of the Holy Spirit. As we consider the implications of this information, some examples may help us navigate the uncertain waters.

> **Example A—Moses:** The text is clear that Moses produced some written documents. God instructs him to write things down and the text reports that he did so.[58] Throughout history, he has been considered the mediating voice of the Torah initially given at Sinai. We have no reason to dispute or distrust the reality of this role, yet we recognize that it carries qualifications based on what it does not claim. The fact that it came to be known as the "Torah, or Law of Moses" is not a claim that he wrote the books that are now in our Bibles. He has a significant role at the headwaters of Torah, and some of the material found there was also written by him. The books that we have, however, were likely the result of a much more complicated history of transmission and composition that cannot be traced given our present state of knowledge.[59] We can accept what the Bible affirms about the role of Moses without going beyond those claims to attribute more to Moses than what is explicitly asserted.

[58]For further reading, see Daniel I. Block, "Recovering the Voice of Moses: The Genesis of Deuteronomy," in *The Gospel According to Moses* (Eugene, OR: Cascade, 2012), 21-67.

[59]I should note here that the familiar source theory known as the JEDP theory, or the Documentary Hypothesis, has also become much more complex as scholars continually make adjustments for the realities summarized in this section. Scholars have increasingly recognized the difficulties in distinguishing the contributions of written sources and in identifying a redactional history. Recent works that both challenge and qualify source theory include Joshua Berman, *Inconsistency in the Torah: Ancient Literary Convention and the Limits of Source Criticism* (Oxford: Oxford University Press, 2017); David M. Carr, *The Formation of the Hebrew Bible: A New Reconstruction* (Oxford: Oxford University Press, 2011); Raymond F. Person and Robert Rezetko, *Empirical Models Challenging Biblical Criticism* (Atlanta, GA: SBL, 2016). Though the concept that at times a variety of sources were used is not inadmissible in theory (Chronicles, for example, admits as much), I am more skeptical of the epistemological confidence that often drives reconstructions of redaction history.

Example B—Jeremiah: As with all the prophets, Jeremiah's messages were delivered orally. Reading Jeremiah 36, however, we are told that Jeremiah is instructed to take a scroll and write down his oracles. We learn that he employed the scribe Baruch to do so, but we also learn that this was an extraordinary occasion. Jeremiah had been banned from the temple precincts and consequently was no longer able to pronounce his oracles there. The alternative was for Baruch to write them down so that he could then read them to the king. Certain oracles were written in this unusual circumstance, but we do not know which ones. Moreover, this is not a claim that Jeremiah shaped the book of oracles that we now have. In fact, when we compare the Hebrew text of Jeremiah with the Greek text, we find that they contain a different assortment of oracles and that they are arranged in different ways.

Example C—Daniel: The book of Daniel presents a complex test case. In earlier decades, some claimed Daniel as the author of the entire book, even though the narratives talk about him in the third person and make no such claims. The visions, in contrast, feature Daniel speaking in the first person. Even that, however, falls short of identifying him as the "author" who compiled the book as a whole. Notice that in Daniel 7:1-2 and Daniel 10:1, even the first-person sections are introduced by a narrator. In contrast to the scholars who claimed Daniel as author were those who saw the book as composed entirely in the second century BC, the time of Antiochus IV Epiphanes, whose reign is described in some of the passages in the visions.

More recently, however, commentators have introduced a more nuanced understanding of the book's composition based on the idea of progressive layers over the centuries. In this view, the narrative court tales have their roots in the setting of the Babylonian exile, then the visions were appended one by one over the centuries as appropriations and reinterpretations until the book reached its final form with the addition of the last vision (Daniel 10–12) in the context of the Maccabean Revolt in the mid-160s. Regardless of whether this new permutation is right or not, this illustrates the complexity of determining the date and authorship of the book. Daniel is a character in the narratives and is presented as the visionary in the latter parts (though that role would be perhaps qualified if the association with Daniel is seen as a rhetorical device, see above, chap. 9). But none of these

> present him as the author, and the Bible never claims him as the author. The evidence consistently suggests otherwise since he is treated in third person by the narrator.

The significance of the information and examples we have presented is that as interpreters of the Old Testament, inquiring as to the date and authorship of books is generally not productive for interpretation—we simply do not have that information, and what we know of the ancient world suggests that we are asking the wrong questions. We have allowed our own culture to determine the approach rather than working from an understanding of literary production in the ancient world.

This book emphasizes throughout the idea that faithful interpretation requires attention to context. At this point, the reader might well be puzzled—how can we take account of context if we do not know when the book was written or who wrote it—are they not the essentials of context? The surprising answer is that they need not be. They are essential elements when we have that information (for example, Paul's prison epistles), but when that information is not available, the situation is not hopeless. The essential contexts this book has promoted are linguistic, literary, cultural, and historical. The linguistic context is determined from the meanings of the words—these rarely change over the period of the Old Testament.[60] The literary context is determined from the work itself and is not dependent on who wrote it or when it was compiled.[61] Certainly, there could be cultural changes taking place over time. For example, in early periods, the use of standing stones was legitimate, but over time, they became problematic and were prohibited. Nevertheless, most major aspects of culture do not change over the Old Testament period and even this example would not have anything to do with authorship and date.

The aspect of context most likely to be affected by author and date considerations is the historical context. Nevertheless, as interpreters we can

---

[60]Some have recognized some development in the meanings of a few words in the later postexilic books, but the examples are few and often disputed.

[61]Occasionally when we notice a book alluding to the content of another book (say, Daniel 9 referring to Jeremiah) it is important to see them in sequence—but that is relative placement, not absolute dating.

gain much advantage by seeking to understand the historical circumstances of the *setting*, regardless of when the account was written in its final form. Therefore, when we are interpreting the book of Judges, it is important for us to understand the history and archaeology of the earliest stages of the Iron Age because that is the setting for the events. This information remains vital even if the book was not written until centuries later.[62] Consequently, we can still be faithful interpreters attuned to the significant aspects of context without having any knowledge of the date and authorship of the book as it finally came to us. In the process of literary production in the ancient world, the writing of the book is generally not toward the beginning, but toward the end. Long periods of oral transmission and perhaps partial documentation precede the final compilation.[63]

15—The Old Testament Is Not About Jesus, but It Drives Us to Jesus

Pastors in training are sometimes told, "If you are not preaching about Jesus in every passage, it is not Christian preaching."[64] Readers will immediately recognize how deeply this conflicts with the concept of accountability to the author's literary intentions that I have been promoting in this book. How can "Jesus sightings" reflect the authority of the text if they are

[62]It is possible that some information will be gained by knowing when it was written in case the perspectives of that time period are reflected in the writing and have influenced the memory and significance of the events. We can benefit from any such information that can be derived from close reading, but we are not in a hopeless situation without it.

[63]Some might consider a complex literary work like Job to be an exception, and maybe it is, but we should remember that the much more complex writings of Homer, *The Iliad* and *The Odyssey*, were composed and recited orally before ever being reduced to writing.

[64]As an aside, I would contend that this statement reflects a reductionistic use of the word "Christian," a word that reflects a commitment to Christ, not a homiletic strategy. Just because a Jewish Rabbi could preach the same message from an Old Testament passage as a Christian pastor need not invalidate that sermon or disqualify it from being Christian. A Rabbi or an Imam could admonish his congregation to love their neighbors and that would not mean that a Christian sermon on the same subject would be less Christian. Our sermons are supposed to reflect the message of the text, and since the Old Testament was originally written by Jews before the time of Christ, it should occasion no surprise and reflect no compromise if Jews and Christians might both draw the same message of truth from a passage.

the product of our own imagination or creativity? When we preach Jesus from any random Old Testament text, are we tracking with the author's intentions? If not, are we not in effect setting the author's message aside and replacing it with another message which he knew nothing about?

Yet pastors might feel conflicted when they read Luke 24:27 and detect a mandate to preach the Old Testament christologically. There are effective ways to bring Jesus into an Old Testament sermon,[65] but we must tread very carefully so that we do justice to our accountability to the Old Testament text itself. Remember that the Old Testament had the authority of God's Word before Jesus came and before the New Testament was written. The guideline of this section offers an alternative strategy that respects the Old Testament author's intentions, accounts for Luke 24, and also respects the central role of Jesus.

I have been proposing that the central revelation found consistently in an author's literary intentions in the Old Testament concerns the plans and purposes of God. Since, from a Christian perspective, Jesus, the Christ, God's Messiah, and our Savior, the incarnate second person of the Trinity, is the centerpiece of God's plans and purposes, it might seem simple to posit an equation:

- The Old Testament reveals God's plans and purposes;
- Jesus is the centerpiece of God's plans and purposes;
- therefore the Old Testament reveals Jesus.

The flaw in the equation is that it accepts the premise that all of God's plans and purposes, their sum total, is found in Jesus. But there are more elements to God's plans and purposes than Jesus, though this does not diminish his significance in any way. There is an old saying, "If the only tool you have is a hammer, you see every problem as a nail." This principle could

---

[65]Numerous books have been written about this, among them Craig G. Bartholomew and David J. H. Beldman, *Hearing the Old Testament* (Grand Rapids, MI: Eerdmans, 2012); Herbert W. Bateman and D. Brent Sandy, eds., *Interpreting the Psalms for Teaching and Preaching* (St. Louis, MO: Chalice, 2010); Rein Bos, *We Have Heard That God Is With You: Preaching the Old Testament* (Grand Rapids, MI: Eerdmans, 2008); Sidney Greidanus, *Preaching Christ From the Old Testament* (Grand Rapids, MI: Eerdmans, 1999); Grenville J. R. Kent, Paul J. Kissling, and Laurence A. Turner, *Reclaiming the Old Testament for Christian Preaching* (Downers Grove, IL: IVP Academic, 2010); Steven D. Mathewson, *The Art of Preaching Old Testament Narrative* (Grand Rapids, MI: Baker, 2021).

sometimes be reflected in the approach of those who want to find Jesus in every passage of the Old Testament. Their "only tool" is christological interpretation, and they therefore treat every passage as requiring that tool. In this illustration, it would be foolish to suggest that the alternative is to discard one's hammer—hammers are useful and necessary. But every tool has its proper use.

We want to identify the full scope of God's plans and purposes in the world. If we believe Scripture reveals that to us, then that becomes our focus, whether or not Jesus is involved at that moment, in that passage. Consequently, our interpretation should begin with what the author's intentions are. In the Old Testament, that would never include Jesus, the incarnate second person of the Trinity—they had no such revelation. It may, however, pertain to the general role of Messiah (as a general job description rather than as an individual résumé), or God's plans to bring redemption (with no reference to the instrument to be used). That starting point reflects our commitment and accountability to the author's intentions, and it should be expected to result in an understanding of the authoritative message of Scripture.

In a later step of interpretation, we will be interested in how that passage has been picked up and reused in later texts, such as the New Testament. There we will sometimes find information about how that Old Testament passage is read in light of Jesus. That becomes, in itself, a significant message of Scripture, as we are accountable to the intentions of the New Testament authors. This brings us back to the guideline of this chapter: we can follow the developing message from the Old Testament to the New Testament in such cases and see how the Old Testament moves us toward Jesus, though the Old Testament authors were unaware of it.[66] Some examples can help us to explore the issues.

Example A—Genesis 22: Genesis 22 contains the well-known episode of Abraham being asked to sacrifice Isaac. Christian readers are often quick to see a comparison in the idea of a father being asked to sacrifice his son. God

[66]In theological terminology, what we are describing is the difference between a *christocentric* approach (it is all about Jesus) and a *christotelic* approach (it is all moving toward Jesus). Both approaches are forms of *christological interpretation*.

offered his Son, Jesus, as a sacrifice, but, in contrast to Abraham, actually went through with it. Given this comparison in contrast, how should we interpret Genesis 22?

At the first level, it is undeniable that such a comparison and contrast *can* be made profitably. Nonetheless, if we desire to track with the author, the question we must ask is whether the author *intends* such a comparison. It is not enough to claim that God (the divine author) intends it—how would you know unless the human author told you? Our interpretation cannot simply reflect our imagination; there is no authority there. In this case, such a comparison might be fruitful, even inspirational, but that does not justify it when we are trying to identify the authoritative message of the text. Our creativity might make for a moving sermon, but if it does not reflect the authority of the text, we cannot claim to be preaching Scripture. If the New Testament had suggested such a comparison and contrast, it could be preached on the authority of the New Testament author's message, but even that is not the case.[67] The New Testament commends Abraham's faith (Hebrews 11:17-19), but does not draw the comparison to Jesus.

Example B—Genesis 6–8: In Genesis 6–8 we find Noah and his small family being saved from death by the ark that he constructed under God's direction. Preaching this passage, we may be tempted to compare the ark as an instrument of salvation, to Jesus as the one who brings salvation. In this case, the bridge is based on the general concept of salvation. The ark saves Noah and his family from the destruction brought on a violent world; Jesus saves all who believe from the judgment brought on sinful people. The comparison can be made clearly, though contrasts are also evident (for example, the ark was only a passive instrument, while Jesus is the active agent). It does not take much imagination to see a parallel, yet it is still the product of imagination, not discernible in the message of any biblical author, Old Testament or New Testament. To preach Jesus from this Genesis text is to preach one's own creativity, not to preach the authoritative message of the Bible.

[67]If, in contrast, we focus on God providing a substitute (the ram in Genesis 22) rather than how Abraham or God felt about sacrificing his son, we are on better ground. This direction does not assume anything the Old Testament author and audience would not have recognized, though they still would not have gone so far as to think about God providing a substitute sacrifice for our sins in Jesus.

Example C—"Types of Christ": We can also find examples in the many prospective "Types of Christ"—characters or objects in the Old Testament for whom some point of comparison to Jesus could be identified. In this case, we may occasionally find New Testament expression of the connection:

- Moses lifting up the serpent in the wilderness (John 3:14-15)
- The stairway in Jacob's dream (John 1:51)
- Melchizedek (Hebrews 7)

Yet interpreters or preachers might often propose types of Christ in commendable characters such as Joseph, Joshua, Boaz, David, Jonathan, Solomon, or any number of others, even though the New Testament does not mention them.

Whether such typology involves a New Testament passage or not, they all face the same obstacle: an effective type requires both sides of the comparison to be known before it is recognizable as a type. That being the case, readers having only one side of a potential typological connection can have no awareness of a typological level of message, and the authors of such Old Testament passages cannot be seen as having the typological connection in their intentions.[68] In contrast, if the New Testament author develops a typology, we then have both sides of the comparison and that very comparison becomes central to the New Testament author's intention and message. Nevertheless, that does not suggest that we read that message back into the Old Testament as if it were also the Old Testament author's message. Typology is the message of the one who draws the comparison, not the message of the one who introduces the initial character or object who will later be used in the comparison. Furthermore, we cannot propose our own typological connections with any confidence that we are representing the Word of God.

Example D—Figures with Christological Significance: Some Old Testament figures eventually take on christological significance: Immanuel, the Suffering Servant, and the Son of Man. There can be no doubt that Jesus is identified with each of these in New Testament contexts. Consequently, when we are interpreting New Testament passages and seeking to understand Jesus' self-presentation, it is important to mine these associations and to investigate

[68]For further reading, John H. Walton, "Inspired Subjectivity and Hermeneutical Objectivity," *The Master's Seminary Journal* 13, no. 1 (2002): 65-77.

how they developed from their launch in the Old Testament, through their development in Second Temple Judaism, to their appropriation by Jesus.

Investigating them each in their original Old Testament context will reveal that none of the three have clear messianic or christological connections in their original contexts. Immanuel is a name given to a child born in the eighth century BC (as Isaiah 7:15-17 indicates). Even if that child is Hezekiah (as some have postulated), he is not the Messiah.[69] The Suffering Servant may be a modified messianic figure in Isaiah 53 to the extent that the Servant profile overlaps considerably with the messianic profile in Isaiah. If that subtle association is accepted, Isaiah may have embedded in his message a reconfiguration of messianic expectation—but only in general terms. Nothing explicitly christological is recognizable or anticipated by the author. Even the concept of a king as a substitute for the sin of the people would have been recognized in an ancient context, but in a far different way than what Jesus does.[70] The "Son of Man," a messianic title adopted by Jesus, is first introduced in Daniel 7:13-14. In that context, it is "one like a son of man" who is referred to, and there are many reasons to doubt that the author is intending even a messianic figure here, let alone a reference to Jesus. In the context, the narrator is contrasting the earlier creatures, which were like certain beasts, to now a being that is human in form. As we try to understand the Daniel passage, proposed interpretations for "son of man" include individuals such as Michael, Gabriel, Melchizedek, or Enoch, as well as representing groups such as faithful Israel or the legitimate high priestly office.[71]

Each of these examples (Immanuel, Suffering Servant, Son of Man) illustrates the development of an idea that eventually finds a significant referent in Jesus. Nevertheless, each one also has a significance in its Old Testament context apart from Jesus—a significance that is part of an authoritative message by the Old Testament author. The authority vested in the Old Testament message must be understood and respected alongside the additional message that eventually develops in the New Testament.

---

[69]For further reading, John H. Walton, "Isaiah 7:14—What Is in a Name?," *Journal of the Evangelical Theological Society* 30 (1987): 289-306.

[70]For further reading, John H. Walton, "The Imagery of the Substitute King Ritual in Isaiah's Fourth Servant Song," *Journal of Biblical Literature* 122 (2003): 734-43.

[71]The literature on this topic is immense. The major academic commentaries all contain extensive discussions and will point readers to further technical bibliography.

Example E—The Angel of the Lord and Others: Consider cases in which an individual appears who later Christian theologians identify as a pre-incarnate appearance of Christ. These include appearances of the Angel of the Lord as well as individuals such as the commander of the Lord's armies (Joshua 5:14-15) and the fourth person in the fiery furnace (Daniel 3:25). None of these cases finds any support in the New Testament. That is, neither any of the New Testament writers nor Jesus himself give any hint that there were any pre-incarnate appearances of Jesus. Furthermore, none of these Old Testament passages indicate that any of these are divine figures. In Daniel 3, it is the Babylonian king who compares the fourth figure to "a son of the gods"—but that is from the perspective of his own religious context and is not confirmed by the narrator. The identification of the Angel of the Lord as Jesus is based on contexts where the angel seems to be speaking in first person as God (for example, Exodus 3 and Judges 6). These can all be accounted for by the way the messengers in the ancient world were considered so closely associated with the one whose message they delivered that they could adopt first-person speech.[72]

Some connections between the Old Testament and New Testament can be explored in the context of what Richard Hays calls "echoes" in a figural reading of the New Testament.[73] The New Testament authors are not tracking with the Old Testament authors in the same way as we are trying to track with them. The New Testament authors are developing ideas such as "Jesus as the new Adam," "Jesus as the new Moses," "Jesus as the new Israel," "Jesus as the new David," and "Jesus as the new temple" in appropriation of the Old Testament. The book of Hebrews is engaged explicitly in this sort of theological development as Jesus is presented as the better high priest and the better sacrifice. These represent important theological developments; they do not represent an attempt to understand what the Old Testament authors' intentions were. They do not overwrite what the Old Testament authors were

---

[72]This concept, as well as the far-reaching theological problems with the idea of pre-incarnate appearances of Christ, are thoroughly treated in William G. MacDonald, "Christology and 'The Angel of the Lord,'" in *Current Issues in Biblical and Patristic Interpretation*, ed. G. F. Hawthorne (Grand Rapids, MI: Eerdmans, 1975), 324-35.

[73]This concept is developed in many of his books including Richard Hays, *Echoes of Scripture in the Gospels* (Waco, TX: Baylor, 2017); *Echoes of Scripture in the Letters of Paul* (New Haven, CT: Yale, 1993); *Reading Backwards* (Waco, TX: Baylor, 2014).

communicating. This does not create a contradiction; the individual messages of the Old Testament and New Testament can stand side by side with equal authority.

Tracking with the canon as a whole will lead us from the Old Testament to Jesus and beyond as we learn more and more about the plans and purposes of God. Nevertheless, to understand the authoritative message of any given Old Testament text, we must track with the author's literary intentions before we move onto the track of the larger canon. The Old Testament is leading us toward Jesus in many important ways that we dare not neglect, but it is not *about* Jesus. Respect for the authority of the authors warns against conflating ideas from the Old Testament with the New Testament. The idea of messianic hope developed gradually. Jesus' fulfillment of that hope was far different from what his first-century audience expected, and was therefore also, unsurprisingly, different from concepts the Old Testament narrators would have held. Progressive revelation needs to be followed step-by-step.

The following distinctions can help us to maintain the distinctives of our Christian theology while still holding ourselves accountable to the authors' intentions in the Old Testament:

- We should begin with text-in-context exegesis, interpreting the texts based on the author's literary intentions as best as we can identify them using all the usual factors by which we understand communication. This is where the authority of Scripture resides.
- The next step is appropriation of the text as Christians. This is what the New Testament authors were doing and explains Luke 24 as well as fulfillment of prophecy. They were not interpreting, they were appropriating, and they saw Christ as the centerpiece of God's plans and purposes—thus, christotelic—everything moving toward Christ. When we read these texts as Christians, they invite christotelic appropriation; they do not demand reinterpretation of the Old Testament as being about Christ.
- Finally, it is the role of the believing community to formulate theology, which will be inevitably christocentric (though that can still be

> overrated if other aspects of theology are neglected in the process). This is where tradition and the creeds, councils, and confessions come into play. We cannot do theology without them.

Consequently, the councils were most interested in *theological* questions, more than *exegetical* ones. The New Testament was dealing with appropriation, not text-in-context interpretation. Biblical authority is not removed from the authors and given to the community, but theology must take place in the community, and we grant it a certain amount of authority (though distinct from biblical authority).

This approach distinguishes authors' intentions (exegesis), christotelic perspective (appropriation), and christocentric theology into three separate acts of the larger enterprise of interpretation leading to theology. It recognizes the central role of community and tradition without giving up the authority of the text to them. As fundamental as the text must be, we recognize that we cannot do theology on text alone.

16—The Holy Spirit Cannot Be Used as an Appeal to Authority

Perhaps you have been in a Bible study where someone offered an interpretation of a particular passage and validated it by claiming that God or the Holy Spirit had given it to them, or maybe you have said something similar. If you have been following the logic so far in this book, you may already be able to explain why that approach to interpretation cannot stand, but this chapter will now work it out step-by-step. What is the role of the Holy Spirit when we interpret the Old Testament?

We believe that the Holy Spirit has been active in the phenomenon of Scripture in numerous and varied ways. First, we believe that the Holy Spirit engaged with the authors of Scripture, prompting them to communicate it, whether orally or in text (2 Peter 1:20-21). In contrast to those who might think that this was simply an act of dictation, the reality was much more subtle and the processes undetectable and variable. In some way they spoke, wrote, or both "in the Spirit." Regardless of the methods used, this means that the Holy Spirit was involved in communicating the message of God's revelation through these human instruments (remember, including tradents, authors, editors, and compilers). This is the chain of communication that was used, and we should not look for another method that would bypass this step (for example, personal communication to us).

Second, we believe that the Holy Spirit not only prompted the authors, but that he inspired the texts. In 2 Timothy 3:16 the textual products specifically are labeled as inspired, not the human instruments that produced them. The main thrust of this affirmation is that these texts, though produced through human agency, find their source in God. They are not just the best thoughts of the best human beings. Therefore, as in our first point, the Holy Spirit was the principal agent in vouchsafing that God's message was preserved in the actual writings that we have, despite the complicated, untraceable process that was involved. So the Holy Spirit was involved at both levels: authors and texts.[74]

That background makes it possible to now discuss the Holy Spirit's role in the last step in the line of communication from God to us: the readers. Here too, the Holy Spirit has an important role to play, but it is not one that offers us the interpretation of any given passage. Interpretation involves understanding the meanings of Hebrew words; the Holy Spirit does not provide that to us. Interpretation involves understanding the literary structure and rhetorical devices that were used; the Holy Spirit does not provide that to us. Interpretation involves understanding aspects of ancient culture; the Holy Spirit does not provide that to us. The Holy Spirit does not give us an understanding of the author's literary intentions above and beyond what we can glean from evidence available to all, yet that is precisely what constitutes faithful interpretation.

At this point, the reader might object—how do you know he doesn't? Maybe when we study and gain insight into something like the literary structure of a passage, it was actually the Holy Spirit who gave us that insight. Fair point. In one sense, we could never know. I like to believe that

---

[74]It is intriguing to imagine how this might also be extended to our understanding of the canon, but that discussion is beyond the purview of this book.

maybe he has helped me on occasion by providing an important insight that unlocks a passage's meaning. But here is where we get to the important point highlighted in the chapter title. Even if the Holy Spirit might do that, we can never claim that our interpretation is correct *because* the Holy Spirit gave it to us. We are obliged to validate our interpretations by evidence; we cannot do so by an appeal to the Holy Spirit's authority.

Why not? The reason we cannot do so is that the claim that the Holy Spirit (rather than the evidence) is the authority for our interpretation is unverifiable and unfalsifiable. It is a conversation-ending claim. If we claim that the Holy Spirit has given us an interpretation that does not find support in the evidence concerning the author's intentions, we are, in effect, claiming that the Holy Spirit has given us an inspired message. That would imply that the author's intentions do not matter. The result of such thinking is that we have replaced what the Holy Spirit gave to the author with what we now claim he gave to us; it amounts to a claim that we have the authority from the Holy Spirit rather than the author having that authority. It posits that the interpreter is an independent instrument of God's authoritative revelation. I would propose that the Holy Spirit is not in the practice of bypassing what he did through the authors to give any of us a personal interpretation of the message that the authors did not have.

The points raised here should not be considered a denial that the Holy Spirit works in us as we read Scripture. Instead, I am calling for a more informed and nuanced understanding of what the Holy Spirit does and does not do. We cannot claim that the Holy Spirit gives us an interpretation that the author did not have, or even that the Holy Spirit validates the interpretation that we have arrived at by analyzing evidence. The Holy Spirit cannot be claimed as the authority to our interpretation of the authoritative message of the text. Once we have identified that message, however, using all the tools and insight to help us develop the evidence for interpretation, the Holy Spirit can lead us to understand ways that the truth of that message can be applied to our lives. The Spirit can convict us of ways that the author's message ought to change our thinking or practice. Only the Holy Spirit can transform us by the power of that message provided through the author. In sum, the Holy Spirit does not tell us the message, but guides us to know what to do with the message and empowers us to respond. The Holy Spirit gave the message through the authors, not through us, but we are responsible to be responsive to that message. It is the role of the Holy Spirit to help that to happen. If we only interpret but fail to respond, our lives are a fallow field. Consequently, the role of the Holy Spirit is vital and robust in the experience of the reader, but it is not the role of providing interpretation. For that, we remain dependent on developing evidence so that we can track with the authors as we reflect our accountability to them.

This brings us back to the dictum already cited a few times, that the strongest interpretation is the one with the strongest evidence. The strongest interpretation is not the one offered by the most spiritual interpreter, or the one with the strongest prayer life or the most disciplined devotional life. A person in very close relationship with God is not thereby guaranteed to have the strongest interpretation.

This means that impressions and ideas that come out of our devotional reading of Scripture must not be confused with interpretation. The biblical messages can give us truth to follow in our lives. Likewise, the Holy Spirit can move us to think and act in certain ways. The Holy Spirit may even actually move us to these thoughts and actions while we are reading Scripture, but that is a different process altogether than interpreting Scripture. After all, the Holy Spirit could prompt us, convict us, or even transform us when we are reading something else—the biography of an inspirational person, or a deeply meaningful poem. When we read our Bibles devotionally, we should be seeking interpretation so we can receive the message from God. During that time, we could also seek the guidance of the Holy Spirit in our lives, but that is not the same thing and should not be seen as a substitute for interpretation.

> **Example—"The Lord Has Given the City":** I once heard the story of a person who was reading his Bible and got to a passage that says, "The Lord has given the city into your hand" (presumably Joshua 6:16; 8:7; or 8:18). As he read that verse, the Spirit impressed on him a new direction for his life and ministry. He would henceforth turn his attention and his efforts toward an urban ministry with the confidence that the Lord would give him a fruitful influence for Christ in the inner city. As time has gone by, he has founded an

> organization that has had a very significant impact, mostly in poverty-stricken urban centers. I have never had the privilege of having a conversation with this person, but I suspect that, if questioned on the specifics, he would not insist that the author of Joshua had urban ministry in mind. It is quite clear from the context that Joshua's armies are going to bring about the destruction of the city of Jericho or Ai. Instead, I would anticipate that he would only claim that the text in Joshua was nothing more than a launching point used by the Spirit that day to call him to his ministry. In other words, I think that he would readily admit that what happened that day had nothing to do with biblical interpretation.[75]

The point I want to make is that while many of us seek God's guidance in our lives and are delighted when we believe that we have received it, that process should not be mistaken for biblical interpretation. Moreover, if that guidance is what we are seeking when we are reading the Bible, we are missing what it is there for. In such an approach, we are not engaging with the authoritative message of God's Word; we are not even looking for it. In its extremes, such an approach simply uses the Bible as some sort of horoscope instead of using it as a repository for the revelation of God's plans and purposes in the world. If we are not tracking with the author (and often not even trying to track with the author), the Bible is not being used to full effect and we are giving only lip service to its authority.

The Spirit's best work is done as we seek guidance for applying the message that he placed in the text through the authors, not in seeking our own personal message apart from what the author was saying. Much more could be said about this, but that is not what this book is about. We are focusing on the Bible's best work. The Bible's best work is done as we seek evidence for sound interpretation so that we may then submit to the authority of God vested in the authors—and then respond to that message. The Holy Spirit helps us respond, and that is the application that we seek once we have properly engaged.

---

[75]I do not use this example to criticize this person—in fact, I admire what he has done. The example illustrates the different ways that God can use Scripture in our lives, and it would be valid for him to say that the verse in Joshua inspired him to move into the direction of urban ministry. He would not be suggesting that that was the message of Joshua.

17—Not Everything Has a "Biblical View"

The final chapter in this unit addresses a fallacy in how we use Scripture. It can be termed a fallacy because it encompasses many of the issues addressed in the foregoing chapters. If we lack a clear understanding of what the Bible is, how it communicates, and what our responsibilities and limitations as readers are, we may begin using the Bible as a "how-to" guide, or a "book of all answers."

We live in a culture where being opinionated is increasingly commended (note the rise of the blogosphere) and where individualism proclaims everyone's personal rights to their opinion. We nevertheless still value appeals to authority to validate our perspectives. The last chapter discussed the question of whether the Spirit could be used in an appeal to authority. This chapter is about using the Bible in an appeal to authority. This is trickier, because the Bible indeed has authority, and therefore an appeal to authority based on the Bible seems not just logical, but essential.

Having said that, we now need to make an important distinction about how an appeal to biblical authority works and what controls need to be applied for such appeals to be meaningful. In short, I will develop the distinction between appealing to the Bible with regard to its own authoritative message and appealing to the Bible as validation for the authority of what we may desire to promote. This is perhaps most often reflected when interpreters develop what may be claimed as the "biblical view of X," where X equals a view on society and its controversies, on theological issues, or on various lifestyles. We have become adept at promoting our own views and preferences by claiming that our conclusions represent a biblical view, which then becomes the basis for arguments and marketing efforts.[76]

The array of topics that fall into this category that I refer to under the rubric of the "biblical view of X" is vast (see table 17.1).

---

[76]This often involves developing a collection of proof texts.

Table 17.1. Biblical views of . . .

CATEGORY	BIBLICAL VIEW OF . . .
Lifestyle	Nutrition, alcohol, dating, social media, sexuality, marriage, wealth management, weight loss, child-rearing, vaccination
Values	Morality, individual rights, ethical use of technology
Qualities	Leadership, teaching
Social issues	Birth control, abortion, euthanasia, gender roles, welfare systems, care for the poor, climate change, racism
Society	Economics (capitalism, communism, etc.), cities, war, slavery, partisan politics, law, creation care
Spiritual practices	Tithing, evangelism, counseling, discipleship, prayer, worship
Theology	Hell, the Rapture, eschatology, predestination, baptism, creation, evolution

This is just a sampling—a comprehensive list would be virtually endless. Everyone would like to claim that the view that they hold dear on something controversial is validated by the Bible. Maybe some of those views can be, at least to some extent, but we must think carefully about how this validation process works and what sorts of things can or cannot be validated by appeal to biblical authority. It is important to explore this considering what I have been maintaining about the essential connection between biblical authority and the literary intentions of the authors. If only the authors' intentions carry authority, we should limit our claims of biblical validation ("the biblical view of X") to cases where the authors are knowingly addressing the particular issues. For example, we could easily construct a "biblical view of wisdom" because we have many passages where the message of the authors is to offer that view.

That being the case, it would seem obvious that the text says nothing about issues such as dating or social media. Dating did not exist in the ancient context of arranged marriages, and social media is a recent technological development. Since the authors of Scripture had no knowledge of these aspects of our modern culture, they could not have included them in their intentions. It is possible, as we think about such issues, that there will be implications that find support in the Bible (perhaps the importance of integrity or honesty), but such general implications are insufficient to construct a "biblical view" if the author's intentions are understood to provide the controls. We do not have the space to engage each of the topics listed above, but we will choose a representative sample in each category to illustrate the issues.

Example A—Lifestyle, such as Nutrition and Diet: In our modern world, hardly anything is valued as highly as health. We therefore desire credible information about maintaining health and have learned that nutrition and diet are fundamental to that objective. Nevertheless, the Bible cannot be understood as a guide to everything, answering all our questions with divine guidance to help us to flourish in every way. But is there a biblical view of nutrition or a biblically endorsed diet?

When we read the Old Testament, we are often baffled by the dietary laws in Leviticus 11 and Deuteronomy 14. In our attempts to make sense of them, it is common for interpreters to understand them as being based on innate properties of the foods that are forbidden because of the dangers they represent. The idea is that God knew what was good for people even if the Israelites were unaware of the nutritional aspects of such dietary regulations. The question we need to ask is whether the authors and their immediate audiences understood these prohibitions as being based on nutritional value or, alternatively, whether they were grounded in a very different premise. The latter is likely, evident even in the fact that violation of the requirements is not cited as having health consequences but are treated as ritual offenses.

As an example of an alternative interpretation, one suggestion has been that all the prohibited meats are defiling because they are connected to animals tainted with death (either because they are predators or because their habitat or diet associates them with the dirt, the habitation of the dead). For Israelites, contact with the dead made them unclean. Whether or not that is a proper understanding, we recognize that these requirements are inherent in God's covenant with Israel, not given to every culture for all time (see further discussion below, chap. 22). Finally, when the dietary laws are set aside in Acts 10:9-15; 15:19-21, it is not because good health and nutrition are no longer being valued.

Others have found biblical diet plans in passages such as Ezekiel 4:9, but it is clear from the context that this does not promote these ingredients as essential for a healthy diet. Instead, it describes the meager foodstuffs that will be available to the exiles, but more importantly, indicates that it will be unclean because they will have to cook their food using human excrement as fuel (Ezekiel 4:12-13). Likewise, Daniel 1 does not stand as a biblically suggested diet. We have already discussed that above (chap. 12), where we saw that it does not represent a choice of vegetables over meat. Daniel's commitment is not to health and nutrition, but to identify with the exilic community instead of with the royal house. No "Daniel diet" is promoted by the Bible as a path to good health. All of this means that anyone who is promoting a biblical diet is not promoting the sound reading of Scripture. The Old Testament does not endorse a particular diet.

Example B—Values, such as Individual Rights:[77] The concept of individual rights stands as a core value in many modern cultures. It is built into the United States Constitution and is one of the main determining factors in judicial verdicts. Its prominent role in American thinking is tied inextricably to the high value we place on individualism. In our culture, we find our identity in ourselves as individuals. It is a defensible premise, though not the only possible one.

In the ancient world, a person's identity was derived from the role and status that they had in the community. Individualism was discouraged and was at times seen as a disruptive influence on society.[78] The Israelites shared this outlook (another example of being embedded, but not indebted). Consequently, we would not expect their literature to take the role of being a champion for individual rights. A passage such as Ezekiel 18 indeed does emphasize individual responsibility, but that is a distinct (though not unrelated) idea.[79] Any text that would be drawn from the Old Testament to support individual rights would have to be carefully weighed for what it is and is not saying. Since the texts do not promote individualism, it would be unexpected that they would promote individual rights—they just do not have that perspective.[80]

---

[77]In this discussion, I want to distinguish this from similar and overlapping categories such as human rights and civil rights, which are also important but have their own conversations.

[78]For important discussion of this issue and its significance see E. Randolph Richards and Richard James, *Misreading Scripture with Individualist Eyes: Patronage, Honor, and Shame in the Biblical World* (Downers Grove, IL: IVP Academic, 2020); John J. Pilch, *Introducing the Cultural Context of the Old Testament* (Mahwah, NJ: Paulist, 1991), 96-98.

[79]Ezekiel 18 may even pertain more toward how each generation is treated rather than each individual, but that does not change this discussion. In any case, Ezekiel is making the point that his generation, which is suffering the exile, is not just being punished for the sins of their forebears.

[80]Note, for example, that both the "image of God" and the "Body of Christ" relate to corporate groups, not individuals.

Example C—Qualities, such as Leadership: The Bible offers no model for successful leadership. It portrays some who, through a combination of natural abilities and the providential blessing of God, become successful leaders. In such presentations, however, the text is descriptive, not prescriptive—it describes what certain leaders did, but stops short of indicating that for anyone to be a successful leader, they must do it that way. Successful leadership may have certain common denominators, but often different situations call for different approaches, different strategies, and different sorts of leaders. When interpreters mine the book of Nehemiah, for example, to offer a "biblical model of leadership," they do so selectively—choosing those elements which they believe are commendable qualities and ignoring others that perhaps are not so replicable (for example, Nehemiah pulling out the hair of his antagonist and beating him, Nehemiah 13:25). Such selective appeal means that the principles of leadership are more those of the modern interpreter than of the biblical author.

Furthermore, the Bible has numerous examples of successful, God-approved leaders whose techniques would not be commended in any leadership book. Joseph's economic policies result in the conversion of private property in Egypt to state control (Genesis 41:46-57). Solomon's successful leadership in gaining the kingdom entailed the execution of his opponents (1 Kings 2). Just because God prospers these efforts does not mean that he is promoting their strategies as a model for all to follow.

Example D—Social Issues, such as Gender Roles: We can gain much information from Old Testament texts about gender roles in ancient Israel. Israelite society was unapologetically hierarchical and patriarchal, but the texts are typically descriptive rather than prescriptive. Descriptive texts are not making affirmations that become the message of the text for all who submit to its authority. The only "biblical view" of gender roles is the one that Israelite society happened to have. Like their views on government or on economics, those views do not come with a biblical mandate—the authors' intentions are not to offer a universally required social structure.

Example E—Society and War: The Bible looks forward to a time when there will be no war, when swords will be beaten into plowshares, and when all will enjoy freedom from oppressors and from the chaos of war. In that sense, we can infer that war is seen as a negative factor of life. Nevertheless, it is difficult to try to build a "biblical view of war" in an effort to promote either pacifism or "just war." Deuteronomy 20 contains Israel's rules for war, and nowhere does it even hint that war is wrong. Furthermore, the Israelites of Joshua's time are led into war by the Lord. In the ancient world, it was understood that war was sometimes necessary to combat evil forces; that it was essential as people sought to overthrow oppressors and to reestablish order when it is threatened by chaos. There are many reasons to oppose war, and many wars are conducted with less than commendable objectives. Nevertheless, the Bible does not offer guidance through those issues to give us a "biblical view of war."

Example F—Spiritual Practice, such as Evangelism: Many believe that the Great Commission and numerous other passages call us to evangelism. This in itself is debatable because the call is to making disciples. A disciple is an apprentice who is being trained to become a master—it is not just any follower or convert. Even so, as a general call to be witnesses (Acts 1:8), it falls short of providing a "how-to" guide. Investigating how Jesus interacted with others can be productive, but others interacted differently. No single "biblical" model can be constructed. It is simply not what the Bible is doing, and not what the authors are intending. Even Jesus interacted with different people in different ways.

Even greater difficulties emerge when people try to use Old Testament passages in a discussion of evangelism. Israel is unquestionably designated as a "light to the nations," but in the context of the covenant, that is not a call for them to be evangelistic. When they serve appropriately as a light to the nations, the nations will come to them; they are not sent to the nations.[81] They serve as a light to the nations as they show what it is like to live in relationship with their covenant God who dwells among them. They do not offer that covenant relationship to others.

Example G—Theology and Hell: Christians have always desired to go to the Bible to develop and defend doctrine and theology. This is not inappropriate, but it is also not always possible. The problem is obvious considering the deep differences held by Christians on theological issues over the centuries as each

[81]Jonah may be the exception. But note that his message is not an evangelistic one, it is a prophetic pronouncement of coming judgment. He offers no indictment, no call to repent or convert, and no hope. No other oracles to the nations in the prophets feature the prophet going to the nations; their pronouncements are messages to Israel.

camp offers biblical support for their theological conclusions. In most cases, select biblical texts can be used to bring information to the theological discussions (that is, to offer support), but if there were a clear "biblical view," the issues would not remain controversial (that is, "support" is not equivalent to "proof"). The most important point to be made here is that we need to beware of using biblical passages to support a particular doctrinal issue in cases where it is not within the purview of the author's intentions to address that issue.

The example of hell is one illustration. In ancient Israel, there was no concept of judgment in the afterlife. One Old Testament passage often cited in the conversation is Isaiah 66:24, but that falls short of addressing a doctrine of judgment in the afterlife, as most commentators agree. If the authors of the Old Testament have no concept of judgment in the afterlife (regardless of the various views of hell in later theology), the passages found in the Old Testament cannot be used to say anything about the doctrine. The Hebrew term *sheol* is simply the netherworld and should not be interpreted as hell—there is no judgment or punishment in *sheol*.

The Old Testament may at times provide perspectives that contribute to our thinking about various issues, and to that extent, we can seek to develop a worldview and a theology that is biblically informed. Nevertheless, that is a different matter than proposing that the Bible offers a systematic position on an issue that derives from the author's intentions about that issue and carries the weight of biblical authority. Again, the point is that we cannot use our accumulated proof texts and tidbits as the basis for an appeal to biblical authority in an attempt to support the position that we are trying to maintain. When the Old Testament offers information on many of these topics, it is generally descriptive, non-systematic, culturally situated, and often addressed specifically to Israel in the context of the covenant.

By this point in the book, some readers will be feeling a sense of despair, wondering what they are supposed to do to be faithful interpreters when they engage in devotional Bible reading or in formal Bible studies. With limited time, limited training, and limited resources, are we simply doomed to wallow in ignorance? The last unit of this book will address this, but there is still more ground to cover before it is possible to receive the full impact of what is proposed there.

PART TWO

GENRE GUIDELINES

SECTION A

PENTATEUCH

The preceding material has set the stage for reading the Bible generally, a necessary preparation for moving into the larger sections of the Old Testament to offer insights for faithful interpretation built on the principles already established. In this section, these will focus specifically on the topics of creation, covenant, and Torah. These are deeply interrelated topics. This section will not deal with the narratives found in the Pentateuch—they will be addressed in the next section on narratives.

18—Creation Is More About Order Than Material

When we read the creation account in Genesis 1:1–2:4, it is easy to approach it with our own modern perceptions. We live in a culture in which science predominates and we have come to believe that creation, whatever the role of God, can be best understood through science. Some accept the modern positions reflected in the scientific mainstream while others reject that narrative and offer an alternative scientific reconstruction. In either case, science provides the canvas and the palette, the tableau by which the masterpiece that is creation is portrayed. We can readily understand, however, that for another culture not so immersed in scientific ways of thinking, they may not find science as providing the best way to talk about creation. We can therefore see that our first question regarding Genesis must be, "What kind of creation account is this?"

From a scientific perspective, creation is primarily about the origin of the material universe (whether God is seen as the agent or not). Universally, cultures are aware of the material world, but not every culture considers the material world as foundational as do those of us who have adopted a scientific perspective. Evidence suggests that in ancient cultures, people believed the gods were responsible for the material aspects of the cosmos. Nevertheless, that is not the major focus of their creation accounts. Though they are aware of what we call matter and would accept the premise that the gods had brought matter into being, in their view, that is not the most important or essential work of creation. Rather than prioritizing the material aspects, the creation narratives that ancient cultures preserve show that they place a higher value on the ordering of the cosmos.[1]

BEGINNINGS

When we try to tell any story "from the beginning" we have to choose some sort of subjective or arbitrary point to start. To tell the story of "how I met my spouse," one could begin when you were first introduced to one another. But what about the circumstances that led you each to that room and event at college? What about the circumstances that led you each to that college? One could even start with, "Ever since I was born . . ." Identifying the beginning is a choice that is determined by many different variables.

Likewise, when a culture offers an account of "how the world began," a decision must be made about where to start: Before your nation existed? Before your ethnic group existed? Before material existed? Before the gods existed? When there was only nothingness? Again, choices are made. In our culture, material stands as the focus, so we tend to talk about how and when the material world came into being. We define "existence" materially and therefore we call bringing material objects into existence, "creation." For us, that discussion is enabled by science.

---

[1]Notice that the seven days feature no terraforming—that is, no creation of rivers, lakes, oceans, mountains, forests, and so on. No mention is made of God creating water; indeed, it already is there before the seven days of creation begin.

But let's consider some alternatives by using an analogy. If we were talking about the origins of the place we live, we might tell the story of how the house was built—its material construction with foundation, frame, roof, electricity, plumbing, and so on. But we could alternatively talk about the origins of the place we live by describing how we made it our home—how each room is furnished and how it functions, how it is ordered with purpose. Both the house story and the home story are "creation" stories. When guests ask us about our place, they are generally more interested in the home story than in the house story. When prospective buyers visit a piece of real estate, some might be very interested in the house, others with how it might work as a home.

In like manner, one could describe how a play began by talking about the writing of the script, the building of the theater, the construction of the set for this play, the choosing of the cast, or the action on the stage once the curtain opened. Any one of these could be a legitimate and correct answer to the question of how the play began. But different people might choose to answer with one or the other of those alternatives.

Consequently, when we pose the question concerning how the world began, we will have our own cultural ways to answer that question. We should nevertheless be hesitant to conclude that it can only be answered one way, or that another culture would answer it the same way that we do. Attentive reading would not seek to merge their account into our way of thinking. Instead, we need to consider how they are answering the question, realizing that it may reflect different values and priorities than ours.

In the creation accounts of the ancient Near Eastern world, order is arguably the highest value, and purpose is the most important question. They were very interested in how each component functioned in the cosmos to bring about order and achieve the purposes of the creator(s). Not only is that a different set of questions than what our culture asks, it is a set of questions beyond the scope of science. When we force our (scientific) priorities on the text, we therefore risk losing any possibility of addressing what was most important to them. Scientists today are not asking "who?" or "why?" Their attention to material origins does not address the who-and-why question. They are interested in mechanisms rather than in an agent, such as God, or his purpose.

I would suggest that in Genesis, as in many creation accounts in the ancient Near East, the author is offering an answer to the who-and-why question, but with different answers than their neighbors, as they are describing in broad strokes how God brought order in the cosmos to achieve his purposes. They are interested in agency, not mechanisms. For Israelites, as with others in the ancient Near East, something only truly exists when it has a role and a purpose in an ordered system. To the extent that this is true, creation (which brings something into existence) is an ordering process when existence is tied to order. In this description, we can see that the Israelites differed from their neighbors regarding the agent and the purpose, though they agreed with their neighbors that those were the important issues.[2] The Israelites differ from our modern view regarding what were the most important issues in the conversation. Their conversation partners were interested in different issues than our conversation partners.

CREATION'S DAYS

This can be seen to be the case in Genesis 1 once we observe how little the text says about material origins. In the first three days, nothing material is brought into existence. On day one, day and night are created through the alternating periods of light and darkness, the foundation of time. Day and night, and time, represent the most fundamental element of order both in the cosmos and in our lives—both in the ancient world and in ours. God ordered the cosmos by means of time, his first act of creation.

On day two, the heavens are organized. The waters above and below are separated by the living space in between.[3] This is organization of the material cosmos—nothing material is *produced*. Day three is similar: dry land

---

[2]Again, we can see the contrast between "embedded" (Israel is exhibiting similar interest in order as a value that is found ubiquitously in the ancient Near East) but not "indebted" (Israel is not just taking up someone else's literature and tweaking it).

[3]Many consider the Hebrew term used here, *raqia,'* to refer to the solid sky, therefore the "firmament." Others translate "expanse," a significantly less material term. I prefer the latter. Though I affirm that the Israelites would have believed in a solid sky, I am not convinced that *raqia'* is that word. For further reading, see John H. Walton, *Genesis 1 as Ancient Cosmology* (Winona Lake, IN: Eisenbrauns, 2011), 155-61.

emerges, and plants are set to growing. Organization and function combine to establish order as people are being provided with the basis for food.

Days four through six take on a different focus, as widely recognized throughout the history of interpretation. In these days, we might find it easier to think that now attention is turning to the origin of material objects, but a closer look shows that not to be the case. On day four, we are told that God said, "Let there be lights," and then that he *made* the two great lights. To our material-attuned ears, that sounds like creating the sun and the moon as material objects, but we must try to step outside of our natural inclinations. First, it calls them lights, and even though the narrator unquestionably refers to the sun and moon, his choice of terms accentuates what they do—they function as lights, and, as such, they rule the day and night. This focus on function should be recognized and respected. Second, it is important to realize that in the ancient world no one was aware that the sun and moon were material objects. Most of the ancient world considered them visible gods. The Israelites were not so inclined but saw them as . . . lights! The fact that we know they are material objects makes no difference. Recall that our question is, what kind of creation account is this in the eyes of the Israelite narrator and audience? The authority is in the author's intentions. If neither author nor audience knew the sun and moon were material objects, then to them, day four does not recount the origin of material objects, but of lights that have a function and role in the cosmos God is ordering. The text affirms that God made *lights*, not material objects.

On day five, fish and birds populate the cosmos. Yet again, however, the text does not make a point of the idea that God materially formed these creatures. If we were able to ask the question of the Israelites, "Did God make these birds and fish as material creatures"? they would undoubtedly affirm that fact. But it is important for us to recognize that that is not what the narrator *says*. God is populating the earth ("teem" and "swarm") and giving these creatures the capacity to be fruitful and multiply. This is about furnishing the home, not manufacturing the furniture.

As this discussion has been proceeding through the biblical account, it has now gone through five days, and there has not yet been a single statement that pertained to creation by manufacturing a material object in the viewpoint of the author and audience. This realization should alert us to the possibility that they are offering a different beginning point and a different focus than what we are generally inclined to suppose. For them, the most important creation account is an ordering account, because only in order is existence truly achieved. Thus, the Genesis account begins in Genesis 1:2 with the absence of order (the description of the earth) and the presence of only darkness and water (the typical features of non-order in the ancient world).

When we arrive at the activities of day six, we may finally see wording that could suggest material creation. Even here, however, in the first act of the day, God says, "Let the land produce living creatures" (Genesis 1:24), and that is how "God made the wild animals" (Genesis 1:25). Clearly, as always, God is the agent, though mechanisms are not the point, and they are not described as being made out of nothing. More important to the narrator is the way that they are organized (according to kinds). As in day five, the text does not focus on individual creatures but on populations. The land had abundantly provided diverse animal populations.

When the narrator comes to people in day six, the focus remains on a population group, humanity (in male and female varieties), created with a particular function—subjugating and ruling alongside God, in whose image they are made. Humanity is created to function as order-bringers, not bringing about their own order, but working alongside God to achieve his order. Materiality is a fact, but it is not the focus of the narrator.

What would a creation account focused on material origins look like? What would we need to see to conclude that Genesis or another creation text is about material creation? I would expect such an account to use the same kind of language that is used in the rest of the Bible when it is talking about the material world:

- Yahweh made the sea and the dry land (Jonah 1:9)—already present in Genesis 1:2
- Laid the foundations of the earth (Psalm 104:5; Job 38:4-7) along with its dimensions and footings
- Stretches out the heavens (Psalm 104:2)

- Forms the mountains (Amos 4:13)—nothing about mountains, lakes, rivers, and so on, in Genesis 1
- Knit and woven together, fearfully made; frame and sinews (Psalm 139:13-15)

These talk about what God has done, but they are not creation accounts, and even many of these pay more attention to order, function, or both. This exercise is not meant to build a theology of creation (for either them or us) but to understand this piece of literature (Genesis 1).

To the extent that the word *origins* stirs up in our minds a scientific perspective, it does not suit this narrative. It likely is closer to the target to refer to this as an account of identity rather than account of origins. One's role and function in the ordered cosmos is what gives one identity. This narrative answers the question "What is the cosmos?" Yet this discussion has still not reached the bottom line in the answer the narrator wishes to give. To understand the purpose behind this ordering of the cosmos, that is, to answer, "For what is it ordered?" requires moving to day seven. But for now there is reason to suggest, as stated in the chapter title, that the account is more about order than about material.

19—The Seventh Day Is the Most Important of the Creation Days

It is not uncommon for people who read the Bible to talk about the "six days of creation." The seventh day is relegated either to insignificance or as the support for some arcane Jewish practice. It is believed to feature inactivity and disengagement and therefore does not qualify as "creation." We have seen that in the six days, there is barely a hint at material creation, instead focusing on order. Viewed from that perspective, the seventh day now takes on a critical role. The seventh day stands as the climax to the creation account and likewise has no material aspect; instead, it turns our attention to purpose.

First, to be clear, the Hebrew term describing what God did on the seventh day, *shabbat*, indisputably pertains to cessation. When God ceased his work of creation (see the previous chapter for the discussion on what that work was), he had completed his ordering of the cosmos.[4] Exodus 20:8-11 supplies an additional significant perspective needed to understand the full nature of this "rest." Chapters twelve and thirteen above discussed the idea that the same English word may sometimes be used to reflect a number of different Hebrew words, and that is the case here. In Genesis 2:2-3, the verbal root *shbt* refers to cessation (that is, God's resting). In Exodus 20:10, the seventh day is a *shabbat* (noun) to the Lord, and Exodus 20:11 tells us that on that day he "rested" (now the Hebrew verb, *nwh*). If *shbt* reflects a contrast to a past behavior, *nwh* reflects a posture that pertains to the present and future. What does it mean when God "rests" (*nwh*)? Psalm 132:14 tells us that God's resting place is in the temple and that he rests on his throne. This in turn indicates that when God rests, he does not do so in a bed, but on a throne—his rest is his rule. It is called "rest" because he has established order and can now settle in to ruling. Ezekiel 28:13 suggests that his initial resting place was the Garden of Eden. When God is resting on his throne, ruling the cosmos, he then brings rest to his people. That does not refer to leisure or naps, but to stability and security—order!

God has been bringing order through his work of creation. He then ceases that work and subsequently assumes the throne to rule the world and sustain the order already established. Furthermore, he creates people in his image to work alongside him and thereby continue the order-bringing process. In light of these ideas, day seven reflects the very important idea of God taking up his reign (that is, his rest).

THE PURPOSE OF CREATION

The preceding discussion makes it now possible to address the purpose of creation in Genesis 1, working from the idea that day seven is the

[4]Note that the cosmos has not been *fully* ordered, but *optimally* ordered. Sea and darkness, the basic elements of non-order, continue to exist; there is an "outside" the garden that is less ordered than inside; people are created to subdue and rule—order-bringing activities. The cosmos is inhabitable ("good" equals "ordered"), but not perfectly or completely ordered. That state will be achieved only in the new creation, where there will be no darkness and no sea (Revelation 21).

theological climax, not a ceremonial footnote—that day seven embodies both the reason for and the outcome of God's creative work. The stream of logic begins with the recognition that God's purpose for creating humanity was that as his image-bearers, humanity would work alongside of him as together they continued to achieve his purposes. This implies relationship. We then discover in Genesis 2 that that relationship (though we are told little about it) features God dwelling with people in the garden. It is a place of his presence. Day seven and the further information we receive about it in Exodus 20 therefore serve as a bridge between relationship (day 6) and presence (Eden). God orders, rules, and dwells. Theologically, this suggests the conclusion that God has created us to be in relationship with him and to dwell among us. This is what the ordering of the cosmos achieved, and day seven is the climax. We miss this if we fail to understand the significance of God's rest (that he rules) and think of creation only in material terms. Order and purpose are more important than the material cosmos and they help us to understand what kind of creation account this is. The "beginning" that is of interest to this narrator and audience is the beginning of the cosmos being ordered for relationship with God and for the presence of God.[5]

The seven days reflects this purpose rather than a material one. All the controversies concerning the length of the days and the significance of that for the question of the age of the earth have assumed that this is a creation account focusing on the material aspect (as our culture would be inclined to do); that it is a house story rather than a home story. In the view presented here, the seven days has significance in Genesis and is used to structure the account because of its parallel in 1 Kings 8. In the seven days of temple inauguration, God's presence came to bring order to the Israelites as he came to dwell among them.[6] The seven days in the Genesis account pertain to the preparation for God's presence, not to the age of the earth. Furthermore, we can now understand that the days are not necessarily

---

[5]For the pervasive theological themes of relationship and presence, see chapters 20 and 37.

[6]The temple inauguration features a seven-day dedication with an additional seven-day feast, 1 Kings 8:65; 2 Chronicles 7:9. For further reading, John H. Walton, *The Lost World of Genesis One* (Downers Grove, IL: IVP Academic, 2009), 86-100.

suggesting a material, chronological sequence (so we don't have to decide how there can be light, day 1, without the sun, day 4).

When we track with the authors and hold ourselves accountable to their intentions, we commit ourselves to understanding the text through their eyes, language, and culture. We want to read it the way they would have wanted their original audiences to read it. This commitment rules out many interpretations. Most importantly, it leads us to the understanding that rather than the seventh day being of negligible importance, it is of ultimate importance. The message of the text could not be accomplished without the seventh day, and all the other days find their purpose in the seventh day. The seventh day is the climax, not only because the ordering work is accomplished, but because God now sits on his throne to rule the world that he has ordered (created). The six days find their purpose in God sitting on his throne ruling the world that he has ordered. The message is not just that God is the Creator, though that is important; it is that God is the ruler of the world by virtue of being the one who ordered it under his rule.

REST AND SABBATH

This interpretation carries significance not only for understanding the creation account in Genesis 1, but for understanding what Sabbath observance would look like. Both Jews and Christians have often read the Sabbath texts and come to the conclusion that their obligation was to imitate God by resting (understanding *rest* to mean relax, don't work). If the most important aspect of Sabbath is God's engagement (in rule) rather than his disengagement (from the ordering work), then imitation is not what is mandated. The alternative is that Sabbath observance calls for participation. Again, not total disengagement, but engagement in God's rule and God's kingdom. Humans rest from our own attempts to order our lives for our own purposes (disengagement), but more importantly we engage in acknowledgment of God's rule as the order-bringer. We recognize that his order is of highest priority, not our own: "Thy kingdom come; thy will be done" (not ours). This idea is prominently observable in Isaiah 58:13-14, where instead of talking about "not working on the Sabbath," it discusses Sabbath observance in terms of the alternative possibilities: keep from doing as you please (far broader than "working") and observe it by not going your own way but by honoring it as "the Lord's holy day." This is further illuminated because earlier in the chapter, when talking about fasting, it contrasted doing as you please with unloosing the chains of injustice, setting the oppressed free, sharing food with the hungry, and providing for the poor (Isaiah 58:6-7). Presumably, those would also be recommended activities for Sabbath observation.

20—Covenant Is More About Yahweh's Presence and Kingship Than About Law, Promise, or Salvation

The covenant Yahweh originated with Abram (Genesis 12:1-3), is the most fundamental element in the Old Testament, and that being the case, interpretation of the Old Testament depends on having a proper understanding of the covenant's nature and purpose. It is widely recognized that the covenant represents a formal agreement and that, as such, it is similar in both form and function to the international treaties known from the ancient world. These similarities are somewhat superficial in that when we delve into the development of the theology inherent in the covenant, we will discover its remarkable uniqueness (for example, in the Old Testament, the agreement is with God). It is nevertheless extremely significant that the covenant takes this form. A treaty is between a king (suzerain or patron) and a vassal (or client). Using such a form for the covenant brings automatic recognition of Yahweh as king. The observation in this chapter's title reflects a proposal concerning the main thrust of the covenant but does so in a statement of contrast to a number of popular conceptions about the covenant. This chapter begins by addressing those missteps and then will turn to an alternative proposal. Applying this interpretive approach to the covenant allows for an improved understanding of the covenant in all its many appearances in the Old Testament.

Many Bible students hold a common perception that the covenant finds one of its primary aspects in law. Chapter twenty-one raises objections to translating *Torah* as "law," but here it is sufficient to say that the covenant does not find its purpose in Torah (whatever translation might be offered). Rather it is the opposite, that Torah finds its purpose in covenant.[7] That is to say, God did not make a covenant with Israel in order to provide a platform for the Torah; the Torah serves the covenant. As is developed below, the Torah gives examples of the order in society that will characterize the covenant community.

Another common focus given to the covenant is that of promise.[8] It is true that in the covenant Yahweh tells Abram what he is willing to do regarding Abram and his family, Israel. Nevertheless, it would be a misunderstanding to conclude that God made a covenant with Abram in order to make promises and then show that he can keep them. In fact, "promise" may not even be the best term to describe what Yahweh offers in the covenant. When two parties enter a formal contract, there are often stated terms to which each party agrees. One could say that, for example, party A agrees to provide a certain quantity of bushels of grain, and party B agrees to pay a certain price per bushel. Those terms could be called promises in that they represent assurances that bind the parties together. But they are more precisely described as an agreement. They are not the same as promises that we make to one another, such as

- I promise that I will come to the next meeting.
- I promise that I will pay back your loan.
- I promise that I will call you tomorrow.

Perhaps this is semantic quibbling, but be that as it may, the main point is that God did not have to make a covenant to make promises, and the covenant was not just a vehicle for promise-making and promise-keeping.

Perhaps more importantly, the covenant Yahweh makes with Abraham and Israel does not provide salvation and was never intended to do so. The Israelites did not anticipate going to heaven (no revelation that they

---

[7]This idea, as well as those expressed throughout the next several chapters, are discussed in more detail in John H. Walton and J. Harvey Walton, *The Lost World of the Torah* (Downers Grove, IL: IVP Academic, 2019).

[8]Classic works such as Thomas Edward McComiskey, *The Covenants of Promise* (Grand Rapids, MI: Baker, 1985) set a course that is still prominent in evangelical thinking today.

had would have suggested the possibility) and did not think in terms of being saved from their sins. The sacrificial system did not make those provisions and Israelites never would have thought of the covenant in those terms. God had delivered them from slavery in Egypt, and later delivered them from exile, but delivering them from their sins was another matter entirely. They were given no such mechanism, had no such revelation, and therefore had no such expectation. Salvation of this sort is not a topic of discussion in the Old Testament. We must look elsewhere for the purpose of the covenant.[9]

The purpose of the covenant, as it can be derived from the understanding of the Old Testament authors, pertains most significantly to Yahweh's presence and Yahweh's kingship. The previously established understanding of creation, particularly the seventh day, provides a better position for understanding the significance of the covenant and how it fits into the metanarrative, that "big picture" of which the Israelite authors and audiences were aware.

PRESENCE

Picking up the thread means going back to Genesis 1, where God's creative activity brought order to the cosmos. On day six, humanity was created as his image to work alongside him and in relationship with him to be orderbringers. As we have already discussed, that working relationship was accomplished as he dwelt among them—his presence acting as a guiding reality. Both relationship and access to his presence were lost in Genesis 3. People made the choice to pursue their own order instead of God's, though they still wanted the benefits provided by his presence. In Genesis 11, humans built a tower inviting God to come down and dwell among them (for relationship and presence to be reestablished), but this was just another attempt to provide order for themselves as they desired to make their own name great.[10]

---

[9]These issues have been dealt with in detail in John H. Walton, *Covenant: God's Purpose, God's Plan* (Grand Rapids, MI: Zondervan, 1994).

[10]Ziggurats in the ancient world were not built for people to climb up to God, but for God to come down and dwell among them. See chap. 4.

God rejected that human initiative and offered his own counter-initiative to reestablish relationship and his presence. It occurs in the next chapter of Genesis, in God's invitation to make a covenant with Abram (Genesis 12:1-3). Here the relationship between creation and covenant becomes evident as both focused on bringing order, relationship, and presence. Covenant is God's primary order-producing instrument. The covenant relationship was formally ratified in Genesis 15, and the remainder of Genesis and Exodus traces its development from Abraham to Moses. At Sinai, Moses is given instructions for building the tabernacle, the place where God's presence would return for him to dwell among those with whom he had formed a relationship. This metanarrative is well-known to the Old Testament authors as its themes are developed in various books.

The metanarrative will be described and traced in chapter thirty-eight below, but this brief summary offers sufficient information to develop an idea of what the covenant is all about. This is important because all the law and the prophets depend on a proper understanding of this theological construct. It also has significance when we eventually want to understand the new covenant in the Gospels and Paul. Based on the guiding premise that the authors' literary intentions are the focus of initial attention in interpretation, Bible readers should be interested in understanding what the covenant meant to Israel before we think beyond those borders to consider what it came to mean in the New Testament or in theological constructions.

God's purpose in making the covenant was to initiate a relationship that would eventually lead to the reestablishment of his presence on earth after humanity had lost access to his presence in Genesis 3. It therefore becomes the vehicle for God to carry out his plans and purposes on earth and in history. The narratives of the Old Testament are largely the story of the covenant. The Torah provides the stipulations of the covenant and offers examples of what order in covenant living would look like (more about this in chap. 21). The wisdom of the Torah shows the path for establishing order as Israel serves as host to the divine presence. The prophets are the champions of the covenant. The exile happens as God's presence leaves the temple (Ezekiel 10). If Israelites thought about the covenant in these terms, then that is how we ought to think about it as we track with the biblical authors.

KINGSHIP

Understanding the central significance of Yahweh's presence also means recognizing that this represents not only the presence of God in their midst, but the presence of their king, a kingship established by the covenant. This additional element will deepen an understanding of the covenant. Recall from the previous discussion of rest that God's rest in his temple is on a throne. Tabernacle and temple were not just the places that recognized him as God; they recognized him as king.

This concept of kingship clarifies the "jealous" nature of God. It has been difficult for many readers to understand the jealousy of God, because, in a modern way of thinking, jealousy is not a positive trait or posture. In a number of passages in the Old Testament, the jealousy of God features prominently: "Do not worship any other god, for the LORD, whose name is Jealous, is a jealous God" (Exodus 34:14). Though this verse refers explicitly to his role as God, the jealousy of Yahweh is related to his role not only as God, but as king, an implicit element here that would not be transparent to modern readers.

To begin, think about polytheism in the ancient world. In the first passage quoted above, notice that God does not state that there are no other gods, but that the Israelites should not worship any other god. Yahweh is supposed to be their only God. In the ancient world, however, this did not make much sense. The polytheism of the ancient world viewed the gods as being a community and each god found his or her identity in the community. Furthermore, in those polytheistic systems, each god had his or her jurisdiction and together they administered the world. For Israelites, it was very difficult to comprehend a God who had no divine community and who did all the divine work himself.

Furthermore, in the ancient world, the rituals and worship were considered the way that humans met the needs of gods, who were dependent on them to do so. In the ancient world, there was no jealousy between the gods. It was recognized that all gods deserved to have their needs met. No god would say, "Feed only me and no other."[11] In the perception of the ancient world, that would be the upshot of saying that you should have no other gods beside me.

The covenant situates Yahweh differently as Israel's one and only God, a God who does not act within a divine community but chooses Israel as his community. He is a God who does not share divine authority or jurisdiction with other gods but insists on being seen as the only effective divine agent that they should acknowledge (Exodus 20:3). He alone makes a covenant with a group of people and chooses to work through them. Furthermore, the distinctiveness of Israel is that their God proclaimed that he had no needs and therefore their rituals were not designed to meet his needs (see Psalm 50:8-15). He alone expresses jealousy as the reason that he demands exclusive attention from his covenant people. The significance of the covenant in all of this needs to be unpacked if we are to track with the biblical authors.

The first requirement is to establish an understanding of the term *jealousy*.[12] The Hebrew term is an "expression of proprietary rights with exclusivistic implications. When someone belongs to someone else it is expected others will recognize that and respect those rights. The basis of 'belonging' is not economic (for example, a possession) but is relational."[13] Israel's covenant relationship with Yahweh established Yahweh's proprietary rights over Israel. Such proprietary rights, as we have just noted, are not characteristic of the relationship between gods and people in the rest of the ancient world. Instead, we will find the closest parallel in the exclusivistic demands that suzerain kings make of their vassals. This leads back to the title of this chapter—that the covenant prominently positions Yahweh not only as Israel's God, but as their king. The covenant eventuates in the tabernacle, where Yahweh dwells among them on his throne as their king. The understanding of divine kingship can then in turn give enhanced meaning to

---

[11]Compare this to our modern system of taxation. The state would not say to people, "don't pay taxes to your county, only pay taxes to me." But one state would not tell residents of another state to pay taxes to them instead of to the state they lived in.

[12]The Hebrew verbal root, *qn,'* is found in passages such as Genesis 37:11; Numbers 25:13; Deuteronomy 32:21; 2 Kings 19:31; Psalm 69:9; Song of Songs 8:6; Isaiah 9:7; Ezekiel 39:25; and Zechariah 8:2.

[13]*The NIV Cultural Background Study Bible* (Grand Rapids, MI: Zondervan, 2016), xx.

various Old Testament passages concerning the covenant at both the theological and exegetical levels, including an understanding of Yahweh's jealousy.

Yahweh must be their only God because, through the covenant (as in an international treaty), he has established himself as their king, and people can only be loyal to one king.[14] In the ancient world at large, a person could serve numerous gods—and they did. It was considered judicious to do so. In that cultural context, then, loyal service to a god was not compromised by also giving loyal service to another god. In contrast, loyal service to a king precluded any service given to another king. Loyalty to a king had exclusivistic expectations. This is made eminently clear in the international treaties from the ancient world, which the covenant in the Old Testament is most like in form and function.

How does this insight affect interpretation of the Old Testament? One advantage is the ability to acknowledge that Yahweh's kingship is more than a metaphor. We find the concept of Yahweh's kingship prominently in individual psalms, especially Psalms 93–99. Beyond that, however, many modern interpreters of Psalms have seen the kingship of Yahweh as the overall subject and message of the book. One evidence of this is found in the climax of the book. Psalms 146–150 serve as a final paean of praise, but Psalm 145 stands as the climax of the book's message.[15] It begins, "I will exalt you, my God the King," and proceeds as an alphabetic acrostic proclaiming all the many aspects of Yahweh's kingship. "Your kingdom is an everlasting kingdom, and your dominion endures through all generations" (Psalm 145:13). The kingdom of God is given pride of place even more explicitly in the book of Daniel, where it will bring an end to human empires and last forever (Daniel 2:44).

How will this shift in perspective away from salvation and promise, and toward presence and kingship, make a difference in interpretation of the

---

[14]Note that this principle is even stated by Jesus when he indicates that no one can serve two masters (Mt 6:24).

[15]Many books could be cited, among them, James Mays, *The Lord Reigns: A Theological Handbook to the Psalms* (Louisville, KY: Westminster John Knox, 1994); Marc Zvi Brettler, *God is King* (Sheffield: Sheffield Academic Press, 1989); John Eaton, *Kingship and the Psalms* (Sheffield: JSOT Press, 1986); J. Clinton McCann, *A Theological Introduction to the Book of Psalms* (Nashville, TN: Abingdon, 1993), 41-50.

text? The difference it will make does not pertain as much to specific verses as it does to the larger perception of what is going on in the Old Testament. For Christians, salvation is sometimes given pride of place as the most important element in our Christianity. It is therefore easy to import that interest into the study of the Old Testament. For an Israelite, however, the most important experiential aspect of their relationship with God was his presence among them—the temple, where he reigned over Israel, the world, and the cosmos from his throne.

Recognition of this will bring new understanding to our reading of the text. Why is half the book of Exodus taken up with the construction of the tabernacle? Perhaps because that is the most important thing that happened at Sinai. Why is so much attention given to the construction of the temple by Solomon in Kings and Chronicles, and by Zerubbabel and Joshua in Haggai, Zechariah, and Ezra? Why is the grand climax of the book of Ezekiel a nine-chapter description of the temple?[16] To a Christian reader the endless details of these accounts can be perceived as tedious, perhaps even boring. But in the Old Testament, the focus is not the cross; it is the temple and its divine throne: preparing a place for God's presence among them carries the highest significance. That presence of God is the fruit of the covenant relationship. That is why failure to uphold covenant order (that is, Torah) in Israel results in the Yahweh's removal of his presence. Readers will not be able to track well with the authors of the Old Testament when studying law (Torah), narrative, or prophecy if they have not adopted these authors' perspective about the covenant.

21—Torah Is More About Instruction That Cultivates Wisdom Than Legislation That Results in Law

The Hebrew word *Torah* is used for the part of the Jewish canon that Christians call the Pentateuch—the first five books of the Bible. But that is a

[16]For that matter, why does the vision of new heavens and new earth in Revelation 21 feature most prominently God's dwelling place (Rev 21:3, though notice that there is no temple there, Rev 21:22)?

secondary development. Within the Old Testament, *Torah* is the word that is often translated "law." That notwithstanding, it is widely acknowledged that the Hebrew word pertains most fundamentally to "instruction." Nevertheless, Christians reading the Old Testament encounter Torah in connection to what they perceive to be law, and that becomes the basis for all sorts of questions:

- If these are God's laws, should they not be laws for everyone?
- Should Christians today seek for their national laws to reflect that which is promulgated in the Torah?
- Some of the laws are very strange or would be irrelevant in today's world—what are we supposed to do with them?
- Should we try to develop legal principles from each law to use as a guide for our behavior?
- Does the law provide a moral system? If so, what about the verses that do not pertain to morality? And what about aspects of morality that are not addressed?
- How do these legal sayings function as Scripture?

Clearly, the ability to interpret these sections of the Old Testament faithfully requires understanding what the Israelite authors and readers understood about the Torah.[17] Addressing that precedes the ability to propose answers to the questions like those listed above, a list that could be expanded almost endlessly. These issues will be addressed from two different perspectives in this chapter and the next.

WHAT KIND OF LAW

In the modern world, when people talk about "law," they subconsciously incorporate into that idea many of the ways that law is represented in their own culture. Most modern readers easily think of law as a body of formal legislation. Such an approach to law is called "statutory law," as described well by Joshua Berman:

---

[17]For further reading, see John H. Walton and J. Harvey Walton, *The Lost World of the Torah* (Downers Grove, IL: IVP Academic, 2019).

> Law, within this conception, is contained in a *codified* text. Only what is written in the code is the law. The law code supersedes all other sources of norms that preceded the formulation of the code. No other sources of authority have validity other than the code itself. Therefore, the courts must pay great attention to the wording of the text and cite the text in their decisions. Where the code lacks explicit legislation, judges must adjudicate with the code as their primary guide.[18]

Berman continues to note that in the history of law, this approach did not become prominent until the early nineteenth century. It is not how anyone in the ancient world thought about law. Instead, law took the form of "common law," also called "customary law." In this form of law, there is no written code to serve as the basis for regulating society or passing down verdicts. Berman again offers a clear description of this alternative way of thinking as involving a judge who makes legal decisions "based on the mores and spirit of the community and its customs" which gradually take shape over time. Norms develop gradually through the distillation and continual restatement of legal doctrine through the decisions of the courts." He concludes by noting that such systems are "consciously and inherently incomplete, fluid, and vague."[19]

The important point to make is that which is specifically indicated in the title of this chapter. Common law, by its very nature, operates on the basis of the wisdom of the community, not on the basis of a legislative body responsible for creating and maintaining a corpus of statutory law. Applied to Torah, even though it is written down, it must be understood as representing communal wisdom rather than legislation.

Nevertheless, one might object, what accounts for the fact that the Torah comes from God (not just a human community or legislative body)? Even though this question identifies an alternative source of Torah, it does not determine the nature of the literature. Is Yahweh identified as the source of this body of literature as legislation (that becomes codified law) or the source of this body of literature as wisdom (that represents common law)?

---

[18]Joshua Berman, "Discrepancies Between Laws in the Torah," in *The Believer and the Modern Study of the Bible*, ed. Ganzel, Tova, Yehudah Brandes, and Chayuta Deutsch (Boston, MA: Academic Studies Press, 2019), 449. Italics original.

[19]Berman, "Discrepancies," 449.

If the ancient world knew nothing of statutory law or codified legislation, readers would do well to assume that God communicated to them in those categories with which they were familiar.[20]

I would therefore agree with Christine Hayes's assessment that the Torah given at Sinai can be characterized as "a body of divine *instruction* that cultivates *wisdom*."[21] This makes sense since, as already noted, the word *Torah* itself derives from a root that at its core refers to instruction. Torah and wisdom overlap considerably in that both give definition to the pathway to order. Scripture itself supports this association as Deuteronomy famously asserts that observing Torah is wisdom (Deuteronomy 4:6) and Proverbs does not hesitate to identify its wisdom as Torah, "Blessed is the one who heeds wisdom's instruction" (that is, Torah, Proverbs 29:18).

Jonathan Burnside expresses this concept concisely, as he indicates that in Israel, doing justice "seems to be primarily a matter of exercising divinely-directed wisdom, not the application of legal rules. . . . Torah makes them wise."[22] After providing several other examples from biblical texts, Burnside concludes, "The role of written law in biblical Israel is considerably removed from that of modern societies. It follows from this that the legislative model of law, based upon the application of statutes in court, is not applicable to biblical Israel and that any attempt to read biblical law in this way will get in the way of its proper understanding."[23]

Modern legislation seeks to be in some way comprehensive, but, in contrast, no matter how extensive the body of wisdom may be, it can never be comprehensive; it can only provide illustrating aspects. This approach can also be seen in the legal provisions found in the stele of Hammurabi, the Babylonian king in the eighteenth century BC. The 282 paragraphs inscribed

---

[20]Hebrew has a variety of words that operate within this instruction, including words that are translated as commands, decrees, statutes, ordinances, and precepts. See Walton and Walton, *Lost World of the Torah*, 40. Each of these words calls for detailed analysis, but all serve as ways that instruction is provided.

[21]Christine Elizabeth Hayes, *What's Divine About Divine Law?* (Princeton, NJ: Princeton, 2015), 29, 38. Italics original. For further, extensive discussion, see Michael LeFebvre, *Collections, Codes, and Torah* (London: T&T Clark, 2006).

[22]Jonathan Burnside, "Write That They May Judge? Applying Written Law in Biblical Israel," in *Write That They May Read*, ed. Daniel I. Block, David C. Deuel, C. John Collins, and Paul J. N. Lawrence (Eugene, OR: Cascade, 2020), 130-31.

[23]Burnside, "Write That They May Judge?," 132.

on that stele in no way provide a comprehensive law collection. Instead, they offer examples of what justice and order would look like from the perspective of the wisdom of the king. In a similar way, the Torah in the Old Testament "refers to a collection of examples that combine to form a description of the desired established order. . . . They embody standards of wisdom for the ordering of society within the covenant relationship that Yahweh had with Israel."[24] The wisdom applies not only to standards of behavior, but also to assessing a judgment that would suit particular crimes. Moreover, it would be a mistake to imagine that the Torah was concerned primarily with criminal justice. Many of its provisions discuss social propriety or ritual purity.

WISDOM FOR ISRAEL'S HOLINESS

These insights about the nature of Israelite society and biblical literature are essential for interpretation. The Torah provides illustrations offering wisdom concerning how Israel's holy status can be reflected in their lives and society. Through the covenant, Israel had been chosen as God's people and given the status of holiness. They were identified with him, and he was identified with them. That holiness was not something that Israel could achieve (it is a given status, see chap. 37), but it is something that they could reflect (or fail to reflect). Both holiness and wisdom are of such a nature that they cannot be comprehensively delineated. That is, no list can suffice, however extensive it may be. Any list can only point in the right direction. That is what Torah does.

Today, one could try to derive principles from each provision and then try to live by those principles, but even that would be inadequate. The provisions are to help Israel understand wisdom for holiness—they do not give a comprehensive list of principles any more than they give a comprehensive legislation. Whatever principles anyone derives may or may not be the appropriate ones, and even if they are, they only give a partial picture. Likewise, anyone could learn the wisdom of certain values inherent in the provisions,[25] but the provisions are not there to teach universal divine

---

[24]Walton and Walton, *Lost World of the Torah*, 45.

[25]We could learn the wisdom behind certain values in good literature that is not in the Bible (for example, Homer, Tolkien, Eliot).

values. Why are the provisions there? They do not consistently offer new information for legislation or morality, so that is not the explanation. Everyone in the ancient world knew most of these things, and Israel knew most of them before Sinai. What makes them God's Word?

Like other parts of Scripture, the Torah conveys God's plans and purposes as they were worked out in his relationship with Israel. As in narrative, the message is not contained in the details of the narrative (see chapters 23–26), but in what God is doing in the described events. Here in the Torah, he is making a vassal treaty with Israel. The provisions of the treaty are descriptive and help readers understand the treaty, but the message of Scripture is not in the stipulations, but in the fact that in God's plans and purposes, he made a treaty with the people he chose. It is not the provisions themselves that are scripturally relevant to us, because much of that content is fairly typical of the ancient world. It is rather the fact that this is how Yahweh has been pursuing his plans and purposes. The treaty was with Israel, not with us; the promises were to Israel, not to us; the curses and blessings were for Israel, not for us. Therefore, the last step is inevitable: the stipulations were for Israel, not for us. Let me hasten to say that that does not mean that thinking about them has no value. Doing so may give us some wisdom as well. But we could have found most of the same kinds of provisions in ancient Near Eastern law and ancient Near Eastern treaties and discovered some wisdom there as well. We may find value in the stipulations, but that does not mean that the stipulations carry God's authoritative message to us. The same thing will be said in the following chapters about the narratives of the Old Testament—we can discover wisdom in the behavior of the characters in the narratives, but the narratives are not given as God's Word for us to do so (chap. 26). Perhaps we could be better people if we considered the characters' behavior and the stipulations of the covenant, but then we are making choices about which ones would make sense to apply and which ones would not. Such choices then become our subjective decisions, not God's authoritative Word.

We cannot have any real understanding of the God of the Bible and the message of the Old Testament without knowing this story of God making a covenant. Consider the covenant that he made with David. It is important *that* he made that covenant, as well as to see how that is contributing to his plans and purposes for kingship. Such understanding eventually leads us to a robust understanding of Jesus as the Christ. As with the Torah, however, the covenant with David is not made with us; the promises to David are not to us; the stipulations for David are not for us.

We cannot cite any given provision of the Torah and claim that this is God's authoritative command to us—and that includes the Decalogue (Ten Commandments). Most of the provisions in the Decalogue were well-known in the ancient world (prohibitions of murder, adultery, theft, false witness, and coveting, as well as warnings about taking God's name lightly and admonitions to honor parents).[26] Having no other God was the same principle as recognizing no other king—a logical extension since Yahweh was Israel's king. The prohibition of images and the call to honor the Sabbath are arguably the only ones that stand as distinctive.

Nevertheless, the fact that Yahweh *made* a treaty is important. The details of what that treaty says do not carry authority outside that covenant. Recognition of the genre tells us this. The Israelite community that compiled the Torah thought that a treaty with Yahweh was important enough to set as part of the foundation of their identity. That community then spent a few centuries thinking about what that meant for them and their relationship with their God, specifically the juxtaposition between favor and exile. When Jesus arrived on the scene, he met his Jewish audience on these terms. He presented himself as a new Israel, primarily through symbolic sign-acts that their own interpretation of their story had given significance. By recapitulating Moses (for example, in the Sermon on the Mount), Jesus did what Moses did, which was to lay the foundation of a new treaty, which in turn meant restoration of favor and the end of exile. As time passed, Gentiles were allowed to participate as well—partners in the new covenant agreement forged by Jesus.[27] That new covenant has no obvious stipulations, yet we still recognize our responsibility to live lives that reflect the holy status God has given us through Christ so that we will bring honor to his name. Wisdom can be gleaned from the Torah, but not legislation.

---

[26]For further reading, Walton and Walton, *Lost World of the Torah*, 104-111, 231-57.

[27]The three previous paragraphs are the result of conversations with J. Harvey Walton.

22—Torah Is Not Establishing an Ideal Social System but Is Speaking Wisdom into Israel's Social System

Modern critique of the "laws" of the Old Testament is rampant, and for many Christians, devastating. A superficial reading leads to the belief that the Torah endorses slavery, encourages violence, and is characterized by misogyny, just to name a few of the more commonly cited indictments.

As I proposed in the last chapter, however, the Torah should not be considered law. Instead, it offers illustrations providing wisdom concerning how Israel's holy status can be reflected in their lives and society under the covenant. Not only does that mean that it is not legislation, it means that it should not be expanded into a legislative system.

THE CONTEXTS OF THE TORAH

The Torah is not offering a universally endorsed social system because it is characterized by several significant contexts that limit its reach. First, as previously noted, it is Yahweh's covenant with Israel. It was binding only with Israel—not with the Canaanites, not with the Babylonians, and not with us. That fact constrains its wider application.

Second, it is situated in the ancient world and therefore reflects old world concepts. That does not mean that its provisions are primitive or inferior; it means that they are culturally sensitive. Cultures are not monolithic. Concepts that we find odious (for example, sacrificing animals) or inequitable (hierarchal structures in society) were meaningful in their culture. Undoubtedly, concepts that we find meaningful would have been problematic for them (for example, our banking system, our prison system, our clothing fashions). We should not judge them for the different shape of their society, and we should certainly not insist on adopting it as the divinely mandated shape for any other society.

Third, the Torah is customized for living life in sacred space. This is why it contains so much information about purity. Moreover, when the Torah was given at Sinai, it included the instructions for the building of the tabernacle. The Torah informed the Israelites how they could construct ordered space in which Yahweh would be pleased to come and dwell, as well as how they could construct an ordered society that would be appropriate as one that served as host to the divine and royal presence. Torah assumed divine presence and gave the protocols for appropriate behavior and treatment when the Creator God, the Divine King, was coming to take up his residence.

Consider the analogy of when the Queen of England, or the President of the United States, or the Pope is planning a visit. Instructions in protocol are necessary, though those instructions would differ with regard to each of those dignitaries. Different still would be the protocols for a prince of Saudi Arabia or the Dalai Lama. When Zacchaeus was told that Jesus was coming to his house, he rushed off; preparation was necessary. The difference when considering Yahweh and Israel is that the divine presence did not just reflect a brief visit—he intended to take up permanent residence. Imagine the strain of having a dignitary present in your home or town permanently!

Torah represents special instructions for special circumstances, constrained by an exclusive covenant relationship, an ancient world context, and a reflection of protocol respective of the divine resident in their midst.

Consequently, the Torah is not endorsing slavery or misogyny any more than it is endorsing an agro-pastoral economic system. Yet we still ask why God would tolerate slavery or patriarchy. Given our modern sensibilities, such tolerance seems to undermine any esteem we might be inclined to hold for him as a God worthy of our worship and admiration. Why does he not fix the system instead of perpetuating it and therefore at least tacitly endorsing it?

NO IDEAL SOCIAL SYSTEM

God has chosen to work through his people, who, working alongside him, will be a force for addressing society's ills. But society is shaped by people, and people are inherently flawed. There is no perfect society, no ideal social system. We may think that ours is better than some in certain respects, and maybe it is, but it is undoubtedly worse than others. The debt slavery and patriarchal hierarchy we observe in ancient Israel were characteristics that brought stability and dealt with social problems in ancient society. But all systems are subject to abuse and collapse of the values that people intend to preserve in that system. The Torah called Israel to operate those familiar systems in the best possible ways; it did not seek to change the systems.

When we track with the authors of Scripture to discover the authoritative message, we will not do so by instituting the social system represented in the Torah. Nor will we seek to adopt its value system and then construct a modern society on its premises. Likewise, we should find no reason to be disconcerted that God worked within the social system that was current in Israel's world. Familiar protocols were appropriate if Israel was to present a positive picture of their God to their world. They are a light to the nations concerning how Yahweh, their God, chose them, took up his dwelling among them as their king, brought his favor to them (not because they met his needs, but because he was a gracious suzerain), and worked out his plans and purposes through them. The order that he called for in their society was exemplary in its time and was intended to establish Yahweh's reputation as Divine King.

TORAH TODAY

Today, in the new covenant, it is not the shape of a particular society that reflects the order that should characterize God's people. It is the shape of the church and its order that testifies to the glory of God and brings honor to Christ, the King. God's presence is within his people, not just in the midst of his people. When we consider applying the Torah to our modern situation, we should be seeking to define what order should look like in the church and how we can show honor to God's presence within us. The Torah neither addresses our modern culture nor the situation in the church. As in Israel's covenant, ours will involve seeking wisdom to reflect Christ to the watching world. Whether we succeed or fail, God is working out his plans and purposes through his church.

Questions we should be asking include:

- What are the best practices that we should recognize in the world around us and adopt as our own?
- What are the inclinations that are commonly accepted in the world but that are unworthy for God's people?
- How can we enhance God's reputation by our attitudes and actions? When the world persecutes us for our faith, we can stand proud in the strength that God gives us to persevere. When the world scoffs at us for adopting positions that do not reflect God's love or dismisses us for the failures fueled by greed, selfishness, or lust, we have failed to learn wisdom and we potentially disgrace the name of our God.

Torah calls us to live wisely, ordered by the reality of God's presence and motivated to bring honor to his name. Reading the Torah may prompt us and give insight into the topics to be considered. The individual provisions inform us of how God's plans and purposes were worked out in Israel, but each individual provision should not be investigated for its individual significance to us. Rather, each individual provision contributes to God's plans and purposes, which then serve as a guide for us (see further discussion in chap. 35). Faithful interpretation may help us to find our way and to avoid some of the pitfalls, so we should pursue it wholeheartedly. These adjustments to common modern perspectives on creation and Torah anticipate this book's final section on a revised understanding on how we should read Scripture. But first, additional genre considerations are in order.

SECTION B

NARRATIVE

Most Christians who grew up in church are very familiar with the narrative literature of the Old Testament—we call them "Bible stories." The very familiarity with this genre, however, breeds a potential for carelessness if we allow our imaginations to enhance the narratives, thus reshaping them, or to treat them as if they are intended to provide role models or behavioral objectives.[1] Why does the Old Testament include Bible stories? What are the authors doing with them? What are we supposed to get out of them? How do they function as Scripture?

Narrative literature can be found throughout the Old Testament, but it is encountered most extensively in the Old Testament literature sometimes referred to as the "Historical Books." That is a logical label because they recount events of the past and the stories of people who were participants in them. In that sense, they can indeed be considered historical; they are accounts of real people in a real past. Nevertheless, modern readers would be mistaken if we therefore believed that their purpose was to *record* history—especially if we adopted the understanding of "history" that is current in our culture. Marc Brettler has expressed this difference between how ancients understood the writing of history differently than people do today by observing,

> There was little, if any, interest in narrating the past for its own sake. Stories were set in the past for a variety of reasons, but antiquarian interest was not one of

---

[1]These issues are treated in-depth in John H. Walton and Kim E. Walton, *The Bible Story Handbook* (Wheaton, IL: Crossway, 2010).

> them. Though sparks of such interest developed in the Renaissance, it came to fruition only in the nineteenth century, and it would be a grave mistake to read the biblical books as the products of those German universities with an interest in recreating history . . . how it really was.[2]

Jean-Jacques Glassner takes the discussion to the next level as he observes that the aim of Mesopotamian literature was not to produce a chronicle of the eras of the past, but "to make a theology of them."[3] Beyond those important observations about how differently various cultures approach writing about the past, we also must recognize the important distinction that "history" is different from "narrative." Not all narratives are history (for example, parables), but the issue is deeper than that. We need to understand how to read the Old Testament narratives in light of these realities.

23—Reality Is Bigger Than History

In current Western culture, though we know it to be merely a convenient fiction, we easily adopt the idea that history is an account of "what really happened." Moreover, we flatter ourselves to think that our investigative research and our empirical methods can encompass reality. In fact, however, deeper reflection will tell us that this is not the case. No gathering of information can be complete, sources often disagree, subjective perspectives are unavoidable, and our demands for empiricism founder in the shoals of our irreparable ignorance. Our attempts at recording history are doomed to fail in their efforts to recover and represent the fullness of the reality. That is one way in which reality is bigger than history.

There is, however, a more important level at which the observation in the title of this chapter is true. The modern practice of understanding and giving account of the past is encumbered with certain assumptions about the world. For example, modern readers have often adopted empiricism as

---

[2]Marc Zvi Brettler, "The Tanakh as History," in *The Believer and the Modern Study of the Bible*, ed. Tova Ganzel, Yehudah Brandes, and Chayuta Deutsch (Boston, MA: Academic Studies Press, 2019), 229-30.
[3]Jean-Jacques Glassner, *Mesopotamian Chronicles*, ed. Benjamin R. Foster (Atlanta, GA: SBL, 2004), 26.

a requirement for reality—that is, "I will believe it when I see it." In a more extreme version, if something is real, we think we should be able to capture it with a video camera.

WHAT THE EYE CANNOT SEE

In contrast, in the ancient world, what an eyewitness was able to see was only on the surface of the reality. For example, an Israelite who witnessed the parting of the Red Sea would not have been content to examine what physical forces and natural phenomena may have been responsible. They would have had neither the means nor any interest in doing so. The reality was that their God had parted the sea to provide deliverance for them. The reality of God's involvement was beyond what they could see or what they could defend empirically; yet the reality of divine action was by far more important to them than the actual physical event that could be captured by a video camera.

In the ancient world, when people remembered or recorded events of the past, they were interested in interpreting the reality beyond the events. They did not want to convey only that the king conquered a particular city; they wanted to convey the reality that the gods gave the king victory and dominion and that this stood as a sign of the favor of the gods and their sponsorship of the king. The most important reality of these accounts was not in what was visible or empirical in nature. It did not depend on eyewitness accounts or objective research. The reality was bigger than the historical accounts that could be produced.

Moreover, when ancient storytellers wanted to convey reality, they did not feel constrained to restrict themselves to observable events of the past. A major body of literature from the ancient world is labeled by modern scholars as *myth*, by which they generally imply that it is made up—a fairy tale about unreal beings and events. Such an assessment reflects modern presuppositions but does not represent ancient ideas accurately. The ancients did not believe that their myths were in some way contrary to reality. Instead, they believed that their myths represented the deepest reality, a reality that transcended the mundane events of human history. The gods were more important than people were. What transpired in human events only held significance in light of what it conveyed about what the gods were doing.

With all of this in mind, modern readers can understand why it may be reductionistic to refer to the narratives of the Old Testament as "historical books." Anyone who desires to track with the authors must understand that these narratives are not just history, and even not most importantly history; they are more than history. They are using historical events of the past as a way of getting at a larger and more important reality—the reality of God's work in the world as he carries out his plans and purposes.[4]

Since most modern readers consider "myth" to be made-up stories, it would be misleading to refer to Old Testament narratives as "myth."[5] Yet, at the same time, the Old Testament narratives clearly filled some of the same functions for Israel that the Babylonian or Egyptian myths filled for those peoples—literary vehicles of a reality that transcends history. To be more specific, the biblical literature reflecting on past events was not primarily interested in those events themselves, or to assert the factuality of those events, as much as it was to reveal the purpose of those events as the work of God in the world. Unlike the literature of their neighbors, however, the Israelite narratives about the work of Yahweh came to be understood as inspired.

The reality that the Old Testament narratives are most interested in, then, is the reality of God's activity rather than the reality of human actions. To say this simply, when we read the narratives of the Old Testament, we are not reading the stories of Abraham, Ruth, David, or Esther; we are reading the story of God working out his plans and purposes in the world through those characters. That is where we will find the authoritative message of the text; that is the story the narrators wish to tell. If we wish to track with the authors and appreciate the narratives as Scripture, we must look to the larger reality. If our primary interest in them focuses on human biography,

---

[4]Though expressed in academic style, one scholar has expressed this by asserting, "The literary translation of their experience was mediated by more elaborate narrative codes than is the case in the modern Western discourse about reality—and in modern historiography." Sylvie Honigman, *Tales of High Priests and Taxes* (Oakland, CA: University of California, 2014), 39.

[5]For discussion see, for example, Paul K.-K. Cho, *Myth, History, and Metaphor in the Hebrew Bible* (Cambridge: Cambridge University Press, 2019), 3-9, 11-17.

we have missed what the text is doing. The reality that is bigger than history is the reality of God carrying out his plans and purposes.

Example A—Joseph: The "Joseph story" is one of the longest sustained narratives in the Old Testament. Its contours are well-known, not only as encountered in the book of Genesis, but in its popular adaptation in a musical, *Joseph and the Amazing Technicolor Dreamcoat.*[6] Even a casual reading of the text of Genesis 37–50 will reveal that the narrator's interest is not so much in Joseph himself but in what Yahweh is doing. Large swaths of narrative pass with occasional, general references to what God can do (for example, Genesis 40:8; 41:16) even as they focus on the plot line of the human characters. Nevertheless, the narrator makes clear that Yahweh is at work. Genesis 37 leaves the reader without guidance regarding Yahweh's involvement as Joseph is mistreated by his brothers and sold into slavery. In Genesis 39, however, the narrator asserts repeatedly that Yahweh's hand is guiding events (Genesis 39:2, 3, 5, 21, 23). In Genesis 45 Joseph declares that it is God who sent him to Egypt (Genesis 45:5-9). God's permission for Jacob to move his family to Egypt is specified (Genesis 46:3-4). The narrator's climax in Genesis 50:20 could hardly be clearer—this is not a Joseph story, but a story of how God worked through Joseph's experiences. That is the most important scriptural reality, but it goes beyond what a historian would be able to say.

Example B—Esther: By way of an objection that some might raise, what can we say about another sustained narrative in the Old Testament, the story of Esther? Problematically, God is never mentioned or referred to by either the narrator or the characters. In fact, the narrator seems to go out of his way to avoid mentioning God (notice Esther 4:14; 6:13; 8:17). Nevertheless, readers have unsurprisingly recognized that God is the one who delivered the Jews and brought success to Mordecai and Esther and, as Mordecai declares, "that you have come to your royal position for such a time as this" (Esther 4:14). He is certainly not simply expressing a belief in impersonal fate. One could even suppose that the narrator has intentionally kept God off stage in the story to convey the idea that God has been working behind the scenes to carry out his plans and purposes. We should be reminded, in conclusion, that the book of

[6]Andrew Lloyd Weber and Tim Rice, *Joseph and the Amazing Technicolor Dreamcoat* (Borough Green, Sevenoaks, Kent: Novello, 1975).

> Esther is exceptional in its failure to mention God. That very fact emphasizes what is evident in reading all the other narratives of the Old Testament: in all accounts, the narrators are most interested in documenting what God is doing. That is the reality that is greater than any eyewitness accounts that populate a narrower approach to historical literature.

When we recognize that reality is bigger than history, we are positioned to track with the narrators of the Old Testament as they communicate a reality larger than just the historical events themselves. Apologetics agendas attempting to prove the historicity of various biblical passages have their place, but we should not confuse those efforts with interpretation. They may help people defend the perceived truth of the text, but they do not offer a path to understanding what the authoritative message of the text is. The message should not be reduced to the idea that the Bible is affirming that these events really happened. The narrators are going beyond that given to affirm the reality of God's active hand—something that our apologetic efforts cannot demonstrate.

24—We Have to Understand a Text Literarily Before We Can Understand It Historically

Based on the last chapter's discussion, a more nuanced statement follows: "historical" literature is more properly described as narrative than as history. It frames events of history, moved by the hand of God, into a literary form. Any literary presentation of events represents a simplification. Narrators choose from a wide range of possible details and approaches as they shape the story to their purposes. As we track with the authors, we want to perceive what is driving those choices.[7]

---

[7]Honigman garbs this idea in academic style as she advises, "Basically, it is essential to identify the structural coherence of a given work in order to understand its author's intentions correctly. Together with the correct identification of the author's rhetorical codes, identifying a structural logic is in turn a prerequisite for assessing whether or not the descriptions found in the sources are reliable facts, and ultimately for reevaluating the factual outline on which modern historical reconstructions are predicated," Sylvie Honigman, *Tales of High Priests and Taxes* (Oakland, CA: University of California, 2014), 33.

COMPILED WITH PURPOSE

The first step, then, when reading one of the narrative books of the Old Testament, is to try to understand the rhetorical strategy of the book as a whole. Books like 1–2 Samuel or Judges have been compiled by weaving together many shorter narratives, which have presumably been transmitted in both oral and written forms, given what is known of literary production in the ancient world. Bible readers do not know who compiled them into a book or when they did so. Nevertheless, these narratives have been selected with intention and compiled with a literary-theological purpose in mind. The book rarely tells us what that purpose was, so we must deduce it from the literary work that we have.

Whatever the compiler's purpose was, we should assume that he has shaped each narrative to contribute to that purpose—that is what a rhetorical strategy is. That is, he has told the story in such a way as to draw out what he believes is important, relegating other details to either a minor passing comment or leaving them out altogether. As mentioned in the introduction, when we "mind the gaps" we want to avoid trying to speculate about details that the narrator left out. Our attention should rather be on what he included, what significance he gave it, and how that contributes to his purpose. We can grow in confidence that we have successfully identified his purpose as we see all the individual narratives functioning together to address that purpose.[8]

This is vital because the most important message of the book is carried by the compiler's purpose rather than autonomously by the individual narratives that he strings together. We have no access to the narratives outside of the shape this compiler has given them. The affirmations of the author must be understood in light of his purpose for the compilation—a literary-theological purpose that incorporates events of the past (that is, history).

At this point, the astute reader may detect a potential flaw in the method. If the authoritative message is to be found in the purpose of the narrator (what I have called the author's literary intention), and that purpose is not

[8]Certainly there is an ongoing danger of what is called "confirmation bias"—that once we get an idea in our head, we engage in sometimes tortuous reasoning to substantiate our working hypothesis. If we can remain aware of this danger, we can seek to avoid it.

generally stated in the book but deduced by the attentive reader, then isn't that identified purpose the result of subjective interpretation, which has been defined in this book as incapable of carrying authority?

Remember that every meaning we can possibly derive from the text requires interpretation. Authority is what the text has, but interpretation is the only way that we can discern the meaning conveyed with that authority. We therefore return to what could almost be called our mantra: the strongest interpretation is the one with the strongest evidence. As at every interpretational level, we must develop evidence concerning the purpose of the compiler, the rhetorical strategy that he has used, and the contribution that each narrative makes to the whole of the book.

The criterion that we use is how well our evidence fits together to explain how the book works toward its purpose. Caution is required here. Just because something fits does not make it right, and, in fact, any number of different proposals could potentially be shown to fit. We are seeking the best possible fit that enjoys the preponderance of evidence. Again, we look to peer review and to community for affirmations (chap. 2).

Note that all of what this chapter addresses defines a literary task, not a historical task. The selectivity of the compiler is not driven by how to present the best portrayal of the history, but how to shape a piece of literature to a theological purpose. Events have been presented through the lens of a literary-theological purpose, which may impede our ability to reconstruct the event from a historical perspective. The tableau may use a historical canvas (recounting events from the past), but the painting is literary-theological. Reconstructing the history is therefore a secondary endeavor at best; understanding the literary presentation and the theological message should be the primary focus. By this I do not imply that there is no historical underpinning—I only refer to our limited ability to reconstruct the history.

ANCIENT LITERARY CONVENTIONS

Second, the literary conventions that are used in a narrative must be taken into consideration before we can understand the historical aspects of its affirmations or message. Cultures have their own conventions for recounting the past and may place value on the past for different reasons. As readers seeking to track with the authors, we must understand the conventions and values of the ancient Israelites lest we impose our own conventions and values on the text and thereby misread it.

A representative list of conventional literary and rhetorical devices in the Old Testament could include these:

Telescoping. The author compresses a long period of time into a few sentences that might make it appear that the events occurred all at the same time. One widely recognized example of this is the report concerning Sennacherib in 2 Kings 19:36-37. In a flat reading, one could easily infer that Sennacherib's withdrawal from Jerusalem was soon followed by his assassination when, in reality, the latter took place nearly twenty years later. Another example is found in Daniel 1:1. Nebuchadnezzar's control of Judah began in the third year of Jehoiakim, 605 and 604 BC, but it did not eventuate in a siege until 597, shortly after the death of Jehoiakim. In these examples, reconstructing the sequence of historical events can be hampered by the literary device employed.

Exaggerating. The author uses hyperbole, overstating for effect. In Zephaniah 1, the prophet is describing the effects of the Babylonian invasion that leads to the destruction of Jerusalem and the temple. The opening lines portray universal annihilation of "everything from the face of the earth"—humans, birds, and fish. The destruction is said to include "all mankind on the face of the earth" (Zephaniah 1:3). This is a clear case of hyperbole since other places in the Old Testament make it clear that some Israelites remained alive and dwelling in the land, while others were taken into Babylonian exile. As another example, the book of Joshua portrays the Israelite conquest of the land as total (for example, Joshua 21:43-45). Yet in Judges 1, many parts of the land clearly remain unconquered. The hyperbole of the book of Joshua is characteristic of conquest accounts in the ancient world and the history of the conquest cannot be reconstructed without recognizing the use of that literary convention. The affirmation made by the biblical author can only be recognized once that convention is understood.

Patterning. The author arranges a series of past eras recognizing common characteristics. When people look back on the past, it is almost unavoidable that they seek to understand it in certain patterns or periods. We easily speak of the Middle Bronze Age or the Iron Age; we refer to the Medieval Period, the Dark Ages, or the Enlightenment. When the historian Manetho looked back at Egyptian history, he divided it into kingdoms, intermediary periods, and dynasties. All of these conventions are artificial. In the Bible, the cycles in the book of Judges represents an obvious, well-recognized example. The narrator himself introduces the pattern in Judges 2. Another example is seen in the use of literary formulas to present the succession of kings in the books of 1–2 Kings. At times these can frustrate our attempts to reconstruct the history (see example 1 below).

Framing. Framing is imposing a framework designed to highlight comparison, contrast, or categories. Perhaps the clearest example of this is in the "*toledoth* framework" of the book of Genesis (for example, "These are the generations [Heb. *toledoth*] of Jacob"), eleven of which punctuate the book.[9] These sections are not in strict chronological sequence. As another example, the seven days of Genesis 1 are framed in a parallel structure in which days one and four are parallel, as are days two and five, and three and six. Once this parallel framing is recognized, it is possible to conclude that the presentation of the days is more literary than representative of a chronological sequence.

Generalizing. The author uses stereotypical language and categories. A good example of this can be seen in the derogatory descriptions of Canaanites, particularly in Leviticus and Deuteronomy. In the ancient world, stereotypical language was frequently used to characterize the otherness and negative attributes of one's opponents.[10]

Using figural devices. The use of literary devices such as metaphor are well-known from the book of Psalms. These pose little problem for most readers. Interpretation becomes more complicated and controversial,

---

[9]Genesis 2:4; 5:1; 6:9; 10:1; 11:10, 27; 25:12, 19; 36:1, 9; 37:2.

[10]For full discussion and footnotes to the literature, see John H. Walton and J. Harvey Walton, *The Lost World of the Israelite Conquest* (Downers Grove, IL: IVP Academic, 2017), 137-56.

however, when discussing whether the fruit and trees of the Garden of Eden are metaphors or not, or even whether the Tower of Babel ought to be understood as a figurative representation of human pride rather than trying to reconstruct the historical time and place of its construction. Regardless of what decision is made in these cases, it is obvious that discerning whether these are figural devices will have a significant impact on how the passages relate to history.

Attributing speech. This refers to putting exact words in the mouths of the characters that approximate the sort of thing they would have said.[11] The book of Job offers one of the clearest examples of this rhetorical device. Even the most conservative scholars readily admit that there would not have been a stenographer present taking down the exact words of each speaker. The speeches are a literary construct. The discussion can easily extend to the book of Jonah (who would not have known what the sailors did or said after he was cast into the stormy sea), and the royal decrees in Ezra, Nehemiah, Daniel (which sound remarkably Jewish in their wording and perspective). But, in fact, given the conventions of the ancient world as well as the classical world (where it is addressed by historians such as Herodotus and Thucydides) nearly every speech in the Old Testament ought to be considered an act of rhetorical attribution to one extent or another.

If Bible readers do not recognize these devices, we are likely to misunderstand what the narrator is claiming at the historical level. The above list only refers to various examples in passing. Two examples, one very minute, and the other wide-ranging, explain specific literary devices in more detail.

> **Example A—Zimri:** 1 Kings 16:9-20 presents the story of King Zimri of Israel. In these twelve verses, Zimri, a high-ranking military commander, assassinates King Elah and seizes the throne of Israel for himself. When word reaches the eastern front, a higher-ranking military commander, Omri, is proclaimed king by the army and promptly leaves the battlefield

[11]Partially addressed in discussions between *ipsissima vox* and *ipsissima verba* (i.e., representing the voice of a character as opposed to reproducing the exact words of a character), but extending beyond it to creating speeches rather than just paraphrasing them.

to march on the capital city. As the city came under attack, Zimri, realizing that he is overmatched and doomed, sets the citadel on fire and perishes in the flames. The text tells us that he reigned for seven days. During those seven days, we can imagine that he was scrambling to consolidate his hold on the throne and prepare for the anticipated attack by Omri and his troops. It would be no surprise if he never ventured outside the city. Yet the narrator of Kings boldly declares that he died "because of the sins he committed, doing evil in the eyes of the LORD and following the ways of Jeroboam and committing the same sin Jeroboam had caused Israel to commit" (1 Kings 16:19). The first two clauses in that indictment are understandable if one considers treachery and rebellion as evil in the eyes of the Lord. However, the narrator did not stop there. He went on to accuse Zimri of the sins of Jeroboam, that is, establishing worship at the calf shrines at Dan and Bethel. As interpreters, we are not called on to explain how Zimri actively supported the calf cult while secluded in the citadel of Tirzah. We are supposed to recognize that all of the kings of the northern kingdom fall under the indictment of Jeroboam. The formula is applied regardless of the historical details.

Example B—Genesis 1–11: Here we encounter a much more complicated issue. How should we assess the events recounted in Genesis 1–11? Though some would disagree, I do not hesitate to identify the people as real people in a real past, and likewise for the events such as the flood and the tower building. Nevertheless, as we have discussed, classifying them as real people and events does not mean that we can engage in flat superficial reading. As the chapter title says, we have to understand these texts literarily before we try to reconstruct the events (which we need not even undertake).

The compiler of Genesis is working with a purpose as he presents the story of the establishment of the covenant. As previously discussed, the covenant is God's order-bringing instrument that is intended to restore his presence in relationship with Abraham and his family, Israel. Genesis 1–11 traces the events that led to that initiative, though its interests are theological, and its framing is highly literary. It is not the compiler's intent to provide what our culture would require for historical verification and reconstruction. Consequently, even when we are willing to affirm that these are real people and events in a real past, that does not mean that we can recover whatever history stands behind the accounts. Furthermore, in our pursuit of authority, we do not need to do so. It is not the people and events that are inspired and authoritative; it is the text and its message. The narrator is interpreting events, and we do not need to reconstruct the events historically to understand his interpretation and thereby receive the authoritative message of the text.

Finally, it is a misstep to begin our investigation of these texts by asking, "Is Genesis 1–11 historical?" Already that reflects a modern predisposition to modern questions and modern conceptions of what it means to write about the past. It encourages a flat reading of these texts rather than a literarily sensitive reading that engages it in accordance with its own purposes and conventions.

Before moving on to the next chapter, consider a variation in this chapter that is also true. This book has been elaborating on the idea that we cannot understand a text historically until we have understood it literarily. The same is true when we turn our attention from historical examination to theological examination. We cannot understand a text theologically until we understand it literarily—and for the same reasons.

25—We Cannot Get Behind the Literary Veil

When narrators offer an account of past events, they can only do so by adopting a literary vehicle for the portrayal. The metaphor of a veil can describe such literary vehicles.[12] The point is that, as readers, we have no access to the events themselves except through what the narrator has given us (except in rare circumstances when a contemporary ancient document also refers to the event[13]). We cannot see the events or the characters; we can only see the veil. Furthermore, and most importantly, the veil represents the

---

[12]One could alternatively use the metaphor of a curtain, a lens, a window, or any number of others. Hopefully readers will not over-read the chosen metaphor but will see the point I am making.

[13]Even in these situations, the information we have from the ancient Near East is generally even less detailed than the biblical account. An exception would be found in Sennacherib's royal inscriptions detailing his invasion of Judah in the time of Hezekiah.

interpretation of events offered by the narrator, which we believe has been given him by God. That means that the veil is what is inspired—not the events themselves. To understand the message from God, we need to understand the veil—not reconstruct the events! Whether we understand the events or not, God's message is in the veil that the narrator has woven and in the interpretation of the events that he has provided. Sylvie Honigman makes a similar point when she observes,

> In Greek as well as in Judean historiographical tradition, works were written not to simply narrate events but to explain them: that is to give them meaning. Ancient historians made it their task to enlighten their readers about the true, deep meaning of past events beneath the superficial, deceptive appearances—'deep causes' behind 'pretexts.' Intentions and meaningful patterns could and had to be deciphered behind apparently random events.[14]

Once we realize that we must attend to the literary account more than to the event itself, we also become aware that we are rarely able to see behind the veil, that is, to gain access to the event independent of the narrator.[15] Our goal as interpreters, then, is not to reconstruct the events. Apologists and historians may have reasons to take on such a task, but interpretation of the biblical text does not require it. A few examples may help to illustrate.

> **Example A—The Flood:** The biblical flood is probably one of the most well-known stories of the Old Testament. In the modern world, great effort has been devoted to geological and hydrological implications of a massive flood to try to reconstruct the event. Many factors come into play.[16] Some may feel the need to reconstruct the event in order to demonstrate to the satisfaction of skeptical friends (or to their own satisfaction) that the Bible is reliable. The point is, however, that the reconstruction of the event is not the same as the interpretation of the passage. The Bible's message is not given to affirm that an event took place (though it assumes that is the case).

---

[14]Sylvie Honigman, *Tales of High Priests and Taxes* (Oakland, CA: University of California, 2014), 72.

[15]Other sources may weave a different veil, but they do not give unfettered access to the event. Archaeology may provide non-literary information, but also is limited in access it offers to the events themselves.

[16]We have already discussed the universalistic terminology above, chap. 9.

Instead, the narrative is offering an interpretation of the well-known event. That interpretation may include theological concepts (that God brought judgment) which differ from other ancient Near Eastern interpretations. It may also (or alternatively) include a message concerning the breakdown of order when people seek to order the world around themselves. In this latter case, the interpretation must be seen as recapitulating creation—a pattern discovered in comparing Genesis 1–3 and Genesis 6–8.[17] These interpretations of the message do not depend on our ability to reconstruct the event. The event is the assumed backstory; the authority resides in the interpretation by the narrator.

Example B—David: The inability to get behind the literary veil pertains not only to events of the narrative, but also to the people in the narratives. Even though we consider them real people in a real past, we cannot get to those people—we can only see them through the narrator's eyes and understand them as the narrator has portrayed them. David is an excellent example. He is famously understood as the godly psalmist and as the hero of a number of narratives. Yet he is also notoriously portrayed as a flawed character, not only in the well-known adultery with Bathsheba and the subsequent arrangement for her husband's death, but in numerous other places where his behavior falls far short of admirable (for example, 1 Samuel 27:8-12). Given this checkered reputation, we may at times have questions whether some of his actions should be considered honorable or morally compromised. One such account is in 1 Samuel 25, where David's men are protecting the sheep of Nabal. At sheep-shearing time, they approach Nabal for payment and he refuses. When they report to David, he gathers his men with intent to punish Nabal's churlishness (1 Samuel 25:13). Some interpreters have viewed David's response as justifiable, having concluded that David's men were due some return for their good work. Others have considered David and his men as engaging in what would today be called a protection racket in which the main protection is from themselves, and this is simply a form of extortion.[18] Is David to be

[17]For more information see Tremper Longman III and John H. Walton, *The Lost World of the Flood* (Downers Grove, IL: IVP Academic, 2018), 112-21.

[18]This view has been described and modified in E. Pfoh, "A Hebrew *Mafioso*: Reading 1 Samuel 25 Anthropologically," in *Patronage in Ancient Palestine and in the Hebrew Bible: A Reader*, ed. E. Pfoh (Sheffield: Sheffield Phoenix, 2022), 317-30.

considered an avenger for justice or a vicious bandit wielding power over those who cannot defend themselves?

In relation to the title of this chapter, we must accept that we cannot get behind the literary veil to discover the "real David." We have only the narrator's assessment. Since we have examples of both good and bad behavior on the part of David, his track record will not solve this for us. Though the biblical text gives strong endorsement to David, it readily acknowledges that his actions are not always honorable. We are therefore not in a position to make our own personal assessment of his motives in this incident. We can note that the narrator does not condemn him for his actions, and Abigail's actions and statements seem rather to affirm her husband's reckless behavior and gives no hint of finding fault with David.

We cannot embark on a psychoanalysis of David in an attempt to profile his personality and motives. He is a literary character portrayed by the narrator and we cannot get to the "real person" behind the character. Our interpretation therefore focuses on what the narrator has told us, not on speculations or suspicions we might have about David. The narrator is interested in showing how David was being accepted as future king among the common folk as God inexorably draws him to the throne. The story of Nabal and Abigail is anecdotal as it uses this event to make its point. We are not in a position to deconstruct the narrator's motives and come to different conclusions.

The narrator's intentions are to tell us God's story, not the stories of the characters that the narrator is using in that effort. We must be content with that. We cannot know what sort of people they were beyond the characterization we have been given. If we spend our time and effort trying to infer or deduce what kind of people Abraham, Sarah, Hagar, Lot, Laban, Jacob, Esau, and Joseph and his brothers were, we are not tracking with the author. We can only know what the author has given us. Perhaps in reality, some of those people were more flawed than we know; perhaps the character of some could be redeemed if we knew more. But that is not our job as interpreters. The events and the characters are illustrations of what God is doing and therein lies the message of the text. This leads us to the next consideration.

26—More Important Than What the Characters Do Is What the Narrator Does with the Characters and What God Is Doing Through the Characters

Though Bible stories are among the most familiar and beloved portions of Scripture, God's people have often not thought carefully enough about how to use them. How do stories of people, some good, some bad, who lived long ago become God's authoritative Word to us? The very common approach is undertaken without serious methodological consideration: we treat the stories as a repository of role models offering behavioral objectives meant to guide us to become better people—more moral, more godly, more pious. One of the consequences of this approach is that we are inclined to put some of the characters on pedestals, glowing idealized people who show no similarity to us or anyone we know. On the opposite end of the spectrum are those characters we consider failures: Cain, Joseph's brothers, Saul, Absalom, Abraham. Wait! Abraham!? Isn't he supposed to be in the pedestal list? True—most of the time he is. But then we get to Genesis 16, where he takes Hagar to his bed to produce an heir, and we are ready to throw him under the bus. Suddenly he is a lust-crazed cretin who has no faith in God to provide the promised heir. We easily jump to such conclusions without bothering to learn about the ancient culture where the primary reason for marriage and the major role of the wife was to produce the next generation. If she could not do so, her status in the family was forfeited, or at least in jeopardy. Some marriage contracts of the time required a barren woman to provide a substitute to provide her husband with offspring in her place. That is precisely what Sarah is doing. Is it a faithless act? Not in the least. Yahweh had told Abraham that a child would come from him (Genesis 15:4), but he had not told him that it would come through Sarah (that does not happen until Genesis 17:19 when Ishmael is thirteen years old). Abraham and Sarah were trying to discern whether faith meant patiently waiting (as they had done for decades) or stepping out and trying to find the path (often what faith calls us to do—step out of the boat!).[19]

The flaw in all of this is found in our haste to derive role models from the narratives of the Old Testament as we make moral judgments about the people as if that is what the stories are there for. We imagine that we can decipher the will of God and guidance for our own lives by decoding the behavior of the people in the stories. Unfortunately, our methods for doing so are subjective and, at times, far too imaginative to believe that they carry the authority of God's Word.

Our principle in this chapter reminds us of one of the fundamental elements of biblical authority. That is, the authority is found in the author's literary intentions as they are represented in texts. It is not the people in the stories who are authoritative—not their actions, not their words, and not the events in which they participate. What carries authority is how the narrator has portrayed them in the text. So, as the chapter title specifies, what matters is what the narrator is doing with the characters and what God is doing through the characters—not what the characters do or say. The characters are not teaching us; the narrator is teaching us. Moreover, as we have said before, he is not teaching us about the characters, he is teaching us about God. That is where the authority of the text is found.

Consequently, we should not be mining the narratives of the Old Testament for role models—that is not why the author has given us this material. The stories are not recounting tales of the heroes and villains of the Bible.[20] We must not reduce the Bible to being an ancient version of Marvel Comics. The people of the Old Testament are real people in a real past, but the narrator (under the direction of the Spirit), by writing about their lives, has turned them into literary characters. And as we indicated last chapter, we cannot get back to the real people, and we do not need

[19]Alternatively, we may find reason to believe that the author invites the reader to critique how Abraham and Sarah treat Hagar, as their actions are juxtaposed to God's care for her and Ishmael. As always, we don't want to miss what the author intends for us to understand, but, at the same time, we don't want to stray from what he is doing to follow our own impressions.

[20]I used to say that the only hero in the Bible is God, but that is also wrong-headed, because to call him a hero is a devaluation that demotes him to the role of super-human.

to—we have what we need. The literary characterizations preserved in the Old Testament are designed to help us see how God is working out his plans and purposes in the world—sometimes through ordinary people like us, occasionally through extraordinary people (though with human flaws and idiosyncrasies nonetheless). Through this, we learn that God does his work through ordinary, flawed people—even perhaps through us.

Example A—David: We have already used David as an example, but we return to him now to explore the dynamics of literary characterization. David is one of those characters of the Old Testament who appears to be a paradox—one moment the godly young man who defeats Goliath and is anointed as God's chosen king, the next moment an adulterer and murderer. Readers sometimes may feel like asking, "Will the real David please stand up?" But we do not need to find the "real David"—we need to understand the narrator's characterization of David (with all his best and worst aspects) and to understand how God can use a complex person like David to carry out his plans. David is not the one from whom we receive the authoritative Word of God in the books of Samuel—the narrator is the instrument of God's revelation.

Example B—Esther: Esther is often seen as the paragon of courage in the Old Testament as she risks her life to save her people. We should not fail to appreciate what it took for her to play that role, but, at the same time, we should recognize that this is not the reason her story is in the Bible. We cannot explore the actual dimensions of her personality that led to her actions. We know from the text that she was recruited against her inclinations and that she was bullied into the act by her uncle's rhetoric. Yet there is no reason to think that that discredits or devalues her courageous act. We can imagine what fears and doubts she must have had, but the very fact that we must imagine them should caution us. Authority is not found in what we can imagine or speculate about her choices, feelings, and motivation. We recognize that she *could* be a role model for us, but so could any character in any literature. The difference about the stories in the Bible is found in what the narrator provides, not what our imagination or personality profiling provides.

Again, then, we must proceed by realizing that this is not an Esther story (and certainly not a Haman, Mordechai, Xerxes, or Vashti story). It is a story of how God delivered his people from a decree of doom deviously pursued by an enemy with a personal agenda and propagated by the most powerful ruler of the time. The authoritative message is about God. The narrator is communicating about God. Our focus should be God, and our interpretation should arrive at what the narrator wants us to learn about God. Our application should follow that same line and lead us to ponder the work of God then and now. If our application only addresses how we should be courageous like Esther, we are not engaging the authority of Scripture.

Example C—Moses: Moses had the privilege of education and status in the household of Pharaoh and therefore the potential to do great things. Providentially spared from death as an infant, he seemed destined to be a deliverer. Instead, an act of violence and a reluctant spirit found him detached from both his people and his upbringing, languishing in the wilderness of Midian for decades. When God eventually pushes him into duty as deliverer, he stumbles through his insecurity and uncertainty to emerge as the founder of a national identity and the instrument by which Yahweh's covenant with Israel was forged. He has a destiny that he resists and is ultimately disappointed as he is forbidden entrance into the land. He has some moments of power and prestige, and others of despondency and discouragement. What are we to make of these inconsistencies? We are not to make anything of them—we are to pay attention to what the narrator is doing with this complicated character.

The narrator does not conceal the less attractive aspects of Moses. Instead, he is simply engaged in showing how God used Moses during this crucial time in Israel's history and in God's plans for Israel and the world. As noted in the previous examples, Moses does not deliver the Bible's message through his words, actions, attitudes, or character; he is the vehicle for the narrator's message and for God's plans and purposes.

All these examples, and many more that could be offered, help us to understand the basic point of this chapter. We are tracking with the author, or narrator—not with the people in the story. We are learning about God's plans and purposes and about how he has worked them out in the world. Moreover, we are learning how we can participate in them. When we move from interpretation of the author's intentions to application, we seek the guidance of the Spirit, personal insight, and community input into how we can better participate given what the narrator has recounted to us about

David, Esther, Moses, and so many others. We may aspire to be like these characters or be warned against falling prey to similar temptations and weaknesses, but that would be a personal reflection, not an application of the biblical message. Such personal reflections can be beneficial, but we can engage in such reflections when reading any literature. Just because they are beneficial does not endow them with biblical authority.

This section has devoted four chapters to the narrative literature of the Old Testament, hoping to discover the nature of the authority represented there and how to tap into that authoritative message. To exercise accountability consistently requires changing what has often been the focus of attention (for example, finding role models, identifying behavioral objectives, reconstructing historical events, building personality profiles, etc.) when reading and teaching Bible stories. When we become aware of these red flags, we may need to change not only the focus of our Bible reading, but also change how we preach sermons, teach Sunday school lessons, and shape curriculum. We may need to take a different direction in our Bible studies and small groups. We will need to stop pandering to behavioral objectives and begin addressing the question of what is required of us if we wish to be instruments rather than obstacles as God works out his plans and purposes in the world. The last part of the book will address new approaches to how these narratives could be understood.

SECTION C

WISDOM AND PSALMS

One of the categories of literature in the Old Testament is generally labeled "Wisdom Literature." It includes numerous genres such as proverbial sayings, some psalms, instructions, and various types of philosophical works such as the books of Job and Ecclesiastes. More important than circumscribing the literature and its genres is to determine what "wisdom" is in an ancient Near Eastern context. As this book has been occasionally noting, we cannot just adopt our modern view of words like "wisdom" and assume that ancient peoples would have associated all the same concepts with that word as we do. We will expect the biblical authors to track closer to their own ancient cultural context than to our modern one. Nevertheless, fundamental concepts such as "the fear of the Lord is the beginning of wisdom" may not find full clarity in either the ancient Near East or in our cognitive environment.

Chapter thirteen briefly discussed the Hebrew words for "fear" and "wisdom." Regarding the former, "fear" refers to holding God (and occasionally humans of authority) in high esteem and therefore treating him (and them) with respect. "Fear" of the Lord accords God his proper place and role and is a response to his authority. "Wisdom" has a different focus than the English word. It does not pertain to intelligence or common sense but is intimately connected with the concept of order. The fear of the Lord is the beginning of wisdom because wisdom is the pursuit of order, and Yahweh is the source and center of both wisdom and order. We will now explore these and other concepts in more depth in three chapters.

27—Wisdom Is the Pathway to Order

As suggested earlier in the book, order is arguably the highest value in the ancient world and in the Old Testament (chap. 18). As a quick review, previous chapters have discussed the idea that creation focused primarily on order rather than on material. That is why wisdom was considered the foundation of creation (Proverbs 8). When Adam and Eve took the fruit from the tree of wisdom, they did so to gain what they considered a fundamental component to their decision to seek their own pathway to order—a pathway that would locate themselves rather than God as the center and source of order. They chose to seek order for their own benefit and purposes rather than to be order-bringers alongside God, pursuing his plans and purposes as his image. The covenant was God's initiative to reestablish his order through a relationship he forged with Abraham and his family as he eventually took up his residence among them (in the tabernacle, then the temple). The Torah offered wisdom for living according to God's order as Israel served as host to the presence of God.

Wisdom perceives what constitutes order and pursues, preserves, promotes, and practices order in every area of life. Relationship with God is primary, but wisdom additionally seeks order in family relationships, response to civil authorities, making good choices, controlling one's tongue, and in many other contexts. These elements are common themes in the book of Proverbs, but they are not unique to the biblical book. The earliest literary texts (early third millennium Sumerian) are lists of proverbial sayings, many of them representing similar concepts of order as our biblical book. This is no surprise since Solomon was noted as one who had a cosmopolitan wisdom that operated in the context of the ancient world at large (1 Kings 4:29-34).

While some concepts associated with order are common across all cultures, order can also take different shapes in different cultures. Some cultures find order and stability in a strictly enforced social hierarchy;

others find such hierarchies debilitating or even abusive and find order and stability in autonomy and personal rights. The respective roles of husbands, wives, and children will vary depending on what a culture understands as the determining factors of order. In a category such as this one, there is no "right" answer and no perfect order to be found. The order we find in the Old Testament is based on how order was perceived among the Israelites in the context of the ancient world. God's message to them is one that encourages them to gain wisdom so that order can be pursued. He is not revealing to them the ultimate shape of what order should look like for any people or culture for all time. Some examples will help us to understand the idea that some aspects of order are culturally situated.

Example A—Disciplining Children: The book of Proverbs talks about the disciplining of children in terms that seem harsh from our modern perspectives. For many today, even spanking a child (a widely accepted disciplinary action just a generation ago) is a form of child abuse. In the context of such modern sensibilities, the Old Testament appears shocking, if not scandalous:

> Do not withhold discipline from a child;
> if you punish them with the rod, they will not die.
> Punish them with the rod
> and save them from death. (Proverbs 23:13-14)

We must not treat the Old Testament as offering "the biblical model for child discipline." More specifically, Proverbs is not commanding that we must use a rod in child discipline. The wisdom that it offers pertains to achieving order in an ancient Israelite cultural setting. Recall from our discussion of Torah (chap. 22) that precepts of order are tailored to the values of any particular culture. When we are tracking with the author, we will understand that order will be achieved when children are appropriately disciplined. Different cultures will have varying opinions about what "appropriate discipline" look like. The Bible indicates what it looks like in ancient Israel; it does not prescribe Israel's practices for all people in every culture.

Example B—Womanly Wisdom: Proverbs 31:10-31 famously describes womanly wisdom. If it seems to women that it sets too high a standard, one impossible to achieve, the passage is being misread. If it seems to men to be offering a job description that can serve as a checklist for their search for a mate, the passage is being misread. This acrostic poem offers a wide range of illustrations about what wisdom would look like in the various activities that an Israelite woman might undertake. It does not prompt her to undertake all of them. A woman will find order in her life as she pursues a path of wisdom in all her endeavors. As in the last example, the list is derived from an Israelite context and what was possible within their culture. The text calls on women to exercise wisdom as a pathway to order in their every pursuit.

Example C—Stereotypes: It is not difficult to find proverbs that seem disparaging to women (Proverbs 19:13; 21:9, 19; 25:24), and on numerous occasions men are warned against the wiles of a wayward woman. Yet we also find proverbs that value women and the influence they can have (Proverbs 5:18; 12:4; 18:22; 19:14). We also find sharp words of condemnation for men easily distracted into promiscuity. The fact is that Wisdom literature recognizes the worst and the best at all levels of society as it seeks to guide readers to value wisdom. It may be that some stereotypical faults may be characteristic of one culture, but not another. Yet many of the stereotypes that we find in Proverbs are commonplace in other cultures as well. Negative and positive examples about the behavior of men and women show the pathway to order.

These examples have been focusing on wisdom as a pathway to order in the book of Proverbs, but we also should recognize this purpose in other Wisdom literature, such as is found in the books of Job and Ecclesiastes. These two books both stand as correctives to particular expectations in life—expectations that wisdom suggests are misguided. We can consider each of them briefly to understand what message the books convey.

Example A—Job: Job is well-known as an ideal character who, though conscientious in righteousness, undergoes extensive suffering. It is not uncommon for readers to think that Job is being presented as a role model for when we encounter suffering, but that is decidedly not the case. God offers severe criticism about Job's response to his suffering (Job 40:8), and Job repents of his response. The character Job does not convey the message of the book.[1] It

[1]For more detailed discussion of the issues surrounding the message and purpose of the book of Job, see John H. Walton and Tremper Longman III, *How to Read Job* (Downers Grove, IL: IVP Academic, 2015).

is not a book about Job, and it is not a book to explain why people suffer. It is a wisdom book that is intended to steer people away from a simplistic view of how God works in the world and guide them to healthy ways of thinking about God when life goes wrong.

Job and his friends believed that the world operated by the "Retribution Principle"—the righteous will prosper and the wicked will suffer. Most of Job's life had affirmed this principle in his mind and outlook. But when he began to suffer, he lost his way—nothing was so clear anymore. He had believed that order in the world was enacted through the retribution principle, that this principle defined God's order-bringing policies. The wisdom insight of the book is that the retribution principle is too simplistic and cannot be used to dictate our expectations of God or our demands on him. God cannot be domesticated to conform to our unrealistic expectations. Yahweh's first speech (Job 38–39) indicates that his order extends to all sorts of places where humans would only see a lack of order. The wisdom pathway to order promoted in the book uses Job and his friends as a foil as it presents a much more sophisticated understanding. In the process it contends that order is not defined by our own comfort or understanding. God's order is often more complicated and sometimes beyond our limited knowledge. The book's advice: Trust God.

As a side note, we find that the psalmist often affirms the retribution principle (for example, Psalm 37), yet the book is also filled with lament psalms in which the principle does not seem to offer explanation for the psalmist's experiences, leaving him to wonder how God is sustaining order. The affirmations of the principle in Psalms and Proverbs should be understood as an expression of sound theology—God maintains order by rewarding the righteous and punishing the wicked. Nevertheless, like all proverbial sayings, it is a generalization not a promise (see next chapter). Consequently, it cannot be read as a promise or a guarantee. The retribution principle cannot stand as the comprehensive explanation of how God works in the world. The book of Job makes that clear.

Example B—Ecclesiastes: Ecclesiastes is a difficult book to read since it can easily leave readers depressed. Its blatant pessimism can lead to thoughts of fatalism and even nihilism—all the more reason to make sure that we are reading it well. The premise behind the book is that most people believe that

> they can achieve order in their lives by a variety of pursuits that pertain to self-fulfillment. We frequently feel that everything would be right in the world "if only. . . ." If only we could have more money; if only we could find more pleasure; if only we could achieve great wisdom; if only we could get that prestigious or well-paying job. The main point in the book is that even were we to succeed in such pursuits, we would find them insufficient to provide lasting self-fulfillment. For Qoheleth, the person conveying the wisdom of the book, order is not derived from self-fulfillment. In fact, self-fulfillment is an empty quest. The book suggests that God's order is not found in pursuit of self-fulfillment. We should expect to experience times of what we perceive as both order and non-order (Ecclesiastes 3:1-8). We should recognize that in God's order, he brings both prosperity and adversity (Ecclesiastes 7:14). Therefore, we should adjust our expectations. When we adopt the wisdom path, we will accept that normal (that is, our sense of order) is not found in a self-fulfilled ideal where we feel that we are flourishing and all our dreams and aspirations have come true. Normal is found in the vicissitudes of life in which, beyond our ability to comprehend, God is bringing about his order. His order does not always look or feel like our perception of order. True wisdom pursues his order, not our own.[2]

Both Job and Ecclesiastes expose the false directions that we so easily adopt and unpack the reality that God's order is often complex and difficult for us to identify. How then can we work beside him as order-bringers in his plans and purposes? We don't have to understand it all in order to participate. These books have shown us that we should not think that we have it all figured out (Job) and that we should not think that pursuit of our own aspirations is going to be satisfying (Ecclesiastes). As participating order-bringers, we do not have to understand everything that God is doing—he has given us enough to be engaged. Furthermore, though we experience adversity and suffering as threats to our sense of order, these books help us to understand that in the larger picture, God's order may yet be served (see Romans 8:22-28).

---

[2]Even Song of Songs can be viewed as a wisdom book based on Song of Songs 8:6-7. That wisdom saying helps us understand that since love and sex constitute a powerful force in our lives, they can drive us to bring great disorder to ourselves and to others. Love and sex themselves are aspects of order; yet they can easily be disruptive if not respected.

Wisdom can be illustrated, and its features can be described in part, but it cannot be exhaustively formulated. That is, no one can draw up a list that can cover every aspect of wisdom for every circumstance and situation in life. Wisdom is a pathway, and a journey. Its destination is order, but we can easily get distracted when we focus on our own perceptions of an order that brings benefit and success to us rather than trying to understand God's order.

28—Proverbial Sayings Are Generalizations, Not Promises

The book of Proverbs is a section of the Old Testament with which many people resonate. We recognize the value of wisdom for our lives and the book strikes us as very practical—certainly not as confusing as Leviticus! Even though we find the content of the book easier to navigate, we must still exercise caution in order to respect the genre for what it is and what it is not. Such respect is essential to our commitment to track with the author.

One of the major fallacies found in interpreting proverbs is in the careless approach that adopts particular proverbs as if they were promises made by God—guarantees for getting through life. This is the mistake made by those who promote a "health and wealth gospel." Sample passages they promote include:

> Do not be wise in your own eyes;
>   fear the LORD and shun evil.
> This will bring health to your body
>   and nourishment to your bones.
> Honor the LORD with your wealth,
>   with the firstfruits of all your crops;
> then your barns will be filled to overflowing,
>   and your vats will brim over with new wine. (Proverbs 3:7-10)
> Commit your actions to the LORD,
>   and your plans will succeed. (Proverbs 16:3 NLT)

> Humility and the fear of the LORD
> bring wealth and honor and life. (Proverbs 22:4 NIV 1984)

These are all expressions of the retribution principle, a concept introduced in the last chapter. A flat reading of these leads those who deeply desire the outcomes of health and wealth to consider them promises. When we read them as proverbial statements, however, we will recognize that, like all proverbs, they are generalizations, not guarantees. Experience and observation tell us this. Further evidence can be found in proverbs which, if not recognized as generalizations, would be contradictory. The prime example is found in Proverbs 26:4-5, where two different strategies are given for responding to a fool. We can see the same dynamics at work in our own modern proverbs. "Look before you leap" encourages patient consideration of options, whereas "he who hesitates is lost" suggests that opportunities should be taken when they present themselves.[3] We could easily find ourselves confused if we decided to always follow one instead of the other. The better approach is to view them as generalizations. The wise person will know which one applies best to their situation.

The nature of generalizations is that they are usually true, to the extent that they contain an important principle; but they are not universally true. Again, to use a modern example, we can truly believe that "crime doesn't pay," yet we could all come up with examples where a person's dishonest or criminal behavior has brought them great success. The truth of the proverb is in the values that it affirms, not in its universal actualization. A few examples can help us see the importance of this principle.

> **Example A—Proverbs 22:6:** Parents experience great distress when their children stray from the core beliefs, principles, and values with which they were raised. Wayward children bring heartbreak to their parents who long for their prodigal to return. In their desperation, they search the Scriptures for some assurance that can give them hope. Some believe they have found it in Proverbs 22:6: "Start children off on the way they should go, / and even when they are old they will not turn from it." In the throes of despair, it is easy to

[3]As another example of apparently contradicting modern proverbs, compare "Many hands make light work" with "Too many cooks spoil the broth."

see how parents might embrace this as God's assurance, or indeed, his promise, that their rebellious son or daughter might come to their senses, like the Prodigal Son in Luke 15:17-20, and come running back home (metaphorically if not physically).

We can surely understand that such hope would be desirable. The problem is that interpreting this proverb as such a promise or assurance reflects a misunderstanding of the genre of proverbial literature. When we recognize this verse as a generalization, we find that it is affirming a principle that the way in which children are raised drives deep roots not easily set aside. We note, then, that the verse does not refer to a child *returning* to the values taught in youth. It rather affirms that even as they reach old age, those instilled values are likely to remain observable and become innate—they will not depart from them. It says nothing about returning to values, practices, or beliefs that they have departed from. Furthermore, this is also not a promise that they will never depart from their upbringing; it is a generalized comment about human nature and the long-lasting effect of one's upbringing.

Example B—Proverbs 3:5-6: We would have to count Proverbs 3:5-6 among the most beloved verses of the book:

> Trust in the Lord with all your heart
> and lean not on your own understanding;
> in all your ways submit to him,
> and he will make your paths straight.

I have heard many testimonials of those who consider it their "life verse." It is indeed a wonderful verse calling faithful people to trust God even when our own knowledge fails and we do not understand how God is working, or even when we feel that he is not working in the way that we would want him to do. Trust and submission are appropriate pathways to follow. But the last phrase can derail our interpretation.

I gave examples above about the health and wealth gospel and how that is derived from taking statements of the retribution principle as promises. Such a misinterpretation feeds what we can identify as a transactional approach to our faith. That is, it represents the idea that if we are faithful to God in our deeds and in our gifts, that we have entered a transaction in which God is now obliged to bring us success. Some might also be inclined to read Proverbs 3:5-6 from a transactional perspective. When the verse indicates that the result of trust and submission are that "he will make your paths straight" or the alternative translation, "he will direct your paths," we must interpret it in light of our understanding of how proverbial literature works, not as an assurance of a transactional relationship.

When life is not following the paths that we hoped for but is filled with crises and trials, we can easily become disappointed with God. In the depths of such frustration, we might be inclined to abandon God, thinking that he is not worthy of our trust—where has it gotten us? These verses assure us that we should continue in trust and submission and that God will then be an encouragement as we follow him—no matter what our circumstances might be. Most importantly, these verses do not suggest that if we trust and submit that God will resolve our troubles. That is not what "making our path straight" refers to. When we understand the nature of proverbial literature as offering generalizations, we will not wander off the rails into transactionalism. Part three will discuss this further.

As an addendum to this chapter, we should note that once we learn how to track with the author in proverbial literature, we will also recognize that proverbs are not offering doctrinal propositions or proof texts. Caring for animals (Proverbs 12:10) is offering wisdom, not a doctrine of creation care. Working the land (Proverbs 12:11) is wisdom because it provides food; it is not offering a theology of work. When Proverbs 12:27 indicates that "the diligent feed on the riches of the hunt," it is not offering biblical support for hunting for sport or arguments about gun control. Instead, it offers wisdom about how persistence and diligence will bring results. The statement that "the eyes of the LORD are everywhere" (Proverbs 15:3) cannot be used as a proof text for omnipresence (it only indicates that nothing is hidden from God), and Proverbs 15:24 cannot be used to inform a doctrine of heaven and hell; the path "upward" is the path of continued life and success, not the path to heaven. Those who would seek to use Proverbs 30:5, "Every word of God is flawless," to support the doctrine of inerrancy are not respecting the genre of the book.[4]

---

[4]This verse refers to all the utterances of God. Such would include written Scripture but is not limited to that, though it may have a defined corpus in view. It refers to them here as refined as if by fire,

29—Psalms Commends Prayer but Does Not Command Prayer

Chapter twenty-four indicated that in order to track with the author, readers need to focus on the rhetorical strategy of the book more than on each individual narrative, and the same is true here in the book of Psalms. Moreover, just as the message of Scripture was not carried in the people or the events in narratives, but in what the narrator did with characters and events (chap. 26), so it is not the psalmists as characters who are supposed to be role models for us. In Psalms, what the final compiler is doing with the book of Psalms, not what each psalm or psalmist is doing, conveys Scripture to us.

If the authority is the result of inspiration (of the text!), we must focus on the *book* of Psalms. Just as the narrators chose individual narratives for Judges or Samuel and wove them together into a book with a purpose, so the individual psalms have been selected and arranged with a purpose in mind and have come into our Bible as a book (with five component books).[5] While each psalm can be considered inspired, we should look to the book with its purpose to receive the message. As with the narrative literature, where each narrative should be investigated with regard to its contribution to the whole, so each psalm should be investigated for its contribution to the purpose of the compiler—first to the compiler of the smaller collection of which it is a part, and second to the book of Psalms as a whole.

The compilers have done their work with a purpose in mind—what is it? This purpose can be determined from the introduction to the book as a whole (Psalms 1–2), from the Psalm that closes each of the books (41, 72, 89, 106), and from the Psalm that stands as the climax of the book (145)

---

indicating that there is no waste or dross. The point is driven home in verse 6, that those who would add to the Word of God would inevitably corrupt it.

[5]The book of Psalms is comprised of five books (1–41; 42–72; 73–89; 90–106; 107–150).

before it moves to the grand finale of praise (146–150). Most who have studied the book in this way agree that the main theme of the book of Psalms is the kingship of Yahweh. His kingship is seen in the lives and struggles of individuals (especially in the individual laments) as well as in his interaction with the nation of Israel and especially with its anointed king.

The result of tracking with the author (that is, compiler) of Psalms is that, in all circumstances, faithful readers will affirm Yahweh's kingship over our lives and over our world. We will come to a deeper understanding of the vicissitudes of life as well as those of history. We will praise him when all is well, and we will come to him with our sorrows in adversity. We will understand that he is the Lord of our lives and that we can place ourselves in his hands. We will find comfort in the fact that he listens, and we can learn to listen to him and look for his plans and purposes being worked out.

We can pray psalms (at least some of them), but that is not what they are there for—that is not how they function as Scripture. Tracking with the compiler does not mean praying the book of Psalms; it means understanding how the psalms show us something important about the kingship of God. This should actually solve some problems for us. Many American Christians would not feel quite right praying psalms like Psalm 109 or 137:9, and the Bible's authority does not suggest we do so. Some African Christians are not comfortable when they are encouraged to use these cursing psalms as giving them power to curse their enemies with powerful incantations.[6] To suggest we do so is also a misunderstanding. These are not model prayers which we are commanded or empowered to pray.

When we turn to theological matters, we must continue to make important distinctions. The book of Psalms alludes to some important theological truths but are not a vehicle for doctrine. Again, this is a matter of respecting the genre. A few examples will illustrate the idea.

Example A—Spirit of the Lord: Psalm 51 is well-known as David's confession of sin after the affair with Bathsheba. Christian readers, while appreciating the need for confession and the power of repentance, have found Psalm 51:11 to pose a considerable obstacle. There David prays that the Holy Spirit not be

---

[6]David Adamo, "Reading Psalm 109 in African Christianity," *Old Testament Exegesis* 21 (2008): 575-92.

taken away from him. Too often this launches a discussion about the doctrine of the eternal security of the believer. But this verse cannot and must not be used as a proof text dealing with salvation.

First, though the term "holy spirit" is used here, the author would not have used this as a reference to the third person of the Trinity. Neither the psalmist nor the compiler was aware of trinitarian theology, and therefore, if we are tracking with them, we cannot bring that doctrine into the discussion here. In the Old Testament, the spirit represented the energizing power of God, not an independent person of the godhead. Here, holiness is used as an adjective because of the nature of David's offense.

Second, the spirit in the Old Testament does not indwell as a result of a person becoming a believer. The endowment of the spirit on David has authorized him as king (1 Samuel 16:13), it has not sealed his salvation. In the Old Testament people did not know anything about being saved from sins by the work of Christ, and that work had not yet been accomplished. This psalm is not giving doctrinal information about the perseverance of the saints—it has nothing to do with David's salvation.

Third, this Old Testament spirit can be taken away.[7] It was given to enable David's kingship, and theoretically that enablement could be retracted. In fact, that is the very thing that happened to his predecessor, Saul (1 Samuel 16:14), and David was fearful that the same might happen to him. There is no doctrinal teaching here about whether the indwelling Holy Spirit can or cannot be taken away from Christians.

Example B—Psalm 139: Psalm 139 was discussed in an earlier chapter with regard to genre (chap. 11). The psalm is often viewed as a treasure trove of doctrine, particularly in its purported references to the omniscience and omnipresence of God (Psalm 139:1-6 and 7-12 respectively). Unquestionably these verses express that God knows human thoughts and that God has access to all places. As important as these affirmations are, they fall far short of establishing fully developed doctrines of omniscience and omnipresence. They allude to the psalmist's affirmations, and we may well conclude that we can affirm the same beliefs and more. They remind us of what we believe, but they do not teach us what to believe—this is not that sort of literature. We can

[7]Note that Samson is endowed with it multiple times.

neither prove nor develop those doctrines from these verses. The psalmist believed some things that we do not and should not believe. For example, the psalmist believed that all go to Sheol, and that there is no other option.[8] The psalmists express often that their destiny is Sheol (for example, Psalm 88:3; 89:48), not heaven (see next example).

Example C—Psalms and Heaven: Psalms 49:15 and 73:24 are often read as attesting to an Israelite belief in a doctrine of heaven, but again we must read carefully. In the NIV, Psalm 49:15 is translated, "But God will redeem me from the realm of the dead; / he will surely take me to himself." That makes it sound like the psalmist expects his final destiny to be heaven as he is redeemed from death. Contrast, however, the ESV: "But God will ransom my soul from the power of Sheol, / for he will receive me." The NET Bible gets even closer to the sense of the Hebrew: "But God will rescue my life from the power of Sheol; / certainly he will pull me to safety." The psalmist expects to be saved from death. The concept of "receiving/taking" me can be seen to refer to having one's life saved in other usage (Psalm 18:16). NIV stands alone in adding "to himself," which is not represented in the Hebrew text and is unwarranted.

Psalm 73:24 is rendered in the NIV as "You guide me with your counsel, / and afterward you will take me into glory." Here the English reader easily equates "glory" with "heaven," but the Hebrew text has no "into" and nowhere else in the Old Testament is "glory" (*kabod*) a reference to heaven. When we compare other translations, the ESV has "to glory" but the NET renders the verse, "You guide me by your wise advice, / and then you will lead me to a position of honor." This is a much more accurate reflection of the Hebrew.[9] This verse talks about God restoring the psalmist after his time of affliction at the hands of his enemies. Consequently, it cannot be used to build a doctrine of an expectation of heaven.

Example D—Psalm 132:13-14: Psalm 132:13-14 is an example of an important way in which psalms *can* allude to a theological idea without using the idea to build doctrine.

---

[8]We should not be misled by the fact that some translations often render the Hebrew word *sheol* as "grave." It refers to the netherworld to which all go—the grave is the portal that leads there.

[9]Notice also the NRSV, "You guide me with your counsel, / and afterward you will receive me with honor."

For the LORD has chosen Zion,
he has desired it for his dwelling, saying,
"This is my resting place for ever and ever;
here I will sit enthroned, for I have desired it."

In this psalm, we learn that God's temple is his resting place. This in turn makes it clear that when he rests in his temple, he is resting on a throne, not on a bed. From that we learn that the Hebrew concept of divine rest reflects God's rule—his engagement in the world, not his disengagement from the world. This is important theologically because it helps us to understand a Hebrew concept that we have long misinterpreted. The result of our misunderstanding the concept of divine rest is that it leads to confusion about the seventh day of creation as well as the observance of Sabbath (chap. 19). This still falls short of providing a theology of divine rest.

How then are we to think about the book of Psalms? This chapter drew an analogy between the psalms and the narrative literature, but we can also benefit from comparing psalms to what we have said about Torah (chapters 21–22). Just as the legal provisions in the Torah were illustrations of what order would look like in the context of God's presence and his covenant relationship with Israel, so the individual psalms stand as illustrations of the many ways in which God's kingship affects his people. Covenant, Torah, and Psalms all operate with reference to God's kingship and prompt us to a broader and deeper understanding of its ramifications. This moves us well beyond the idea of model prayers.

SECTION D

PROPHECY AND APOCALYPTIC

Prophetic and apocalyptic literature make up almost 40 percent of the Old Testament and more than a quarter of the Bible. It has nearly as many words as the entire New Testament.[1] Despite the continuing prevalence of prophecy conferences and the public interest in the end times, the prophetic and apocalyptic literatures of the Bible are underrepresented in the sermons preached in today's churches. Attention to the prophets in the church is generally centered on two primary interests: apologetics and eschatology. Regarding apologetics, readers comb the prophetic and apocalyptic literature for prophecies about Jesus so these can be used to prove that God knew the future and predicted many aspects of Jesus' life and ministry. This is then used to defend the ideas that the Bible is indeed the Word of God, and that Jesus is indeed the Son of God. Regarding eschatology, readers comb the prophetic and apocalyptic literature for indications of the Last Days with an interest in gleaning details of what to look for, how the future will unfold, and how their present times may be identified as those Last Days.

These are not meaningless pursuits, though they can at times be extreme. We treasure the Bible and are eager to show ways in which its divine source

[1]Statistics are based on word counts in the original languages.

can be demonstrated. We anticipate the return of Christ and the coming kingdom of God and new creation. The Bible and the role of Jesus stand as the foundation of our faith, and the coming kingdom of God is the foundation of our hope. It is no surprise, then, that we seek affirmations in the prophetic literature.

The burning question, however, concerns whether this is what the focus should be when readers want to read the text in context. This book so far has been presenting an approach that fulfills our accountability to the authority of the text by diligently tracking with the author. The oracles of the prophets provide the content of these books, though there is little reason to think that the prophets themselves were the authors who collected, compiled, and authored the books that we have in our Bibles. It is more likely that others did that at a later period as the prophecies were recognized for their lasting significance. In that regard, we will be tracking with the prophet, (who is not necessarily the author, but the source of the content) through the compiler, to see what understanding that will give us.[2] What new perspectives will that suggest for our understanding of God's Word? As has been the case in previous units, we can find our sense of direction by identifying missteps that are all too easy to take. We will pursue these in the next five chapters.

30—Prophecy Is More About Revealing God's Plans and Purposes Than Revealing the Future

To gain a proper understanding of how to read prophetic literature, we must first examine the nature of the prophetic role and message. The prophets are the spokespersons for God. They were charged with delivering the messages that he gave them. The messages were not their own and some prophets were uncomfortable with the messages they were called to announce. Yet they were under the compulsion of their calling, so

[2]The next five chapters are condensed versions of the longer study that I will provide in *The Lost World of Prophecy* (Downers Grove, IL: IVP Academic, forthcoming).

resistance was not successful (see Jonah, who tried to flee). Prophets were not always exemplary people, and they were often despised by those whom they served. Some served honorably in the courts of kings (for example, Isaiah with Hezekiah) while others had to flee for their lives (Elijah) and suffered imprisonment (Jeremiah).

The role of prophets was not unique to Israel.[3] As early as the first half of the second millennium BC, not long after the time of Abraham, prophetic messages were being sent to the king of the town of Mari along the Euphrates River. It was not unusual for kings of the ancient world to have prophets among their advisors and consultants. Rulers always believed that it was advantageous to have information from the gods as they made decisions, and prophets provided one way of getting such guidance. Prophets worked in tandem with the various divination specialists who also provided information from the gods.

Even though biblical prophecy fits broadly into this larger cultural context, the prophets that we encounter in the collections of oracles in the Bible—we will refer to them as the "classical prophets"[4]—were distinct from their ancient Near Eastern counterparts in a number of important ways.[5] Most significantly, the classical prophets were often out among the people declaring their messages instead of focusing their attention primarily on the king. Consequently, their messages involved how God was working with respect to the people of Israel as a whole, not just giving direction to the king. We therefore find messages in the prophetic literature about coming invaders who will bring about destruction and will carry the Israelites into exile. Such messages are not found in the oracles of the

---

[3]The primary literature pertaining to the prophetic texts in the ancient Near East has been conveniently gathered and translated in Martti Nissinen, *Prophets and Prophecy in the Ancient Near East* (Atlanta, GA: SBL, 2003). For broader discussion see Nissinen, *Ancient Prophecy* (Oxford: Oxford University, 2017). I will discuss these issues at greater length in *The Lost World of Prophecy*.

[4]I am drawing a line of distinction here between prophets whose oracles are preserved for us in books associated with them in the Bible (the earliest of whom lived in the eighth century BC), and "pre-classical" prophets whose activities are reported in the narrative literature, but whose oracles have not been preserved (for example, Deborah, Nathan, Elijah, Elisha). The pre-classical prophets generally gave messages to leaders and were not inherently related to covenant faithfulness, though they sometimes could be.

[5]For more detailed comparison and contrast, see John H. Walton, *Ancient Near Eastern Thought and the Old Testament*, 2nd ed. (Grand Rapids, MI: Baker, 2018), 213-51.

prophets of the ancient Near East. Another significant difference is that the prophets in Israel were often critical of their kings, whereas that was a rarity in the oracles from the ancient Near East.

The messages of the prophets fall into four general categories:

- Indictment—identifying what the people were doing wrong
- Judgment—indicating what God was doing to remediate or punish the deviant behavior
- Instruction—directing the people to a particular sort of response (for example, repent, return to the Lord, do justice, keep the covenant)
- Aftermath—confirming and describing God's continuing relationship with Israel that will result in return and restoration

Nearly every prophetic oracle can be associated with at least one of these categories. We can see then that the prophets are not primarily dealing with the future. They are interested in the past, present, and future. They are proclaiming how God has been working out his plans and purposes among his people and how he will continue to do so. We could call them champions of the covenant because they call the people to covenant faithfulness, pronounce the judgment of God based on the covenant curses (Deuteronomy 27–28), and console the people with the hope based on God's faithfulness to the covenant that will bring restoration.

When God's plans and purposes were revealed in these oracles, the people came to understand more about who God is and how he worked among them. As the chapter title indicates, these messages are more about the plans and purposes of God than about the future. God holds the future of his people and the world in his hands, and he directs the course of history. These are affirmed not so that God's people become privy to details of the future, but so that they understand the sort of God they serve and what he wants from them.

When I distribute my course syllabi to my students, I unavoidably provide information about the future as I indicate what the content of the lecture will be on any particular day of the semester. That is not because I can tell the future; it is because I have a plan and am generally in a position to carry it out. They can use the syllabus to learn more about me as their professor, but that is not what the syllabus is for either. The purpose of the syllabus is not to tell the future, it is to help the student understand how they can successfully participate in the course. They are informed of my objectives and of their requirements. What it says about the future is not unimportant, but it is subject to variation. That is, perhaps the questions the students have or the difficulties that they encounter may lead me to spend an extra class period on a difficult topic. My plans are designed to unfold in a way that is aware of and sensitive to student needs and responses. Despite the possibility of alterations to the course schedule, my objectives remain the same, and they will be accomplished. All these observations provide apt analogies for considering the nature of God's plans and purposes as they are articulated in prophetic literature. A few examples can illustrate these points.

Example A—Jonah: When God sends Jonah to Nineveh, what message does the prophet carry? The text is forthright about this: "Forty more days and Nineveh will be overthrown" (Jonah 3:4)—a message of judgment. Despite this remarkable clarity, from children's Bible story books to Sunday school curriculum, and from devotionals and Bible studies to sermons, a very different story is told. Many times, Jonah is portrayed as giving instruction and hope: "God loves you and wants you to worship him alone;" "God will forgive your sins if you stop being so mean and violent." Those who make such suggestions are not tracking with the author. The fact that the Ninevites repent and that God does spare them does not mean that Jonah's message gave that instruction or hope. God's plan was to destroy them, but instead, we find that their response brought a change—God decided not to do so (Jonah 3:10). The text cannot be clearer on that point. That means that the oracle, though not framed in conditional language, had alternative possible outcomes. This stands as a straightforward case in which God's statement about the future is altered. The portrait of the future was not assured but indicated the inevitable result if the Ninevites continued on the path they were following. Jonah's oracle did not say that a change of course would affect the outcome, but, as it turns out, it did. God's objective remained unchanged but the pathway to getting there was revised. It is God's prerogative to do so. His objectives are assured; the pathway is not—therefore he is not telling the future, he is announcing his plans.

Example B—Micah: The prophet Micah makes an astounding statement in Micah 5:2 when he proclaims that the ruler over Israel, the long-anticipated messiah, will be born in Bethlehem. This is an unusual and, in fact, unprecedented sort of detail for a prophetic oracle. It has the appearance of a random, arbitrary factoid. Furthermore, it seems that later interpreters took it seriously (Matthew 2:4-6). But let's not be hasty. When we investigate the role of Bethlehem in Israel's past history, we recall that though it was a small, nondescript village, it carried a notable distinction—it was King David's hometown. Nevertheless, David himself had made Jerusalem his capital city, and all his descendant successors, the kings of Judah, were born in Jerusalem. We would therefore expect that his heir, who would be the ideal king, would likewise be born in Jerusalem. Yet Micah indicates that is not the case.

Now we are in a position to ask the crucial question, "Why does Micah designate Bethlehem (and not Jerusalem)?" What does this signify? And here we learn something important about God's plans and purposes, not just a detail about the future. There will be a lapse in succession to the throne—a period without a king. This ideal, future, Davidic king will represent a fresh start, in some sense, a "do-over"; a reset button for kingship. Far from being an arbitrary factoid, this statement plays a significant role in charting the course of God's objectives. The prophecy will be fulfilled not based on a birth certificate stamped "Bethlehem" but based on the way God's plan unfolds in a new David, not just a successor to the throne. The more significant element of the prophecy has little to do with the physical place of birth; what is important is what that place stands for. Hopefully this helps us to see the important nuanced difference between laying out a plan and telling the future.

Example C—Isaiah 13:19-22: We can gain further insight when we examine instances where it might seem that prophecies were not fulfilled. Isaiah 13:19 indicates that Babylon "will be overthrown by God like Sodom and Gomorrah." Such a statement paints a clear picture of judgment in the minds of any who know the familiar story from Genesis 19: fire from heaven and total destruction. But is that what happened to Babylon at the hand of the Medes? Not at all. From every indication in contemporary accounts and from all the data gleaned from archaeological excavation, the Medes and Persians took the city of Babylon without even a battle. Furthermore, Isaiah indicates that as a result of this presumably fiery destruction, "she will never be inhabited or lived in through all generations" (Isaiah 13:20-22). In contrast, the new lords of the city occupied Babylon and counted it among their most important capitals. After two centuries of Persian rule, Alexander took control of the city, as did the Seleucid rulers that followed him in the Hellenistic period. Over time, as the course of the Euphrates shifted and Babylon no longer enjoyed the advantage of easy river access, the city gradually wasted away and was finally abandoned.

So was Isaiah wrong? Did he tell a false future? The problem here is with the assumption that his oracle against Babylon was telling the future. Just because God's plans for Babylon held a destiny of being judged just like God's plans for Sodom and Gomorrah did, we are not therefore obliged to think that the way they arrived at that destiny would necessarily be the same (though readers might have defensibly expected such an outcome). It is not the specific future of Babylon that Isaiah declared, but the destiny that God had declared as part of his plans and purposes. If someone of Isaiah's time tried to give specific shape to the future of Babylon from these verses, they likely would have been wrong. But God's Word had not thereby failed.

Readers are accountable to the messages of the prophets that carry the authority of the text. When we attend to the message of any given oracle, we will focus less on the shape of the future and more on understanding what God is doing and how he is working out his plans and purposes in history. Prophecy is not predicting the future, and that is the focus of the next chapter.

31—Prophecy Is Not Prediction

It is not uncommon to hear people talk about "predictive prophecy" when they are talking about the way that the prophetic or apocalyptic literature tells us of the future. But let's think for a moment what we mean when we use the word "prediction." I am particularly interested in exploring the relationship between prediction and causation. If I were holding a pen and told the people around me that I predicted that before the next minute passed, the pen would fall to the ground, and seconds later I dropped it intentionally, they would not be impressed. Why not? I had predicted the future! If questioned, I suspect they would contend that if I could make the pen fall, then the term "prediction" would no longer carry any meaning. If I were to predict that a certain stock would dramatically drop in value, but could do something to cause that to happen, it would no longer qualify as prediction. A person who can cause something to happen cannot refer to that which they cause as something that they predict. In short, prediction and causation are mutually exclusive, by definition.

When we apply this important distinction to prophetic literature, we must conclude that "prediction" is not a useful description. In fact, we would have to insist that God, since he is at some level the cause of everything, cannot be said to predict. Since God is an agent engaged in cause, prediction is never an apt description of what he is saying. As an aside, we should also note that it would also be inappropriate to refer to the prophets themselves as predicting, because the message is God's, not theirs. Consequently, "predictive prophecy" is an oxymoron. Yet prophetic messages given by God unquestionably at times refer to the future. If we have found the word "prediction" to be inadequate, how do we talk about what God is doing?

We have other vocabulary to talk about projections into the future. For example, when we describe what the meteorologist is doing, we do not say she is "predicting the weather." Instead, we say that she is "forecasting the weather." The difference is that the meteorologist is using all sorts of tools and observations, combined with weather patterns, past behavior of weather systems, and recent movements of systems to offer her wisdom on what will unfold in the coming hours and days. An economic forecast works in similar ways. These forecasts are not mystical insight, they depend on hard evidence. They depend on the concept that past trends and knowledge of the present will lead to sound estimates of the future. If God were not so directly involved, "forecast" might well describe what the prophets were doing. They were working with data, observations, and wisdom. But this does not account for what God is doing.

Another word that we might hear when people are talking about the future is *foretelling*. In fact, it is not uncommon to hear people say that prophetic literature is "forthtelling" rather than "foretelling" as they try to give nuance to what is going on in this literature. *Forthtelling* emphasizes the declarative nature of the pronouncement. Prophecy is a declaration, but it is more than that. Nevertheless, *foretelling*, in contrast, sounds a little too much like tarot cards, palm-readers, and horoscopes, and we dare not reduce prophetic literature to such categories. Remember that how we define prophecy is not going to be in relation to the practitioners, who are simply messengers, but must relate to what God is doing.

When we characterize prophecy in relation to God's intentions (working through his spokespersons, the prophets), it means he is revealing various aspects of his plans and purposes in order to generate a response regarding what Israelites are doing wrong. The prophet's message often specifies what his audience was doing wrong and indicates the judgment that such behavior will bring. They sometimes also offer hope regarding the direction of the future. All of these relate to their covenant relationship with Yahweh as he calls them to covenant faithfulness. These prophecies at times refer back to God's actions in the past—his track record as well as Israel's; at times they address present situations and behavior; yes, at times, they project a future based on the past and present, but also as guided by God's overall objectives, which themselves are unalterable.

> **Example A—Jonah:** Jonah was used as an example in the previous chapter and warrants turning to again. The book tells us plainly what Jonah's message to Nineveh was, but what was Jonah's message to Israel? Jonah pronounced God's judgment on Nineveh, they responded, and God "changed his mind." We know the message of the prophet Jonah to Nineveh. But what was the message of the book to its Israelite audience? We can infer it to be that the sequence of events at Nineveh is consistent with the nature of prophecy and paradigmatic of how God works. That would mean that when the prophets pronounce judgment oracles on Israel, the response of the

audience could change the course that had been proclaimed. The announced judgment is presumably then not inherently fixed in the plans and purposes of God; it is merely the inevitable result of the course that the people are following. God can respond by withdrawing the threat without changing his larger plans and purposes. This in turn says something about the nature of prophecy, and here is the important point. If prophetic oracles have this level of flexibility, then they would be a precarious basis for formulating a precise view of the future, though the general direction of God's future plans and purposes is discernible.

Example B—1 Samuel 2:30: The previous example dealt with a judgment oracle. But what about the oracles that offer hope and restoration or that speak of God's positive plans for the future? An example to consider is found in the prophetic oracle 1 Samuel 2:30: "Therefore the LORD, the God of Israel, declares: 'I promised that members of your family would minister before me forever.' But now the LORD declares: 'Far be it from me! Those who honor me I will honor, but those who despise me will be disdained.'" According to this verse, God had apparently communicated a future destiny to Eli's ancestors (whether by prophetic word or not, we are not told). It is a destiny of honor and status. Yet now God is retracting it through a prophetic pronouncement. Apparently, he can do that based on how people act. Presumably this does not alter God's overall plans and purposes (the existence of priestly mediators for Israel?), but it changes the role of Eli's family. They would be mistaken to take the previous word from God to be a prediction of an inexorable future.

Example C—Daniel's Seventy Weeks: Daniel's seventy weeks provides a third example, this time not of something that is being undone, but of something that is taking a different shape than could have possibly been anticipated. Scholars take varying points of view concerning whether Jeremiah's prophecy of seventy years (Jeremiah 25:11-12; 29:10) is being replaced in Daniel 9:24-27 with a longer period, or whether a distinction is now being made between return (after seventy years) and restoration (a period extended by seven times based on Leviticus 26:18). Regardless, what the passage demonstrates is that there is some degree of flexibility in how prophecies will turn out.

The point of all of this is that prophecy cannot be used to determine what the future will look like. If behaviors change, some of the results may change. Even when they do not, fulfillment may take a very different shape than what people might have anticipated (see chap. 34). Prophecy does not create an absolute future; it projects God's plans and purposes based on a current course, and that course is subject to change, though his plans and purposes are not. Prophecy is not a way for God to give us tomorrow's headlines today. Instead, it is calling the Israelites to a response to God's message and giving them hope. Prophecy is God's mechanism to remind the people of their covenant relationship, especially after the kings failed so miserably in that department. God tells them what they aren't doing, what they need to do to get back on track and carry out their covenant responsibilities and affirms that he (God) will be/still is faithful to the covenant, thus giving them hope.

As a conclusion to this chapter, we might consider, "What do prophecies to Israel mean to us?" If the prophecies are addressed to Israel in their historical context as God's covenant people, they identify Israel's offenses within that time and place. We cannot assume that we are guilty of the same offenses. Even if our offenses fall into similar categories, that does not mean that we are subject to the same judgment (though we may be subject to similar action by God). If the instruction to Israel pertains to covenant faithfulness, we must recognize that we are not in that same covenant. Most of the aftermath prophecies refer to Israel's restoration, which has no direct relevance to us. What we learn from the prophecies is that God has plans and purposes and that he is carrying them out. We are instructed as we observe how God works, and we learn about what it means to participate in God's plans and purposes, while gaining brief glimpses into their direction. But we ought not take the prophecies as prediction of the future.

32—Apocalyptic Is Not Prophecy

Up until this point in the unit, the chapters have been focusing primarily on prophetic literature. This chapter turns its attention to apocalyptic literature with the proposition that apocalyptic is not simply a subcategory of prophetic literature that depends more on visions than oracles. Instead, despite some identifiable overlap between prophecy and apocalyptic, they should be considered separate genres with separate ways of communicating. Academics adopted a consensus definition of apocalyptic literature decades ago, and it is still often quoted, though it is also subject to pushback in a variety of ways large and small, so even though our discussion will not be dependent on that definition, it is helpful for offering a general description:

> A genre of revelatory literature with a narrative framework, in which a revelation is mediated by an otherworldly being to a human recipient, disclosing a transcendent reality which is both temporal, insofar as it envisages eschatological salvation, and spatial insofar as it involves another, supernatural world intended to interpret present, earthly circumstances in light of the supernatural world and of the future, and to influence both the understanding and the behavior of the audience by means of divine authority.[6]

As we seek to understand apocalyptic literature, we can easily identify several similarities and continuities with prophetic literature. They both at times project a particular sort of future and both are seen as having their source in God (that is, they represent divine revelation) and are mediated by select humans. They offer hope and affirm that God is in control of history. They both offer insights into God's plans and purposes. The roots of apocalyptic literature can be found in a variety of cultures and literatures from early in the first millennium BC, but the genre finds its greatest popularity in Jewish and Christian literature between the second century BC and the second century AD. So much for similarities; some of the most important distinctions can be seen in Table 33.1.[7]

---

[6]First defined in John J. Collins, ed., *Apocalypse: The Morphology of a Genre*, Semeia 14 (Missoula, MT: Scholars Press, 1979); and later revised in Adele Yarbro Collins, "Introduction: Early Christian Apocalypticism," *Semeia* 36 (1986): 7.

[7]This chart summarizes the discussion of contrasts in the introduction of Aubrey E. Buster and John H. Walton, *Daniel*, New International Commentary on the Old Testament (Grand Rapids, MI: Eerdmans, forthcoming), where a more detailed nuancing can be found.

Table 33.1. Prophecy and apocalyptic contrasted

PROPHECY IN THE HEBREW BIBLE	APOCALYPTIC
Direct divine revelation ("Thus says the Lord")	Mediated revelation through visions or heavenly beings
Word from God to be proclaimed	Vision from God to be understood
Prophet speaks oracles	Visionary records the vision and its interpretation
Oracles that claim to reproduce the speech of God directly	Revelatory visions that claim to unveil mysteries about the past, the present, and the future
Projects a plan for Israel's history	Projects a pattern of universal history
Driven by indictment leading to restoration	Driven by pattern leading to kingdom of God
Rooted in time and history	Transcends time and history with cosmic scope
Exhortation to return to covenant faithfulness: reverse course	Exhortation to be faithful to the covenant in crisis: steady on
Ethical urgency for changing course of events	Historical determinism
Projects the consequences of Israel's covenant failures rooted in the blessings and curses of the covenant	Projects a certain kind of future, rooted in the patterns of the past, to re-orient the readers' thinking about present
Focus on God's rule over Israel established by the covenant	Focus on God's rule over the kingdoms of the world
Announces exile (offenses leading to it, result of judgment, restoration coming from it)	Resolves exile (kings and empires are transitory)
Divine judgment leads to salvation or destruction in this world	Extends the timeline of divine judgment to include post-mortem judgment for the wicked and reward for the righteous

In summary, the primary purpose of apocalyptic literature is not to foretell the future but to communicate God's plans and purposes, both in space and in time. Rather than being impressed by accurate predictions, readers should educate themselves in God's plans for bringing order to the cosmos and in history.

Example A—Daniel 10: Daniel is never referred to as a prophet in the book. As time went on, anyone in the Bible who talked about the future and, eventually, anyone who was considered to have been a mediator of revelation in Scripture was labeled a prophet, but those were later developments. Daniel is presented as a visionary (differentiated from a prophet in the above chart). So, for example, the historical résumé of Daniel 10 is not introduced by a formula indicating the word of the Lord—there is no "thus says the Lord . . ." Instead, he has a vision—not a vision of the events, but of a man in linen (Daniel 10:5) who is speaking words (Daniel 10:6, 9). An envoy then speaks to Daniel (Daniel 10:10) to tell him (not show him) what is written in a particular document (Daniel 10:21). The document is sometimes identified as the "Book of Truth" (for example, NIV, ESV, NLT, NRSV), or a "dependable book" (NET).[8] This is a book of fate, known in the literature of the Hellenistic period (for example, Jubilees) and comparable to the tablet of Destinies known in Assyrian and Babylonian literature. It contains the divine decrees that set the course of history. The visionary named Daniel is not prophesying these events. It is rather the man in linen who is apparently decreeing these events, and the envoy is conveying them to Daniel. They are framed in the future because that is how destiny is decreed. But it should not be considered either as prophesying the future or as reciting the past. In apocalyptic literature, the course of history has been decreed and Daniel is being told of those parts of the book of Fate that have covered from the fifth century to the second century BC, regardless of where in time he is standing. His vision is not telling the future in an act of predictive prophecy (recall the problem with that terminology) but revealing the destiny of the empires as it had been decreed by the heavenly figure.

Example B—Daniel 7: Daniel 7 gives another opportunity to discern the difference between apocalyptic and prophecy. Consistent with apocalyptic visions, the chapter never indicates that a word of the Lord came to Daniel and never offers a spoken message portrayed as "thus says the Lord." He is never told to convey his message to any audience. No mention is made of the covenant as a basis for indictment, judgment, instruction, or future restoration. Instead, the little horn is indicted and judged. Moreover, there is no talk of restoration, even though the kingdom is given over to the holy ones. All of these differentiate the chapter from covenant-focused classical prophecy, as does the nature of the vision. The beasts coming out of the sea and the seating of the heavenly court are not foretelling future events; they are casting a vision that projects the general shape of God's unfolding plan. The message does not tell us the future but tells us that God holds the future.[9] The beastly empires will not prevail; they will be judged, and the kingdom of God will come.

---

[8]The latter is supported in Buster and Walton, *Daniel*, with the translation the "Reliable Book."

[9]Notice that it does not offer identification of the four empires that are represented by the beasts. Some might claim that the identifications are transparent, but that is a spurious claim given the variety of identifications present in the history of interpretation.

> Furthermore, when we read the Daniel 7 text in context, we should not just jump to the conclusion that the use of the description "one like a son of man" is intended by the author as a prophecy of Jesus (The Son of Man). When Daniel 7:13-14 talks about "one like a son of man," it indicates that the figure in the vision is human in nature in contrast to the beasts at the beginning of the chapter. Centuries later, this description will come to be connected to a messianic expectation, and it is therefore appropriate that Jesus picks it up. But that is a re-appropriation that is not reflecting what the intentions of the author were in the context of Daniel 7.[10] Based on the New Testament, Daniel 7 can be viewed as having been fulfilled in Jesus, but fulfillment does not generally find identification by tracking with the Old Testament author (this will be the focus of chap. 34).

The significance of the title of this chapter is that it steers us away from simply equating prophetic and apocalyptic literatures. Both continuity and discontinuity can be identified in comparison. Moreover, previous chapters have contended that prophecy itself should not be reduced to a future-looking enterprise but is focused on the plans and purposes of God for his covenant people. Apocalyptic enlarges the perspective from the covenant people to the kingdoms of the world. Neither constructing an eschatology of the end times, nor formulating apologetic defenses of God's foreknowledge regarding fulfillment of prophecy in Jesus, nor the reliability of Scripture represent the appropriate response to apocalyptic. Readers who have been following the logic of this book could write the next line themselves. The appropriate response to apocalyptic is found in grasping the truth that God is working out his plans and purposes in the world of empires (contrast prophecy, "in the world of the covenant"). We trust his wisdom and find hope in the coming kingdom. When we try to make more of it (eschatology and apologetics) we run the risk of diminishing or reducing the authority of God's Word to the level of our own speculations or logical proofs.

---

[10]Re-appropriation is not the same as interpretation. It refers to bringing the biblical passage into a new context rather than trying to understand the text in context.

33—In Apocalyptic Literature, the Visions Are Not the Message but the Occasion for the Message

We have already discussed the nature of the message in prophetic literature (chap. 30), which generally falls into the categories of indictment, judgment, instruction, aftermath, or a combination of these. Those messages were conveyed to the prophet as the "word of the Lord" and the prophet then conveyed that word to his immediate audience. The process is relatively straightforward. But since apocalyptic literature, in contrast, does not frame its message as "the word of the Lord," it is reasonable to inquire how the visions convey a message.

When reading the book of Revelation, it is easy to adopt the idea that the message is that the events of the vision will take place at some time in the future: bowls will be emptied, trumpets will sound, battles will be fought, Satan and his angels will be expelled from heaven, the rider of the white horse will come, and so on. We are focusing on the Old Testament in this book, so we will look at Old Testament apocalyptic rather than that of the New Testament, but the example of Revelation helps to make the point of this chapter. Instead of considering the vision itself to be the message, we need to understand that the vision merely serves as an occasion for the message that the text conveys.[11]

The vision happens in the experience of the seer, not in the unfolding of history. In Daniel 7, the audience is not being directed to camp out on the beach and watch for beasts to emerge from the sea (and no one would think that). The beasts are symbols of empires and there is no vantage point in either time or space where that which is represented by the symbols can be viewed. Furthermore, not every symbol in a vision calls for interpretation and identification. For example, when Daniel 7:5 describes three ribs in the bear's mouth, the number three may not necessarily refer to three

[11]In Revelation, that message pertains to the primacy of Christ.

conquered countries (as often assumed). They might only represent a high quantity of devouring referred to in the second part of the verse. Moreover, even if it does represent three conquests, we have no way of knowing which three it might mean. The history of interpretation has demonstrated that there are numerous possibilities. When the text does not provide an interpretation of a symbol, we must be content to resist our own speculative interpretation and even consider the possibility that it has no symbolic significance. In either case, it does not carry the message of the text. The narrator will make clear what the message is.

Example A—Zechariah's Visions: Some individuals serve both as prophets and as visionaries. The book of Zechariah is not considered apocalyptic, though the prophet does have a series of visions that are comparable in many ways to those found in apocalyptic literature.[12] His prophetic oracles are introduced as "The word of the LORD came to me" (Zechariah 6:9; see also Zechariah 7:1; 8:1) and other such introductions. Furthermore, the series of visions is introduced as the word of the Lord that came to him (Zechariah 1:7-8) and prophetic pronouncements punctuate the visions (Zechariah 4:1-14). Nevertheless, the message of the visions comes through an interpreting angel (for example, Zechariah 1:9) as in Daniel.

In Zechariah's first vision (Zechariah 1:7-17), he sees a man on a red horse standing among myrtle trees in a ravine, accompanied by other different colored horses, reporting to the Angel of the Lord. Zechariah and an interpreting angel are looking on. The horseman gives a brief report and the Angel of the Lord replies with dismay. The description of the vision (vv. 7-12) is followed by the message that the prophet receives and is then to proclaim (vv. 13-17).

Notice first that though there are many potentially symbolic elements in the vision, they do not receive interpretation, neither are they necessarily symbolic. Neither Zechariah nor his audience is given any meaning behind the myrtle trees or the ravine. Even the colored horses are not given symbolic meaning.[13] Since the narrator does not identify these as symbolic, and does not explain any such symbolism, we do not need to know. We could only

[12]It is sometimes referred to as "proto-apocalyptic."

[13]Note that this is dissimilar to the book of Revelation, where the four horsemen of the Apocalypse are on four different colored horses. In Zechariah, there are not just four, the colors are different from Revelation, and they are not given symbolic meaning as in Revelation (plague, etc.). John *uses*

speculate, but we do not need to do so, because the message is not related to those symbols. When we track with the author, we are following his lead. We are not supposed to find a myrtle grove in a ravine and look for colored horses.

In this case, the message is given to us clearly and has nothing to do with any of those potentially symbolic elements. God is still concerned for Jerusalem, is angry with the nations who plundered her, and will return with favor on his people, who remain his covenant people (Zech 1:14-17). This is an important message, for this group that has recently returned from exile and has found that the return is not all that they expected it to be. As our chapter title indicates, the vision is important as the occasion for Zechariah being given the message; it is not the message itself. Furthermore, the message is not opaque or obscure—it is perfectly clear and simple. I would contend that this is consistently true of apocalyptic visions. We ought to be looking for the clear message stated in the passage rather than seeking it in speculative interpretation of the assumed symbols of the vision.

Example B—Daniel 8: Daniel 8 contains the vision of the ram and the goat with their respective horns. In this case, the specific identification of the animals is given by the narrator (Daniel 8:20-21), but the horns are identified only in part—they represent kingdoms, but no specific identification is provided. Understanding the message is not determined by the identification of the major players. The vision pertains to the unfolding of history, but the message is not intended to reveal all the particular details of that unfolding. It is true that once the goat is identified as Greece, there would be little mystery for a post-Alexander audience to identify four successor kingdoms (though they may well disagree as to which four they may be, and it doesn't matter). The king who will arise and eventually be destroyed (Daniel 8:23-25) is not named. Again, a second-century audience would have felt reasonably certain that it was Antiochus IV Epiphanes, but other generations may have had different opinions. Every generation who is being terrorized by a tyrant would want to place themselves as that generation.

Nevertheless, we must recall that we are dealing with the message of the vision, not its fulfillment (that distinction is the subject of the next chapter).

some of the symbolism of Zechariah but gives it his own particular twist. He does not identify the horses or horsemen in Zechariah.

> The message retains its significance regardless of which tyrant fulfills it (or which tyrants, since fulfillment can happen multiple times). The message is not found in providing identifications or in the audience's ability to posit those identifications with confidence; in fact, even the fulfillment is not dependent on such identification but on the way the message is fulfilled. The message transcends the identification details. The message is that the tyrant and his empire will be overthrown. In this case (unlike Daniel 2 and 7), the message does not pertain to the coming of the kingdom of God, but only to the destruction of the tyrant. Before getting to that point, the vision also indicates that a couple more kingdoms will rise and fall in the march of empires through history. In that way, it connects to Daniel 2 and 7, and in the process, it identifies two more kingdoms (represented by the ram and goat), but still leaves much unsaid.

When we recognize that the message is not the vision, but that the vision is the occasion for the message, we find relief from the pressure to interpret the meanings of symbols. Even if they have symbolic value (and they may not), we do not need to penetrate the symbolism to receive the message of the text. To say it another way, tracking with the author does not require us to decode the symbols. The opacity or obscurity of the symbols in the vision need not deter us from having confidence that we can understand the authoritative message of the text.

34—Fulfillment Is Distinct from Message

In the church, there has typically been more interest in fulfillment than in the prophecies that are being fulfilled. That is understandable to a degree because it is a natural human tendency to focus on that which seems most pertinent. Though understandable, it is unfortunate because it has resulted in the confusion that sees the fulfillment as the place where the authority of the text resides. That is the misunderstanding this chapter corrects.

The message of the prophet was always known to the prophet, and it was believed to be something that the audience would also understand, even if they chose to ignore its warnings or distrust the hope that it gave.

Furthermore, the message carried authority even in times when the fulfillment had not yet taken place. But first, some definitions.

The "message" is the word given to the prophet and proclaimed to his audience. As mentioned earlier, this falls neatly into the categories of indictment (what they were doing wrong), judgment (what God would do in response to their offenses), instruction (what he expected them to do in response), and aftermath (the messages of hope, deliverance, and restoration). None of this was impenetrable to the audience—they understood exactly what the prophets were talking about. The "fulfillment," in contrast, is how the prophetic message might unfold in history and most logically is generally pertinent to judgment and aftermath oracles.[14] Fulfillment is usually found in events or, in the case of Messiah, in a person (though, even then, often in the events that transpire around him). Accordingly, the message is the authoritative word from God and the fulfillment is the unfolding of God's plan to which the message can be connected. That connection was not known ahead of time by the prophet, though the prophets would not be surprised that such connections would unfold. The fulfillment was not part of the revelation that the prophet received, and, in fact, the connection could be quite obtuse.

Fulfillment can take many different directions and does not always happen in the way or in the time that readers might have considered essential and obvious. It could often only be identified in hindsight. This is transparent when we read the New Testament. Jesus was fulfilling prophecy in entirely unanticipated ways, and he was not at all the sort of Messiah that anyone expected.

It is very important, then, to recognize that the fulfillment is not something in the author's intention, so no amount of tracking with the author will uncover the fulfillment. Instead, when we are tracking with the author, we are trying to understand the message—that is what has authority, so that is our goal. Identification of fulfillment is part of the New Testament author's intention, so when we track with the New Testament authors, that is what we are seeking.

---

[14]I have qualified this as "generally" because sometimes the New Testament identifies fulfillment of other sorts of oracles, for example, Hosea 11:1, which will be discussed below.

When we seek to interpret the message of the prophetic oracles as text in context, we are trying to track with what those prophets knew and communicated. In contrast, the New Testament authors are not trying to track with the Old Testament authors to uncover their true message as they identify a fulfillment. Moreover, the message does not change because of the direction that fulfillment takes. The message cannot change—it is God's message. The New Testament authors are doing something entirely different when they identify fulfillment. They are indicating how God's plan has unfolded in their time, often through Jesus, in connection to the Old Testament prophecies. In message and fulfillment, we have two sides of the prophetic coin, and neither negates the other. They do not stand in contradiction to one another but work together as complementary aspects.

The message of the New Testament author offers an authoritative identification of fulfillment. The message of the Old Testament author offers an authoritative word from God. To neglect either one of them is to neglect a word from God. Furthermore, we do not have to bring them into conformity with one another, because they are doing different things. The Old Testament author's word finds validation in its source (from God)—it is not validated by trying to figure out how he could be saying the same thing that fulfillment expounds. Sometimes the fulfillment might be precisely what the Old Testament author said (Micah 5:2); sometimes it will follow the same path in unexpected ways (Isaiah 53); sometimes it will follow a pattern from the Old Testament (Jesus as new Adam, new Israel, new covenant, or new temple). Sometimes it is difficult to figure out how to connect the dots.

The church's preference for elevating fulfillment over message is due to the fact that the message is generally to Israel and therefore may seem irrelevant to us. In contrast, the fulfillment is often seen to relate to Jesus or the end times—now those are things we can get excited about! This is unfortunate because only a very small percentage of Old Testament prophecies actually have the option for fulfillments, because prophecy is focused on God's plans and purposes, not simply on the future. Consequently, not only are the messages that are fulfilled neglected, those that have no connecting lines to fulfillments are relegated to obscurity, in which case authoritative messages from God are being silenced.

Example A—Hosea 11: In Hosea 11 the prophet is reflecting the voice of Yahweh, who speaks in the first person in a soliloquy that laments Israel's covenant violations despite the obvious love that Yahweh had shown them. The chapter intersperses indictment and judgment oracles. In the introduction to this sweeping critique Yahweh says, "When Israel was a child, I loved him, / and out of Egypt I called my son." The message concerning God's love for Israel and his action on their behalf is clear; so is the picture of Israel's unfaithfulness.

How surprising it is, then, when Matthew asserts that this prophecy was fulfilled when Jesus was brought out of Egypt by his parents (Matthew 2:15). Even the casual reader of Hosea would not think that his prophetic oracle called for fulfillment. It was a statement about the past, with nothing even vaguely messianic about it. If the Jews of the first century AD had made a list of messianic expectations, the idea that the Messiah had to come out of Egypt would not have been on it. Furthermore, the context of Israel's faithlessness and rebellion lends cognitive dissonance to the connection, since no indictment is connected to Jesus coming out of Egypt.

Some have maintained that the line of connection is justifiable once we recognize that the Gospel writers are portraying Jesus as a new Israel—one who gets it right. He is therefore walking in Israel's footprints. To the extent that such a case can be made, it is able to relieve the tension that we may feel about these contrasting passages. Nevertheless, it does not thereby clarify the relationship between prophecy and fulfillment.

This chapter title, however, contends that fulfillment is a phenomenon distinct from prophecy, though dependent on it. Hosea 11:1 is not a problem if we recognize that Matthew is appropriating Hosea, not interpreting Hosea. Matthew is perfectly free to use the words of Hosea as a launching point to draw his own connection in his own way. We accept his creative connection because we recognize his authority—not his authority to rewrite what Hosea meant, but his authority to identify fulfillment, whatever oblique route it might take.

The connection that Matthew makes does not demand that we read Hosea's oracle differently than Hosea and his audience would have read it. Hosea's message is not messianic, even though Matthew finds it fulfilled in Jesus. These are two sides of the coin, and both can stand in their own integrity and authority. We do not have to unify them in order to protect the reputation of Scripture. The message and fulfillment are different. The fulfillment ought not be superimposed on the message and the message should not stand as critique of the fulfillment.

Example B—Isaiah 7:14: Isaiah 7:14 became a well-loved passage once it was identified as fulfilled in the virgin birth of Jesus (Matthew 1:22-23). In both Isaiah and Matthew, the child is designated as Immanuel, although that does not seem to have been the actual name of either one. For all the significance of the virgin birth and our affirmation of it, however, we face a dilemma. As referred to earlier (chap. 15), an actual child was born in fulfillment of the prophecy in the eighth-century time of Isaiah. To have that child born of a virgin will not do. The theological integrity of the virgin birth will not be threatened by careful consideration of what each of these passages claims and by the application of sound methodology to explain the nature of their connection.

We begin with the unarguable blunt fact: Isaiah gives no hint that he was talking about the virgin birth of a messiah to be born eight centuries in the future. Therefore, if we are accountable to the author's intentions, we cannot assume the connection to either Messiah in general or Jesus in particular. If Isaiah is referring to a contemporary mother giving birth in the prophet's own time, we should be wary of identifying her as a virgin. To our relief, the Hebrew word so translated does not mean that. Hebrew does not use labels for women that identify their sexual status (that is, the way English uses "virgin"). Two Hebrew words are at times translated as "virgin" (*'almah* here and *betulah*, often). Both these terms, however, refer to social and family status, not sexual status. An *'almah* is a woman who has not yet had a child. She ceases being an *'almah* when she becomes a mother. It is usually the case in the ancient world that women in this category were also virgins, except in the generally brief time between marriage and conception. The *betulah* is a woman who is still under the guardianship of her father. When she is transferred to the guardianship of her husband, she ceases being a *betulah* and becomes a wife. Likewise, those in the category of *betulah* would generally be virgins, but, again, that is not what the word means.[15]

[15]For a detailed study of these two words and their usage, see John H. Walton, "*Betulah*," in *New International Dictionary of Old Testament Theology and Exegesis*, ed. W. VanGemeren (Grand Rapids,

When Isaiah announces that the *ʾalmah* is pregnant (yes, it is an adjective here), he is not indicating that a woman has become pregnant without knowing a man, but that a woman who has not yet borne a child has become pregnant—an occasion of great rejoicing.[16] The son she will bear is not identified as having a special role—the sign is his name, not his birth or his identity. The prophecy takes place in a time of dire jeopardy at the hands of potential invaders. The name, "God is with us," when given, will serve as an indication that God has delivered them from invasion. The very point of the prophecy is that all of this will happen very soon—she is already pregnant!

With this analysis before us, we are now ready to turn to Matthew 1:22-23. Matthew's identification of fulfillment in the virgin birth of Jesus, the Messiah, does not require that Isaiah was talking about the Messiah or about a virgin birth; neither does it require that he was talking about Mary or Jesus. Fulfillment can take a very different direction than that indicated by the prophet's message. Isaiah's message was true in the eighth century and was fulfilled in the eighth century BC. But Matthew recognized it as having been fulfilled again, and in a very different way, in the first century AD.[17] We do not have to force conformity between Isaiah's message and Matthew's fulfillment to validate either one of them. They are free to operate autonomously, yet they are not fully independent—the spoken words draw them together even though the meaning and context given to those words differ.

Some readers may find this loose connection uncomfortable, but it is a more viable option than pulling the two passages so tightly together that the author's intention in one or the other is compromised. The authority of both can be maintained even in their diverse referentiality when we recognize the distinction between message and fulfillment.

We can now see how important it is to maintain the distinction between message and fulfillment. When we fail to do so, we sacrifice the authoritative message given to the prophets—the text in context—having reduced

---

MI: Zondervan, 1997), 1:781-84. As an aside, note also that this is the only passage where NIV translates *ʾalmah* as "virgin."

[16]This would especially be true if the woman is of the royal household, as some propose.

[17]The New Testament authors are not unique in this approach to connecting the dots. It was done by the community at Qumran and in general by Jewish readers around this time. See Richard N. Longenecker, *Biblical Exegesis in the Apostolic Period* (Grand Rapids, MI: Eerdmans, 1975).

it to the fulfillment. Interpretation of the prophetic literature calls us to focus our attention on the message if we are trying to remain accountable to the author's literary intentions. The prophets had no knowledge of the details of fulfillment, so we are not respecting their intentions when we concern ourselves only with fulfillment. Fulfillment becomes the proper object of our study in the context in which it is identified—whether that takes place later in the Old Testament or in the New Testament. As a concluding note, we need also mention that when fulfillment is not identified in the pages of Scripture, our attempts to identify it can only be speculative and of questionable value.

PART THREE

A WAY FORWARD

SECTION A

CHARACTERISTICS OF FAITHFUL READING

35—Reading Scripture Well

So far, this book has discussed a lot of "red flags" (remember the illustration of *Tootle* in the preface). Now we need to make sure we see the "green flag." We have seen that we need to "always stay on the rails no matter what," but now we need to attend to where the rails are taking us as we "track with the author."

This book has discussed ways that we engage in the act of interpretation. But reading the Bible well also requires talking about the transition from interpretation to application. We have learned that in interpretation we must move beyond our own voice (that is, our cultural lenses) to seek the Israelite voice. Now turning our attention to application, we similarly need to move beyond our own voice to seek out other contemporary voices. How do we integrate many voices into our perspectives?

It is therefore important to draw some distinctions between interpretation and application. In interpretation, we are to be guided by the voice of the author, but at the level of application, we benefit most from many voices. In the end, we want both to understand the message of Scripture (through interpretation) and to find its relevance for our lives, our culture, and our world based on who we are and the issues we face (through application). Different people will find that in different ways. But if we recognize that a variety of readers will have a variety of perspectives, how do we maintain the authority of the text?

We begin by recognizing that the movement from interpretation to application involves multiple steps. Arguably, the first step in that process is the most important so that we can ensure that we are being directed by Scripture. It is practically a truism that we cannot remove ourselves from our interpretation—our minds are deeply and subtly influenced by all the aspects of our identity and culture. But at the first stage of interpretation, we can make the attempt and we must, because the message of God is at stake. If we consciously make the effort to attune to the author, we will have some success, and every little bit helps.

Consequently, in that first step of interpretation, we don't want to read like a White person, like a Black person, like an Asian person, or like a Latinx person; we want to read like an ancient Israelite. We don't want to read like a man or a woman; we don't want to read like a wealthy person or a poor person; we don't want to read like a colonizer or like a refugee; we don't want to read like the Rabbis, Augustine, Calvin, or our pastor—we want to read like the audience to whom the author was communicating. If the only voice that we can possibly hear is that of the reader, we are left without an authoritative message from God.

Different voices can contribute to this first stage of interpretation because of the different observations they can make in a text and the different perspectives they represent. For example, an Asian reader might understand aspects of community identity that an American reader would never detect. An African reader may have greater insight into polytheistic cultures. A reader who is a refugee will have greater insight into the plight of Israelites in several periods of their history. Nevertheless, when we take that first step in interpretation, we want to maximize the insights any reader may have into the Israelite world but minimize the voice of the reader as we make the voice of the author a priority. We value the voices of many interpreters at that stage not so we can read the text through their identity and culture, but because they can bring additional important perspectives to discerning the author's intentions.

When we get to later stages of application, all those other perspectives will be worthy of attention, but in the first step, our goal is to understand as deeply as is possible the historical context, situation, and perspective of an ancient Israelite. Attempting to prioritize an identity that is not our own, but that of the ancient Israelites, is a stance of humility that prepares us well for the humility required to listen to other contemporary communities of Scripture readers.[1] In the last stages, we will read like the person we are, but should also appreciate the readings of those who are not like us. At that stage we need to hear the many insights that different readers will draw from the text. Such variety unlocks the dynamics and dimensions of a text that transforms and can ever provide rich insight through the cross-fertilization of readers in community.

How shall we focus the application process? Figures 35.1 and 35.2 will help us to explore this issue.

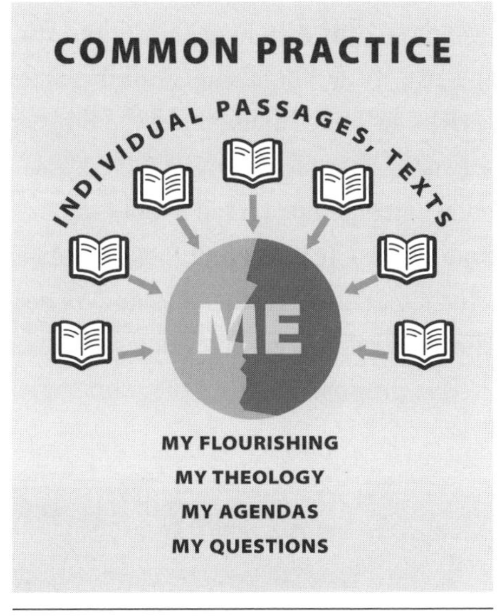

Figure 35.1. Common practice

In this diagram of the practice here labeled "common practice," a problem arises when we are struck with the difficulties of interpretation (Hebrew words, impenetrable culture). If each individual passage is supposed to carry innate meaning that affects our lives, we can easily despair of ever being able to read the Old Testament successfully. What if we miss the red flag? If the readers of this book have been persuaded of the danger represented in all the red flags, it may seem that the Old Testament has become totally inaccessible, and they have become skeptical of ever being able to use it again. While caution is commendable when so much is at stake, that is not the desired response. The fact

[1] I am grateful to my colleague Aubrey Buster for this insight.

is, even if we got all the passages figured out in terms of language and culture, this diagram of common practice represents an arguably flawed perspective—a potentially misguided understanding of what God's Word is and how it is supposed to work. Each individual passage does not feed directly into the "me" circle (my flourishing, my theology, my agendas, my questions). If we think that we must learn all sorts of language and culture to get the right instruction for "me," we are missing the point.

Sometimes we are not just led astray by seeking guidance or theological truth in misguided ways. Sometimes we have a cause or an agenda that we want to promote, or even a specific theological position for which we want to advocate that might lead us away from what the text is actually doing. We must be extra careful not to commandeer the Bible when we are in these situations. The third commandment tells us that we should not take the name of the Lord in vain. That is what we are doing if we are using God's name to advance our own agendas to our own benefit. Modern use of the Bible too often reflects a perspective of one-upmanship—mining details in the Bible to prove that your view is right. As I have maintained, the Bible is not a "how-to" book, not a "rules of the road" manual, and not a GPS device to get you to God's will, God's favor, and success in life. It is all about God, not about me. Many of the factors that undermine Christian unity and reputation come from making the Bible do what it was never intended to do. We need to respect the Bible by refusing to commandeer it to validate our own opinions or to assure our own success in life.

This proposed revised diagram suggests the alternative.

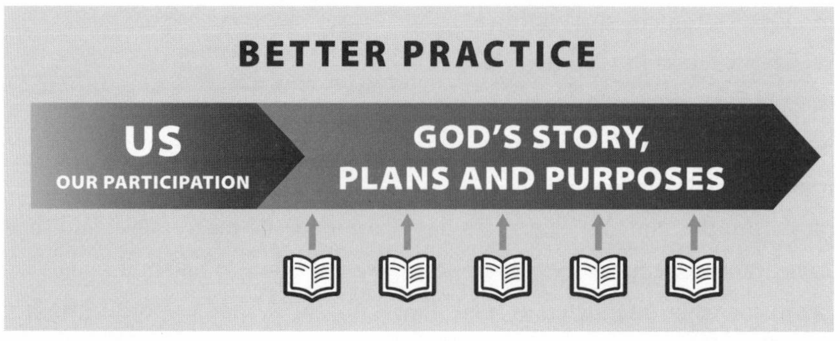

Figure 35.2. Better practice

In this diagram, all the individual passages are seen to contribute to our understanding of God's story and ultimately, his plans and purposes in the world and in us. The individual parts feed directly into that, not into the "me" circle as on the previous diagram. The better we understand all the individual parts, the clearer our understanding will be of God's story and his plans and purposes. Nevertheless, if some remain obscure, or even if we get them wrong, they will not derail us too badly, as long as we see the larger picture taking shape.

For example, if we think that the Tower of Babel is about the city builders, in their pride, trying to get to heaven, we will have missed an important insight into the theme of God's presence. When we become aware of the alternative interpretation based on cultural insights (chap. 20), it will improve our understanding of the contribution of the passage to God's plans and purposes but will not alter that understanding. Consequently, the cultural and linguistic challenges that we encounter in interpreting individual passages, and awareness of how easily we can misunderstand, should not make us fearful of reading the Bible and using it.

Since the plans and purposes of God are affirmed in many ways throughout Scripture—through its variety of genres and across the testaments—if we go astray on one or two passages, our overall understanding will not easily be undermined. Nevertheless, even in this broader perspective, misguided reading could cause a serious problem. For example, if we read a passage like Jeremiah 29:11 as an indication that God's plans and purposes are directed toward our individual flourishing, we need the corrective of other parts of Scripture to disabuse us of that misperception.

When the Reformers spoke of the "perspicuity" (clarity) of the Bible, they were insisting that the gospel was clear to any reader regardless of their level of education or training. Moreover, far more passages are easy and straightforward than are complicated and obscure. I am expanding that idea beyond the gospel, to God's story as it unfolds his plans and purposes. Moreover, the basic concepts of God's desire for relationship with his people and his intention to dwell with us are unmistakable. If we live in light of those, rather than wandering off the rails in all of the various pursuits that we have warned against throughout the book, we will find the Bible a source of comfort and insight.

All this now also makes it possible to circle back to the question concerning the role of Jesus in our reading of the Old Testament. If all the passages are supposed to inform our understanding of the plans and purposes of God and to tell us his story, it is no surprise that our thoughts often turn to Jesus as we read. Nevertheless, we can also now understand that if we want to grasp the fullness of God's plans and purposes and the depth of God's story, we cannot just be content with seeing Jesus. We need the Old Testament because the more completely we can understand God's story and see how he has worked out his plans and purposes, the better we will be able to see how we can participate in them (as well as seeing more clearly how they come to fruition in Jesus). It is what we were created to do. Furthermore, we should note an additional revision in the diagram. Perhaps we need to expand our view to see that our participation is not just about "me" but about "us"—the corporate people of God, his church. Just as each of the passages of the Old Testament contribute to the greater understanding of God's plans and purposes, so each one of us contributes to how God's people as a whole should be participating in the plans and purposes of God. We each need to play our part to fulfill the role of the whole.

36—Five Tendencies to Avoid

In a practical vein, based on these contrasting diagrams, there are five common tendencies in Old Testament Bible study that we should avoid.

SEARCHING FOR PROOF TEXTS TO EXPLOIT

Often when we are dealing with questions of theology or practice, we reasonably want to know what the Bible has to say. In many cases, the Bible has nothing to say in answer to our questions, but that, unfortunately, has not stopped interpreters from attempts to bring the purported biblical testimony to bear on the issue. I remember once reading a theology book that was proposing a particular theological affirmation. It listed a couple of dozen references in support. I took the time to look through each one and found, to my surprise, that none of them, when read in context and with all the variables of interpretation for each, actually substantiated the affirmation. A reader who did not look them up could have easily accepted the theologian's affirmation, thinking that there were dozens of passages that supported it. Such was not the case.

Example A—Women in Ministry: The record has shown that those who promote either complementarian or egalitarian positions regarding women in ministry can produce texts that appear to support their view. Each side is accused by the other of being selective in the texts that they choose. This is only one of many examples that could be mentioned regarding how proof texts are used in modern discourse. When approaching such important yet divisive issues, the point I am making is that we are too prone to go looking for the texts that we feel will support our particular view and, at the same time, can easily neglect verses that support a different view. The problem with this selective approach is that when we use it, we are often seeking verses that we can engage, or sometimes exploit, for our own issues rather than tracking with the author. To track with the author, we would have to give attention to the precise meaning of words that he used and consider the contexts (cultural and literary) in which the statements were made.[2] Such conscientiousness may lead us to a more reserved and nuanced use of what Scripture has to say about gender roles and we may find that it does not resolve the issues that we are discussing.

Example 2—2 Samuel 12:23: When pastors or other counselors are faced with the unhappy circumstance of a young child who has died, and the parents are seeking comfort about whether they will see their child in heaven, it is not uncommon for interpreters to open to 2 Samuel 12:23. David's child by Bathsheba has just died. While the ill child still lived, David was mourning, but when the child died, David stopped. His attendants wondered why. His reply was, "I will go to him, but he will not return to me." This verse is then used as a proof text that children go to heaven when they die.

Unfortunately, though we would sincerely desire to provide the parents with comfort, this is flawed interpretation of the passage. It assumes that

[2]Such issues require book-length treatments to do them justice and can therefore not be treated in any detail in a book such as this.

David has confidence that he will go to heaven when he dies, so if he will then see his child, the child has also gone to heaven. The flaw here is that in the Old Testament, the Israelites had no such confidence that they would go to heaven. David expects to go to Sheol, the non-descript netherworld where all go. That is the location where he expects to join his dead child—in death, not in heaven. When this proof text is given to bereaved parents, the interpreter has failed to take full account of the cultural and theological background of the author, and the result is that he or she is misusing that text.[3]

SEARCHING FOR INSPIRATIONAL NUGGETS

When people open their Bibles, they often do so hoping to find guidance for their lives or to be inspired to grow more mature in their faith. This is not misguided, and the Holy Spirit can work in our lives through our Bible reading. Nevertheless, in our zeal to grow, we must be careful that what we are drawing from the Bible is something that the Bible is actually saying.

Example A—"After God's Own Heart": One of the most widely recognized phrases that people have drawn from the Old Testament for inspiration is the aspiration to be a person "after God's own heart" (see 1 Samuel 13:14). We know that the person being referred to is David and, with the psalmist in mind, we desire to also be someone who pursues the heart of God. At the same time, we often have that nagging question in the back of our minds—how could someone who committed adultery, murder, and many other crimes, as David did, be so described? Here the problem is that we have misunderstood the verse in our desire to spiritualize it. From the use of the same phrase in 1 Samuel 14:7; Psalm 20:4; and Jeremiah 3:15, we can see that it does not refer to David pursuing the heart of God, but to God using his own criterion in the selection of David (the verse refers to God's choice following his own heart rather than David following God's heart).[4] In 1 Samuel 13:14, the contrast is between Saul, who was chosen according to the criteria of the people, and David, who was chosen according to God's criteria (without delineating what

---

[3]A good resource for an understanding of developing perception of the afterlife can be found in P. Johnston, *Shades of Sheol* (Downers Grove, IL: IVP Academic, 2002).

[4]It is a phrase regularly used in Akkadian royal inscriptions as the kings of old declare that the god has deemed to choose him to be king using his own criteria.

those criteria were). The point does not concern David's qualities but how God intends to bring about his plans and purposes through David.

Example B—Nineveh's Repentance: We often find inspiration in what we perceive to be the conversion of the Ninevites under the preaching of Jonah. But let's not be hasty. Jonah's message was one of impending judgment (Jonah 3:4). He did not offer instruction concerning Yahweh, the covenant, or the Torah. He did not rebuke them for their images or many gods. He did not instruct them in doing good and turning away from evil. Furthermore, while they did turn from their violent ways, the text gives no indication that they converted to the Israelite God. Repentance is not the same as conversion. The fact is, the Ninevites did far less than readers often imagine. We may find it inspirational to think that these Assyrians came to a true knowledge of God, but the text suggests nothing of the kind. Not only did they take a very small step, it is important to the interpretation of the book to recognize that fact. The greater the transformation of the Ninevites, the smaller the compassion of God, and vice versa. When we overstate the response of Nineveh, we minimize God's grace. When we recognize how small a step the Ninevites took, we discover how immense was God's compassion (and also come to a greater understanding of Jonah's anger).[5]

SEARCHING FOR PROMISES FOR GOD TO KEEP

Christian readers of the Bible know that God does make promises. We know that he will keep them, and we treasure them for the hope that they give. Nevertheless, it is easy to take an extreme approach to this and seek promises in all sorts of passages.

Example A—Passages That Aren't Promises: Sometimes these passages are not even promises: "The Lord is my shepherd; I shall not want" (Psalm 23:1 ESV). Though this should be great encouragement to a believer, it is not a promise that a believer will never go hungry. It is certainly not a promise that God will give you whatever you want. In fact, it is not a promise at all, but a metaphor,

[5]For further reading, see John H. Walton, "Jonah," in *The Expositor's Bible Commentary*, rev. ed., ed. Tremper Longman III and David Garland (Grand Rapids, MI: Zondervan, 2008), 451-90; John H. Walton, "The Object Lesson of Jonah 4:5-7 and the Purpose of the Book of Jonah," *Bulletin for Biblical Research* 2 (1992): 47-57.

along with its implications. The shepherd is responsible for the provision and protection for his sheep, and they in turn trust the shepherd and follow him.

Example B—Promises to Israel: Sometimes they are promises to Israel but not to us: "'For I know the plans I have for you,' declares the LORD, 'plans to prosper you and not to harm you, plans to give you hope and a future'" (Jeremiah 29:11). This is a promise to Israel related to their particular and unique covenant relationship to Yahweh. God is the hope of all his people, but this is not a promise made to all his people. Instead, it should be viewed as offering insight into the nature of God's plans and purposes. Furthermore, it is a promise given in the context of the Babylonian exile and therefore related to a specific historical moment where God is asking Israel to go into exile.

Example C—Promises for a Defined Situation: Sometimes the promises pertain to a defined situation: "If my people, who are called by my name, will humble themselves and pray and seek my face and turn from their wicked ways, then I will hear from heaven, and I will forgive their sin and will heal their land" (2 Chronicles 7:14). This verse is similar to Jeremiah 29:11 in that it is addressed to Israel in the context of the covenant and the covenant land, but it has the added feature that it is talking about coming to God at the temple. That is a particular cultural situation, not paralleled by anyone today who happens to pray. We cannot interpret it as God's message to our country or use it to support a nationalistic fervor.

Example D—Promises for a Particular Task: Some promises pertain to a person who has been commissioned by God for a particular task: "Be strong and courageous . . . for the LORD your God will be with you" (Joshua 1:9). This does not promise that anyone who is strong and courageous in what they undertake will have God's presence with them. God's exhortation to Joshua to be strong and courageous relates to his ability to complete the particular task for which he has been commissioned.

SEARCHING FOR COMMANDS TO OBEY

Yes, there are commands in the Bible that we ought to obey. We need to be careful, however, for the Bible ought not be construed as simply a repository of commands.

> **Example—The Ten "Words":** As discussed in chapter four, even something as basic as the "Ten Commandments" provides an intriguing case—the Bible never calls them "commandments." They are the ten "words," and they are to be *heeded*. Sometimes heeding may require more than simple obedience. We might wonder whether the rich young ruler (Matthew 19:16-21) was guilty of simply obeying the law rather than heeding it in all its implications. Recall that Jesus' Sermon on the Mount makes it clear that obeying the command not to murder does not mean that one is now heeding all that the law calls for (Matthew 5:21-22). If we just go searching for promises or commands, we may ultimately be engaging in reductionism as we focus only on what we are looking for rather than on what the Bible's own message is in each passage. To avoid this, we should focus on the wisdom and values that underlie the message and seek to incorporate them into our lives.

SEARCHING FOR JESUS OR THE GOSPEL

Luke 24:27 indicates that, "Beginning with Moses and all the Prophets, he explained to them what was said in all the Scriptures concerning himself." In extreme cases, some have taken that to mean that every passage and verse concerns Jesus, so they go searching for Jesus passage by passage. We must, however, be cautious about the interpretation of this verse. It does not say that every Scripture concerns him, but he showed them what was there that did so. We do not know which verses he used or how he used them. If we try to find Jesus in every Old Testament passage, it is difficult to be accountable to the author's literary intentions. If the author was not intentionally talking about Jesus, then to read it that way, especially if the New Testament does not read that particular passage that way, is to depart from our accountability. If we can freely use our imagination when finding Jesus, what prevents us from doing the same thing for other ends? The commitment to consistency is jeopardized. When we avoid this tendency, we do not diminish Jesus, but if we indulge in these speculations, we risk diminishing the authority of God's Word in the Old Testament.

> **Example A—Song of Songs:** The early Christian writer Origen is famous for his allegorical interpretation of the Song of Songs in his ten-volume commentary. Many of the interpretations that he offers understand the text

in reference to Christ. Song of Songs 2:3 reads, "Like an apple tree among the trees of the forest is my beloved among the young men. I delight to sit in his shade, and his fruit is sweet to my taste." Origen explains that the outstanding quality of the groom suggests the way that Christ is outstanding among other heavenly beings. He further comments that the qualities of the apple compare to Christ as the bread of life.[6] These fanciful suggestions have no foundation in the author's intentions. Moreover, others might devise alternative suggestions, just as fanciful. Though Origen may be considered extreme, examples like this demonstrate the need to have controls designed to track with the author's intentions found in the author's historical and cultural context. If we don't, then what is to stop us from doing what Origen did?

Example B—The Tabernacle: Though Hebrews 9:1-9 discusses the tabernacle in connection with Jesus, it offers no interpretations of the various components of the tabernacle as representing Christ. Interpreters, however, have not been so shy. Instead, they exercise considerable imagination purporting the ways that Christ is typified or allegorized in the tabernacle. Even the colors and the materials are at times given christological significance.[7] Such interpretation can only represent speculation, and different interpreters could offer vastly different connections with little support in evidence.[8]

Our search should be for the author's literary intentions, taking all aspects of context into consideration. Too often, when we go "searching" for something of our own devising, we run the risk of re-contextualizing the communication of the author, with the result that it no longer reflects his intentions. When that happens, we have traded away the authority of the text (found in the author's literary intention) for our own insights. We

[6]This example was taken from Duane A. Garrett, *Song of Songs* (Grand Rapids, MI: Zondervan, 2004), 64-65, where the reader will also find further examples and discussion.

[7]Evidenced in Henry Soltau, *The Tabernacle, The Priesthood, and The Offerings* (Grand Rapids, MI: Kregel, 1972), 144-45 (originally published in the latter part of the nineteenth century in London: A. S. Rouse, n.d.); similar typology in Paul Kiene, *The Tabernacle of God in the Wilderness of Sinai* (Grand Rapids, MI: Zondervan, 1977). These examples are extreme, but the same sort of connections are common in popular Bible study and even in preaching, even though scholars today are much more nuanced.

[8]Similar discussion surrounds the relationship of Jesus to the sacrificial system, where the New Testament draws a few connecting lines. For further reading, see John H. Walton, *Old Testament Theology for Christians* (Downers Grove, IL: IVP Academic, 2017), 261-63.

risk reneging on our accountability to the author as his intentions are represented in the biblical text.

Throughout the chapters of this book, and particularly in these last five sections, it seems that there is no end to red flags! By now readers may be asking, "Where are the green flags?" The green flag has been in sight and guiding us all along—the author's literary intentions. That is the green flag that we follow. Many red flags compete to distract us. We only need to doggedly pursue one green flag. We "stay on the tracks, no matter what" when we track with the author's literary intentions.

SECTION B

LIVING LIFE

37—Living Life in Light of Scripture

For those of us who take the Bible seriously as God's Word, we can never be content with reading the Bible impersonally as simply an analytical exercise. If it does not ripple into our lives, we are treating it as nothing more than antiquarian literature. It cannot even be recognized simply as a book containing a theology that we believe to be true. Reading it should be a life-transforming experience. Faithful interpretation should lead to faithful lives. Nevertheless, its impact on our lives can be skewed if we are not following sound methods of interpretation.

In the early 2000s, sociologist Christian Smith of Notre Dame conducted research to discover what characterized the Christianity of young people. His findings were enlightening, but perhaps not surprising. He concluded that what most characterized the young Christians of that time was what he termed "Moralistic, Therapeutic Deism" (MTD).[1] Whether we accept Smith's research and characterization or not, we can see that, to the extent that it is accurate, those characteristics are fed by our missteps in reading the Bible (or maybe they have dictated that we read the Bible the way we do). People want the Bible to guide them to doing right (like a moral form of "rules of the road" manual or "Roberts Rules of Order"), to give them a GPS-like path toward success, prosperity, and flourishing

---

[1]Christian Smith and Melina Lundquist Denton, *Soul Searching: The Religious and Spiritual Lives of American Teenagers* (New York: Oxford University Press, 2005).

(therapeutic self-help), even as they keep God at a distance. If they have any inclinations toward MTD, they will tend to use the Bible as providing the lens for that perspective. Smith's categories will be helpful as I try to redirect our reading strategies.

This book (1) has suggested that the Bible does not guide us by moralizing (either through narrative or law); (2) has denied the validity of transactionalism (our own benefits and flourishing are not foremost); and (3) has called for relationship with God and being continually aware of his engaging presence (the opposite of deism). If God is the source and center of order—and morality is one facet of order—then God could defensibly be considered the source and center of morality. But that does not mean that he gave us a moral system in the Bible or that we can deduce morality from what we know of him. The goal of the Bible is not to make us moral, flourishing people; rather, it is to help us understand God's plans and purposes and participate in them to his honor and glory ("Hallowed be your name"), to the flourishing of his kingdom ("your kingdom come"), and to recognize him as the source of order ("your will be done on earth as it is in heaven"). In the subheadings below we will explore how the best practices of faithful interpretation that we have discussed will help us to live as God's people.

GETTING THE BIG PICTURE: PRESENCE AND RELATIONSHIP

When we understand that the big picture of the Bible is found in the ways that it unfolds the plans and purposes of God, it leads us to inquire what those plans and purposes are. Why did God create us? What is he doing in the world? We build this big picture from all the little parts of Scripture; the forest is made up of trees. We have been talking about how to approach reading all the parts (and how not to). If we fail to read them well, the larger picture may become blurred. Alternatively, if we employ sound methodology, we will see how the parts contribute to the whole, and the resulting picture will provide insight for how we should focus our lives.

I contend that God has created us to be in relationship with him. That means that biblical Christianity cannot settle for deism that keeps God disengaged from our world and at arm's length from our lives. Furthermore, the relationship that he has created us for is characterized by his presence with us. Immanuel is not just a Christmas story—it is God's story and the Bible's story. What he is doing in the world is moving toward a future time when he will dwell with us in perfect relationship. This is the description of new creation in Revelation 21.

This big picture is evident throughout the Old Testament. God's purpose in ordering the world in creation was to dwell among us. His rest on the seventh day completed his work of creation but also led to his taking up his residence among us on his throne (note his presence in Eden and the terminology of Exodus 20:8-11 combined with Psalm 132:13-14). The covenant inaugurated a relationship that resulted in God's presence (the tabernacle, Exodus 40; see also Leviticus 26:11-12). God's presence reached new levels in the incarnation of Jesus to live among us (John 1:14) and at Pentecost (Acts 2:4) as God's people became the temple (1 Corinthians 3:16), with the presence of God within us. Consequently, we can see that these plans and purposes continued to develop in the New Testament—they are not just Israelite issues. The Israelites of the Old Testament did not anticipate these later developments, but it is clear that throughout the Old Testament they understood the issues of relationship (covenant) and presence (temple). These are the great themes of the Old Testament that serve as the scaffolding for God's plans and purposes.

What does it mean, then, for us to live in the light of God's presence and in relationship with him? The Bible gives us hints, insights, and wisdom, but the implications for our lives are too multifaceted to enumerate. Nevertheless, living our lives should be informed by those realities day-by-day and moment-by-moment. This cannot be achieved by simply trying to keep a list of rules or by constructing a morality. It is an existential reality that should penetrate every molecule of our being and thought of our mind. Two brief examples will have to suffice.

> **Example A—Christian Role in the World:** As people living in the light of God's presence, what do we have to give the world? When we understand our response to Scripture as seeking to bring honor to God's name (his presence)

by becoming participants in his plans and purposes, we will perhaps see that it is not the place of God's people to judge the world or to rule the world. We may desire for people of every nation, tribe, and tongue to come to know our God and to experience relationship with him, but that does not happen through imperialism or colonization. We want to be perceived as humble servants, not as those who desire the power and perquisites of rule. We want to be perceived as wise and caring, not as those who disdain wisdom and resist submitting ourselves to others. We are to be those who give up our rights and transcend our fears. The behavior of the church can bring honor to the reputation of our God or it can bring dishonor. When we recognize that the agenda must be God's agenda (his plans and purposes) not our own, perhaps the world will begin to find us to be the wise and caring people that we are called to be. We should not be defined by the things we fight against, but by the way we love in a cruel world. These would sound like stale clichés if we did not so often fail at this very basic level. Sadly, some of these behavioral missteps are sustained by claiming biblical proof texts, illustrating that flawed methodology is not harmless. When even people of faith do not want to associate with the church because of the bad reputation that it has in the world, we are off the rails.

Example B—Unity in the Church: As people living in the light of God's presence, what do we need to give one another? One would think that God's people would see the benefit of providing a united front to the world. Yet as the world peers through the stained-glass windows of the church they may understandably be repelled by the rancor and belligerence that they observe. Apologists and theologians treat brutally those Christians who disagree with them. Bloggers seek out people to attack and try to destroy them. Denominations excoriate other denominations for proclaimed compromise or heresy (too often surrounding practices of biblical interpretation discussed in this book). Our track record with regard to race and gender is our shame. If justice exists anywhere in this world, it should be evident in the church, but sadly this is not the case.

This sort of infighting bears little resemblance to how the Bible characterizes what God's people should look like. What ought to characterize us, instead, is giving others the benefit of the doubt and treating brothers and sisters with kindness, charity, and fairness. It is a sad commentary that such behavior is so rare and therefore appears remarkable when observed.

Furthermore, as was the case with the builders of the Tower of Babel, we continue to be engaged in making a name for ourselves rather than to exalt God's name through our actions. This tendency extends beyond individual Christians to our institutions. When churches, Christian schools, or Christian companies treat their bottom line as more important than the welfare of their parishioners, students, or employees, we should recognize that our priorities have drifted. When people in authority in these institutions value their own power above the mission and consider paramount their personal reputations and status, and the financial success of their organization, we repeat the scene in the Garden of Eden. That is, we still seek to position ourselves (and our institutions) as the center of order reaping the benefits of order as we see it. In contrast, reading Scripture well should constantly remind us that it is all about God, not all about us.

WHAT DOES GOD WANT FROM US?

God wants us to be participants in his plans and purposes. He created us in his image with that in mind, he continually sought us out when we strayed into the pursuit of our own plans and purposes, and he tolerated our waywardness in grace and restored us in mercy. He provided a means for re-establishing relationship with him through the death of Christ and is preparing a place where we can dwell with him in new creation. He wants us to be his faithful people, to love him because he has loved us and to serve him because he is worthy, not just of our attention, but of our very lives. The following enumeration will give some specificity to this larger statement.

Holiness. Holiness is a status, not a pursuit, achievement, or accomplishment. God did not call the Israelites to "be holy" but told them that they were holy (proper translation of Leviticus 19:2: "You will be holy for I the Lord your God am holy").[2] They were holy because God said they were,

[2]See full discussion in Walton and Walton, *Lost World of the Israelite Conquest*, 104-8, and Walton and Walton, *Lost World of the Torah*, 54-55, 204-205. The same grammatical conclusions are expressed in T. W. Mann, *The Book of the Torah* (Atlanta, GA: John Knox, 1988), 117. It is represented in Young's literal translation. Others, such as the NRSV, represent it as "You shall be holy" rather than "Be holy," as in most translations.

and such status can neither be gained on our own nor lost through offense. This concept is appropriated for Christians in 1 Peter 1:15. Consequently, instead of thinking that we must try to be holy (Does that mean pious? moral? spiritual?) to please God or gain his favor, we need to concentrate our best efforts on finding the most effective ways to be his people, reflecting his glory in an often-dark world. Recognizing the status that we have been given in God, we should be living in hope and giving hope to others. We have received his grace and, as a result, we should be passing it on to others. We were never intended to be cisterns, collecting the ever-flowing grace of God, but to be aqueducts, channeling that grace to others as it flows through us. Such grace would intrinsically include seeking justice for others.

Justice. Unarguably, God desires justice and therefore we ought to be engaged in bringing justice wherever and however we can. We can see that in Micah 6:8,

> He has shown you, O mortal, what is good.
> And what does the LORD require of you?
> To act justly and to love mercy
> and to walk humbly with your God.[3]

The facets of response to God mentioned by Micah are important, but they represent the low bar. Many of us would admit to knowing unbelievers who work toward justice and mercy more actively than anyone we know at church. If Micah offers the low bar, what is the high bar? We can get a glimpse of it in Deuteronomy 10:12-21, where "fearing the Lord" is central in God's expectations of his people.

> And now, Israel, what does the LORD your God ask of you but to fear the LORD your God, to walk in obedience to him, to love him, to serve the LORD your God with all your heart and with all your soul, and to observe the LORD's commands and decrees that I am giving you today for your own good?
>
> To the LORD your God belong the heavens, even the highest heavens, the earth and everything in it. Yet the LORD set his affection on your ancestors and loved them, and he chose you, their descendants, above all the nations—as it is

---

[3]Note that this is addressed to humanity, not just to Israel.

> today. Circumcise your hearts, therefore, and do not be stiff-necked any longer. For the LORD your God is God of gods and Lord of lords, the great God, mighty and awesome, who shows no partiality and accepts no bribes. He defends the cause of the fatherless and the widow, and loves the foreigner residing among you, giving them food and clothing. And you are to love those who are foreigners, for you yourselves were foreigners in Egypt. Fear the LORD your God and serve him. Hold fast to him and take your oaths in his name. He is the one you praise; he is your God, who performed for you those great and awesome wonders you saw with your own eyes.

Here, doing justice is clearly part of the response, but it is only one example of how people fear the Lord. That is the high bar. We have previously discussed the word *fear* (chap. 13), where we noted that instead of referring to fear that people would naturally have toward those who abuse power, this is fear that is reflected in submission to benevolent authority. It is captured in the two great commandments: loving God and loving your neighbor as yourself. The latter is one expression of the former.[4]

Following the will of God. God wants us to live in his will, but we should understand that his will is reflected in his plans and purposes, not in a particular, personalized path (including details such as where we go to college, whom we marry, what job we get). Various alternatives in each of those areas could be pursued without departing from the will of God. The Bible helps us to know the will of God at the larger level—what our participation in his plans and purposes might look like. It does not guide us through the intricacies of decisions that we make that set a course in life.

One of the most memorable sermons I ever heard was preached by Clayton Keenon.[5] It had a lasting impact on me concerning how we think about the will of God. One of the points he made was that God's expectations for our lives are never hidden, so we don't have to feel like we have to put pressure on him until he lets us in on the secret. Another insight

---

[4]Note that the appropriation of these verses to Christians do not run the same risks as many of the passages discussed throughout this book. These are not promises made to Israel that we are misappropriating—they refer instead to what characterizes God (who does not change) and what he expects from his people, who we now are.

[5]Preached at Wheaton College grad chapel by Clayton Keenon. "Clayton Keenon | What If God's Will Is Not a Secret?," Wheaton College, video, 26:12, November 30, 2011, www.youtube.com/watch?v=oblk6flds2o.

Keenon offered was that God's will for our lives is more focused on what kind of people we become than on what tasks we do. The end result is that on those finer points of life, as well as on the big decisions, we have to trust God to guide our thinking—to give us wisdom (James 1:5), either through our own mental processes or through the advice of wise people in our family or community. We will not find it by giving new, personalized meanings to biblical phrases that we pluck out of context.

Finding our identity as the people of God. God wants us to find our identity in him. *Holy* is a word that defines our identity, as is *image*. God has formed our human identity and we find our true identity in relationship with him and participation with him. Our true identity is not found in our family, our social status, our positions, our achievements, our sexuality, our personality, our acclaim, or our past experiences (whether successes or failures). We are "in Christ" and no other aspect of our identity is as important as that (Galatians 3:28). We experience nothing but trouble and confusion when we elevate any of those other facets of our lesser identity to a place of primacy.

Abandoning the quest. God wants us to seek him rather than being on a quest for our own self-fulfillment and flourishing.[6] As the book of Ecclesiastes develops this idea, we find that our quests for fulfillment that center on pleasure, wealth, wisdom, work, family, and even religious duty are futile. Furthermore, the book has no alternate quest for self-fulfillment to propose. Instead, it indicates, in effect, that we should expect ups and downs in life—life is less like a smooth ride on a monorail and more like a roller coaster as we experience both the good and the bad that come our way (Ecclesiastes 3:1-8). God brings both good times, for which we are grateful, and crises, in which we depend on him for strength to endure. God wants us to find joy in being his people, regardless of what we are experiencing in life. Seeking self-fulfillment is just another way that we try to forge order and meaning for ourselves apart from God. Abandoning the quest does not call for self-denial (though that may at times be appropriate), but for re-focusing our efforts in life.

---

[6]For an excellent article that unfolds this idea powerfully, see Mark Buchanan, "Stuck on the Road to Emmaus: The Secret to Why We Are Not Fulfilled," *Christianity Today* 43, no. 8 (July 12, 1999): 55-57.

Being responsive. God wants us to be people who are responsive to his initiatives. His initiatives are found (1) in the act of creation itself; (2) in commissioning us, humanity, to be his image-bearers; (3) in stepping down to live among us; (4) in forging a relationship with us through covenant; (5) in revealing his plans and purposes to us; (6) in bestowing mercy and grace on us; (7) in sending his Son to provide salvation, relationship, and life—in sum, in all the ways that he has loved us. This incumbent responsiveness reflects a view of an engaged God that is the opposite of the deism that too often characterizes the human walk through life.

We should be responsive not only to what we know of God, but to what we find in the Bible, even the Old Testament!

- We respond to Torah by recognizing that God desires his order to be reflected in how we conduct ourselves in the world.
- We respond to narrative by realizing how he has unfolded his story though history and by finding our place in it, as well as by recognizing how his plans and purposes are carried out by means of people like you and me. Some of these people were cooperative and God did great things through them as his instruments (for example, Daniel). Some chose to be obstacles, though they did not thereby hinder God's work through them (for example, Samson). Some were the poorest and most humble of people (Ruth); others were rich and powerful (Solomon). Some were brought low (Nebuchadnezzar); others raised up (Esther). And God was steadily carrying out his plans. We should aspire to be instruments rather than obstacles and to serve in whatever role God gives us.
- We respond to Psalms by joining the ranks of the psalmists as they seek to understand the work of God in their lives and their world. We also come before him, sometimes humbled by his majesty and worthiness, sometimes confused by the turmoil around us. And we are comforted to know that he listens and that he welcomes our company.
- We respond to Wisdom literature by adopting the adjusted view of what constitutes God's order in the world and coming to new insight and appreciation concerning what a life of wisdom might look like when founded on the fear of the Lord.

- We respond to the prophets by observing how God worked out his plans and purposes for Israel. The indictments warn us that unfaithfulness, whatever its nature, will not be taken lightly by God. The oracles of judgment stand as testimony that God disciplines those whom he loves. The oracles of instruction remind us of the sort of response that will bring restoration or relationship. The aftermath oracles testify to the inexorability of the destiny that God has set forth for Israel, but also for us—a destiny that should fill us with hope even when we experience the judgment of God or the crises of history.

The responsiveness outlined here coincides well with what is affirmed in 2 Timothy 3:16-17. There Scripture is described as "useful for teaching, rebuking, correcting and training in righteousness, so that the servant of God may be thoroughly equipped for every good work." Previously it was noted that this enumeration does not delineate the purpose of Scripture, but identifies some of the ways that it functions. These are the very functions that we have enumerated.

More specifically, how does that help us to know how to read, say, Leviticus or Nahum? When we approach them as contributing to an understanding of God's plans and purposes, how do they work? I would propose that Leviticus provides details of the system that Yahweh established in Israel so that they could preserve the purity that his presence required. In all this detail, God made it possible for them to have access to him even though no permanent solution for their impurity and sinfulness had been provided. These resound with God's grace, but also make clear that cavalier attitudes toward their rituals would fall short of showing the respect that he deserves. Reading them, we can be reminded that we dare not be cavalier, and we should be aware of his great grace toward us as well. They give us ample reminder that purity is appropriate when encountering the presence of God.

A book like Nahum contains a judgment oracle against Nineveh and the Assyrians. What we learned about the nature of prophetic literature comes into play here. Specifically, we see this oracle as evidence that God holds the world powers accountable and will bring judgment at the proper time.

This book therefore gives us further insight into how God carries out his plans and purposes.

WHAT DO WE WANT FROM GOD?

Now things get dicey. What do we as Christian believers expect as a result of our service to God? The correct answer is "nothing." God does not owe us anything. He has no needs—he does not need our money, he does not need our service, he does not need our church attendance, he does not need our praise, and he does not need our love. He. Does. Not. Need. Us. He never stands in our debt. We may well want his favor, but we do not deserve it, and we cannot earn it.

We would do well to stand in the dock alongside of Job here. The question posed to God in the first chapter of Job asked, "Does Job serve God for nothing?" And that is the question that we should all continually ask ourselves. We have mentioned the travesty of transactionalism several times in this book. Many Christians have unfortunately treated their adoption of Christianity as entering a transaction with God: we act on his behalf (serving, giving, etc.) and he is then considered obligated to respond to us. This is not what biblical Christianity is—God is not a vending machine. If there is any transaction that defines Christianity, it is found in Christ dying for us and thereby securing our redemption. But that is a gift, not a reciprocal transaction. Because of what he has done for us (in every way, not just in our redemption), we owe him our lives unconditionally.

When we approach our Christianity as a transaction, we too easily assume that we have received a very healthy benefits package: forgiveness of sin, eternal life, an easy path through life. The first two are provided by God, the last is not. But even the first two must not define our faith. Ideally, we should adopt the viewpoint that even if we did not have those benefits, we would choose faith in Christ. As Andraé Crouch sang years ago, "If heaven never was promised to me . . . it's been worth just having the Lord in my life."[7]

It is strange how even our prayers can so easily become self-serving. What we want from God are answers! We so often speak of answered prayer.

---

[7]Andraé Crouch, "If Heaven Was Never Promised to Me," track 6 on *Just Andraé*, Light Records, 1972.

It is true that God hears our prayers and at times we see dramatic answers, but we must not conclude that prayer is about getting answers, that is, about getting results. Prayer is about communing with God more than communicating to him. Prayer should feature more listening and less talking (not unlike our human relationships).[8] Our prayers should focus more on requests for God to help us become the people we ought to be than attempts to coax out of him what we want.

We will be learning appropriately from Scripture when we understand that it is not about us. It is about God, and his plans and purposes. If we imagine ourselves as drivers through life who have picked up Jesus hitchhiking alongside of the road and invited him into the car to help us navigate toward all we want to achieve in life to flourish and prosper, we have the wrong idea. He calls us to abandon our car and our ambitions for life, and to board his train. We should view ourselves as passengers on his "Plans and Purposes Express" rather than imagining that he is a passenger in our personal car with us at the wheel. This is also a helpful contrast when we think of the role of Scripture.

In the end, we can want no more from God or his Word than what he has freely given: relationship, wisdom, comfort, encouragement. These are more abstract than tangible, and though we may desire more (in our innate selfishness), these are what we need most. We do better to strive to live by the wisdom the Holy Spirit gives rather than trying to find substantiating proof texts. None of our pressing controversial issues have been resolved by appeal to biblical proof texts.

HOW DO WE MANAGE CRISES?

Life often goes wrong. Neither relationship with God nor the truth of his Word guarantee a smooth path through life. When the inevitable happens (and sometimes it is not just a blip on the screen, but is what life has become or even what it always was), how do we respond as those participating in God's plans and purposes?

---

[8]These ideas are well-developed in Skye Jethani, *What If Jesus Was Serious About Prayer?* (Chicago, IL: Moody, 2021).

When life goes wrong, we find a good perspective in the teaching of Jesus. When he and his disciples encountered a man who was born blind (John 9), the disciples seek an explanation for the man's condition and ask whether the presumed sin was this man's or his parents'. They assumed that his condition was the result of someone's sin. This was a common assumption both in the Old Testament and in the New Testament, as well as throughout the history of Christianity. It is how we often think today as well. Jesus offers his disciples (and us) the important insight that rather than looking to the past for a cause or reason for suffering, we should look to the present and future to try to discern a purpose or an opportunity. In this sense, we are called to seek ways to participate in God's plans and purposes even in the context of our trials, disabilities, crises, illnesses, and losses. This does not change when we think of how we might experience poverty, persecution, or dysfunctional relationships. God neither promises to protect his people from such circumstances nor to deliver us from them; but he does say that he will be with us through them.

Both Old Testament and New Testament call us to a life of trusting in God. This stands in stark contrast to what we often seek: clear answers and full explanations. Trust steps in where knowledge fails. We most need to trust when we are puzzled or disappointed. We may often wonder how we can go on; how life can possibly make sense; how God can allow such things to happen. Instead of being given answers, we are encouraged to trust his wisdom, even though we despair of discovering how our experiences or observations could be the result of wisdom. We dare not adopt a view that we could do it better. We cannot out-god God, we cannot domesticate him, and we cannot stand in judgment on him. Many of our missteps in interpreting Scripture have led us to misunderstand what God is doing, and then to criticize him for what is actually a mistaken conclusion. If we love him and believe that he loves us, we will trust his wisdom.

Finally, though neither God nor Scripture promise relief, that is what we may find when keeping our eyes focused on participation in God's plans and purposes. This will give us a pathway to the rest, peace, and coherence that God gives, which may be different from what we anticipate. To understand, we must define our terms carefully.[9]

Perceive Rest. We discussed the word "rest" and the concepts behind it in chapters thirteen and nineteen, where we identified it as characterized by stability, security, and equilibrium. It refers to a perspective that transcends any turmoil in our *circumstances*, rising above unrest. It is what God gives when his people look beyond their difficult circumstances to recognize the greater reality of God's kingdom. This is what Jesus means when he says "Come to me, all you who are weary and burdened, and I will give you rest. Take my yoke upon you and learn from me, for I am gentle and humble in heart, and you will find rest for your souls" (Matthew 11:28-29). The rest he offers does not eliminate difficulties we are experiencing but helps us to look beyond them.[10]

Find Peace. In the Old Testament God offers peace (*shalom*, Isaiah 26:3) as does Jesus in the New Testament (John 14:27; 16:33). As John 14 indicates, this is not the sort of peace that we often desire. The peace that the Bible speaks of offers freedom from fear and revitalizes our *feelings*. Again, it is available as we look beyond the circumstances that fill us with fear and feel nothing like peace, and can help us to solidify in our minds the perspective of God's plans and purposes. We find peace by participating in them as best as we can, even though our circumstances may be terrifying.

Redefine Coherence. Coherence may be defined as finding order not in our ability to understand and explain everything, but by trusting God. When our reference point is God and his kingdom, our *thinking* can rise above the confusion swirling around us. Both Old Testament and New Testament indicate that coherence is provided by God, and we have identified the foundation of it throughout this book—the concept of order.[11] We must learn to look beyond our own sense of what brings order for us and see the larger picture of God's order. Adopting God's perspective can help us to navigate through what life brings.

---

[9]These are more fully developed in John H. Walton and Tremper Longman III, *How to Read Job* (Downers Grove, IL: IVP Academic, 2015), 168-78.

[10]Important Old Testament references include Deuteronomy 12:10; Joshua 21:44; 1 Kings 8:56; and Isaiah 32:18.

[11]For some of the most important references, see Proverbs 3:5; Isaiah 50:10; Colossians 1:17.

CONCLUDING CHALLENGE

In the musical *Wicked*, one of the characters revels in his commitment to live the "unexamined life"—have no cares and no worries, live life as it comes, be spontaneous, don't think too hard about things, follow your inclinations.[12] Many Christians today have adopted an "unexamined methodology" in approaching biblical interpretation that they have pieced together from what they learned in Sunday school and in Bible studies and sermons. They have not thought much about it and as a result have a very carefree approach to interpretation, following their inclinations wherever they lead. Though they may eagerly do research about how to fix their plumbing, mend their roof, or make the best chocolate chip cookies, they don't want to spend time researching the Bible. They will plan carefully for their trip to Scotland or Greece but are not willing to expend the same level of energy to read the Bible. They prefer to be spontaneous and intuitive. Application is what interests them, and they often fail to distinguish between interpretation and application. Though it has created problems for both the church and individual Christians in the past, we refuse to learn the lessons of history. We cannot afford to adopt an unexamined methodology. Too much is at stake.

In 1980, James Sire published a book with InterVarsity Press titled *Scripture Twisting: 20 Ways the Cults Misread the Bible*. I had just gotten my first teaching job and was assigned to teach a course on Bible study methods. I decided to use Sire's book as one of the textbooks for the course because, as I read it, I realized that most of the misreading he identified in the cults could also be found in traditional Christian interpretation. This prompted the question, Why are we any different from the cults? If we seek to critique what others do with Scripture, we had better make sure that our own house is in order.

When we fail to use consistent methods and controls to reflect our accountability to the authors' literary intentions, the result can easily be flawed theology, skewed perspectives, and practices that reflect our own desires rather than honoring God. We all have in our heads a methodology

---

[12]"Dancing Through Life," from Stephen Schwartz, *Wicked* (New York: Decca Broadway, 2003).

for reading Scripture, though it is often an unexamined one. The cost for carelessness is potentially high since it can compromise our ability to be the church, shining the light of Christ to the world. Our methods can render our light dim and our salt spoiled. It can bring dishonor to the name of our God rather than testifying to his glory.

Yet we must not now be afraid to read our Bibles. Many resources are available to help us become more knowledgeable interpreters. These tools include study Bibles, Bible atlases, Bible dictionaries and encyclopedias, commentaries on biblical books, word study books, background commentaries, books on biblical history or theology, and a host of ever-proliferating online resources—from sermons to Bible studies and from podcasts to seminars. All these provide ample information to improve and inform our interpretation.

Nevertheless, the important point is that the most significant challenge to our faithful interpretation is not posed by details we do not know; it is rather in our lack of understanding of what the Old Testament is and how it works to deliver God's Word. Hopefully this book has provided some insights that can remedy that. With that understanding, we can read the Old Testament with more confidence. Even if details of language and culture are beyond our grasp, we can always answer the most important questions: "What is this passage teaching me about God? What is God doing? How is God using this person, people group, or situation to carry out his plan?" We frame those answers within the larger picture of God desiring to be with the people he has created and loves, and carrying out his plan to see that accomplished. We are able to read Scripture and embrace our role as God's people. He has provided all that we need to participate in his plans and purposes and has made relationship available through Christ as we live in the light of his indwelling presence.

When we are learning God's story and seeking to understand his plans and purposes (the function of Scripture), we are seeking the face of God.[13] We might therefore draw a fruitful analogy to how our modern facial recognition programs work. A facial recognition program compiles the data

[13]For similar ideas, see Tim Stafford, *Knowing the Face of God* (Grand Rapids, MI: Zondervan, 1986) and C. S. Lewis, *Till We Have Faces* (New York: Harcourt Brace and Company, 1957).

about your face by making minute adjustments every time it engages. The more you use it, the more sophisticated and precise its knowledge of your face. That means that it becomes less susceptible to errors and more capable of overlooking oddities (a black eye or a scratch on the face) as well as adjusting to variables (a new haircut, glasses, dyed hair). The more data points it has, the surer its identification. Similarly, every time we read Scripture—every narrative, every prophecy, every psalm, every legal provision—we are adding more data points that give us more insight as we grow to know the face of God. Passages that appear to us as oddities about God will not distort our perception and we will learn from variables. The more we use Scripture to understand the full range of God's story and the nature of his plans and purposes, the more we will recognize the face of God as we live day-by-day. This is why we read Scripture and it is why we need to read all of Scripture. If we only read the New Testament, we will not have the data necessary to know his whole face.

APPENDIX

WHAT TO DO WITH THE OLD TESTAMENT

Table A.1.

WHEN YOU ARE TEMPTED TO . . .	PAUSE TO CONSIDER	DO THIS INSTEAD	CHAPTER(S)
Use a biblical character as a role model	Is there any indication that the author is presenting the character as a role model?	Consider how the author is showing the role that the character played as God was unfolding his plans and purposes. We are learning what God is like, not what the biblical characters are like.	27
Derive a lesson on ethical behavior from a biblical character	Does the author draw the character's ethical decisions to the reader's attention?	Recognize that characters may be able to be used as illustrations of good or bad behavior, but that our first priority is to track with the author and his message.	27
Draw a moral conclusion from the Torah	The Torah is not intended to provide a moral system.	Seek to discern the wisdom of what the Torah offers that may benefit our own current moral decisions.	21–22
Extract a principle from Torah	Undoubtedly principles undergirded the provisions of the Torah, but those principles are not always easily recognizable and are not necessarily universal.	Seek the wisdom of the provision and discern how we can also practice wisdom.	21
Extract a verse from its context	Removing a text from its context can lead to distortion and misuse, and risks missing the author's message.	Read the entire chapter (or even the entire book) to determine what the author's message is and how the verse contributes to it.	4
Use a narrative to determine God's will for you	Narrators are not addressing the particulars of God's direction in your life.	Pray for wisdom to make good decisions and consult with wise friends and family as you seek the most effective ways to participate in God's plans and purposes.	26, 27, 38
Pray a psalm	The Psalms do not come with a mandate to use them for our own prayers.	Remember that God stands willing to hear any prayer that we pray, even ones that are unworthy, but we do well to pray thoughtfully, whether we use a psalm or not.	30

WHEN YOU ARE TEMPTED TO . . .	PAUSE TO CONSIDER	DO THIS INSTEAD	CHAPTER(S)
Use a prophecy to point to Jesus	The prophets knew nothing of Jesus and their messages are not to be equated with fulfillments.	Seek to understand the prophet's message first and then supplement that with the fulfillment identified by the New Testament author. Be reluctant to devise your own fulfillments.	35
Use a character as a type of Christ	Types need both endpoints in order to build a connection, and the OT authors did not have both, so they are not developing characters as types.	Seek the author's message and intention first, and only adopt a later connection to Christ if the New Testament authors offer it.	15
See Jesus in an OT passage	Is the proposed connection to Jesus something that the author would have intended?	Think about how the message of the author can lead us to something we see in Jesus, rather than being about Jesus.	15
Determine what the end times will hold by charting a future from a prophetic or apocalyptic passage	The focus of prophecy and apocalyptic is on God's plans and purposes rather than predicting a specific future.	Be content to trust God as you anticipate his coming kingdom rather than trying to understand the present as fulfillment, or to construct the shape of the future.	33–35
Extract a promise from a biblical passage	Many promises that we find in Scripture are not made to us.	Read the promise in context to discover who it was made to and under what circumstances. Then think about what it might tell us about God's plans and purposes or what God is like.	37
Use an OT passage to establish a theological concept	Were the Israelites aware of this point of theology? Was the author seeking to establish a theological point?	Draw a distinction between how a passage may support a theological concept developed through other means rather than using it to establish that point.	30, 37
Interpret a symbol in a vision	Not everything in a vision carries symbolic value, and not all symbols are decipherable.	Be content with the interpretation of symbols provided by the biblical authors rather than trying to expand beyond what they offer.	34
Use the Torah to support a particular social issue or cause	The provisions of the Torah are situated in the ancient world and in the covenant between Yahweh and Israel. They may not represent the ideal or the universal.	Ask yourself whether you would use any Torah provision in the same way. Seek wisdom for understanding social order that would honor God today.	21-22
Use a New Testament idea to interpret an Old Testament verse or concept	Was that New Testament idea known to the Old Testament author and was it his intention to address it?	Allow each testament to stand on its own so that the authority of the Old Testament author is not neglected.	6, 35 and throughout

WHEN YOU ARE TEMPTED TO . . .	PAUSE TO CONSIDER	DO THIS INSTEAD	CHAPTER(S)
Propose a "biblical" view of something	Not everything has a "biblical" view; we must remain aware of cultural context of the authors.	Be content to focus on wisdom in discerning a way to think that will honor God.	17
Promote "lessons from the life of X"	The biblical authors are rarely interested in teaching lessons from the lives of characters.	Observe how the author is using the characters to show how God is working out his plans and purposes and telling us his story so that we can be in relationship with him.	27
Comment on the meaning of a word in the text based on English synonyms or definitions	English and Hebrew package ideas differently and often there are not clear equivalences.	Use resources to gain as much information about the Hebrew word as you can.	12–13
Read modern science between the lines	The authors have no knowledge of our modern science and therefore are not addressing that.	Nurture a sense of wonder concerning God's work in the world seen through Israelite eyes.	18
Become discouraged when the latest archaeological finds are used to discredit the Bible	Archaeology as a discipline has its limitations and involves a degree of interpretation.	Investigate ways that you may have been making false assumptions about the biblical passage that could be adjusted by the new archaeological information.	25–26

FAQs

Q: What should I do when it seems that my pastor is using what you have identified as "missteps"?
A: Receive the sermon as application because that is often what pastors are doing anyway. It is unlikely that what is being preached is dangerous, even when it cannot be traced back to the interpretation of the author's message. Remember, our goal is to understand how to best participate in God's plans and purposes as his people in his story. Strive to be charitable rather than critical.

Q: Are you suggesting that many of the interpreters over the centuries of Christian history have been wrong?
A: Many Christian writers of the past have been engaged in appropriation and application more than in the level of engagement with the text that I have been calling interpretation. They often did not know the original languages, and until about a century ago, they had no access to the cultural background of the ancient world. It is not difficult to find statements in any ancient Christian writer that we entirely reject today for good reasons. But modern interpreters also have blind spots and biases—we all must recognize our fallibility.

Q: What do you recommend for my daily Bible reading practice?
A: Whatever biblical book you are reading through, begin by using resources to understand the purpose and structure of the book.[1] Then read a chapter each day meditating on how that chapter contributes to the

[1]Available in accessible and readable form in, for example, John H. Walton, Mark L. Strauss, and Ted Cooper Jr., *The Essential Bible Companion* (Grand Rapids, MI: Zondervan, 2006), where each biblical book is addressed in one spread.

author's purpose and how you can understand God's plans and purposes through it.

Q: What should I look for in a devotional guide?
A: The best devotional guide will show awareness of the author's message, even if most attention is given to inspirational insights for application.

Q: I find my devotional guide insightful and inspiring, but it seems to be characterized by what you have called "missteps." Do I have to stop using it?
A: Not necessarily, but I would recommend that you daily evaluate the interpretation methods that the guide is using to determine whether your reading for the day would be somehow undermined. Then take to heart whatever helpful application they might offer. If you now find yourself daily distracted by interpretation methods with which you do not agree, it may be advisable to seek out a different guide.

Q: How can I share these reading strategies with others at my church?
A: One way to do this would be to use this book as the basis for a Bible study or small group series so that the various points can be discussed. Another way is to use some of the resources already mentioned in the process of group Bible study.

Q: How can I help my child learn to interpret the Bible with more attention to the author's intention?
A: My wife and I began teaching these principles to our children in their early years as we read Bible stories to them. Those principles that particularly relate to Bible stories can also be incorporated in family Bible times making use of the *Bible Story Handbook*.[2] Children are spiritual beings just like adults and have the ability to encounter God and learn about him on their level. Keeping a focus on what we learn about God and his long-term plans and steering conversations in this direction will not only help them understand the purpose of the texts but lead them to know God better

---

[2]John and Kim Walton, *The Bible Story Handbook* (Wheaton, IL: Crossway, 2010).

Q: How can I keep my Bible reading "on track"?
A: Remember that the main green flag is to stay on the tracks, which we have identified as attending to the author's literary intentions. We can track with the author when we make it a practice to ask the question, "What do I learn about God and about his plans and purposes from this passage?" Application may at times suggest action that we need to take, but perhaps even more often it pertains to adjustments we need to make in our beliefs. Proper action is commendable, but our actions will be shaped to some extent by our beliefs, so we may need to strengthen our beliefs as preparation for taking the right actions, whether this week or twenty years from now. Reading Scripture well should train our minds to be more instinctive in acting in ways that reflect sound belief, like a concert pianist who has trained her fingers to play a difficult piece well without having to think where each finger is placed.

SCRIPTURE INDEX

THE LOST WORLD SERIES

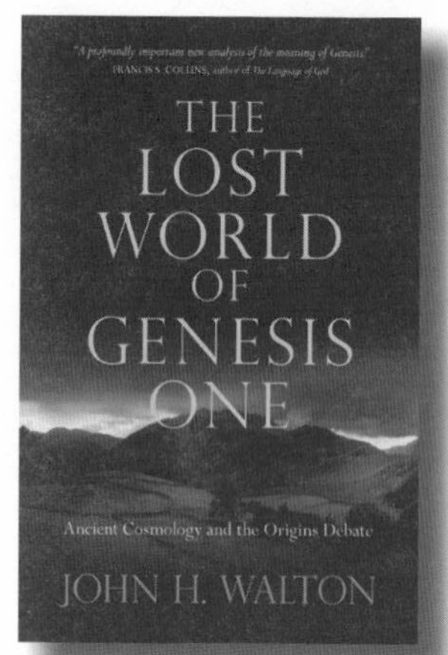

The Lost World of Genesis One
978-0-8308-3704-5

The Lost World of Adam and Eve
978-0-8308-2461-8

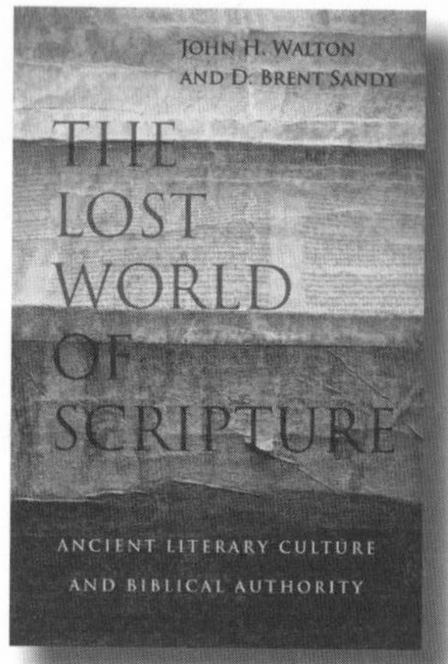

The Lost World of Scripture
978-0-8308-4032-8

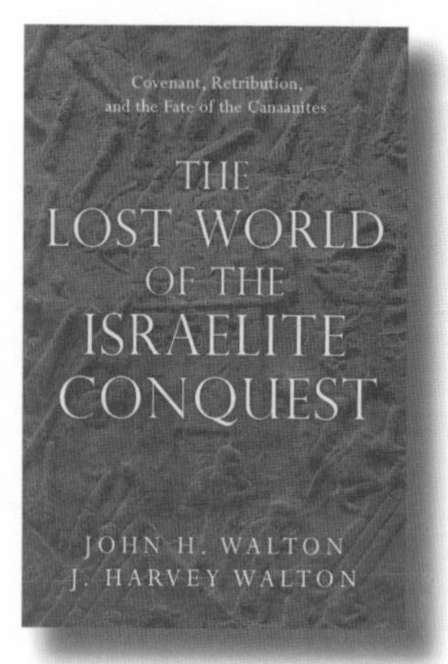

The Lost World of the Israelite Conquest
978-0-8308-5184-3

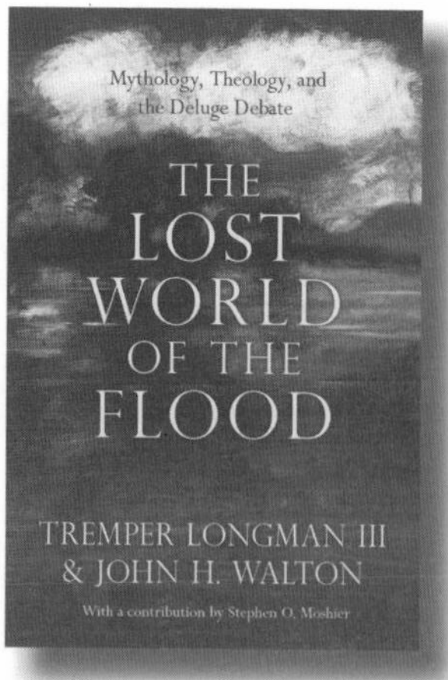

The Lost World of the Flood
978-0-8308-5200-0

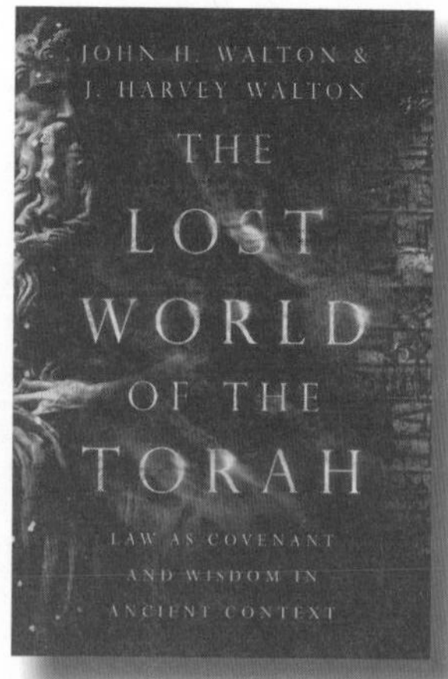

The Lost World of the Torah
978-0-8308-5241-3